Studies
in
Utilitarianism

THE CENTURY PHILOSOPHY SERIES
Justus Buchler, Editor

Studies
in
Utilitarianism

Edited by
Thomas K. Hearn, Jr.
College of William and Mary

New York

APPLETON-CENTURY-CROFTS

Educational Division

MEREDITH CORPORATION

This book, or parts thereof, must not be used or reproduced
in any manner without written permission. For information
address the publisher, Appleton-Century-Crofts, Educational
Division, Meredith Corporation, 440 Park Avenue South,
New York, N.Y. 10016.

721-1

Library of Congress Card Number: 79-151031

PRINTED IN THE UNITED STATES OF AMERICA
390-42805-1

Contents

Acknowledgments   vii

Introduction   1

Selections from *An Introduction to the Principles
of Morals and Legislation*
Jeremy Bentham   15

Utilitarianism
J. S. Mill   39

Selections from *Principia Ethica*
G. E. Moore   103

The "Proof" of Utility in Bentham and Mill
Everett W. Hall   123

The Interpretation of the Moral Philosophy of J. S. Mill
J. O. Urmson   151

Interpretations of Mill's *Utilitarianism*
J. D. Mabbott   161

Some Merits of One Form of Rule-Utilitarianism
Richard Brandt   169

Two Concepts of Rules
John Rawls   201

An Examination of Restricted Utilitarianism
H. J. McCloskey   231

Extreme and Restricted Utilitarianism
J. J. C. Smart   251

Suggestions for Further Reading   265

Reference Guide to Selected Topics   269

Acknowledgments

I should like to thank the authors and publishers of the materials reprinted in this volume for permitting them to appear. In the planning and preparation of this volume I was helped by Professors Justus Buchler, Frank MacDonald, Alan Fuchs, William Cobb, and John Lachs. The following former students assisted me: Lizabeth Beegle, Judith Johnson, Olivian Boggs, Jeanne Forrer, and Sarah Mays. To these, and to the many students who gave these materials classroom testing, I am deeply grateful. Special thanks also to Mrs. Gordon Galow.

Page numbers in brackets refer to this volume.

T. K. H., Jr.

Studies
in
Utilitarianism

Introduction

Interest in utilitarianism on the part of moral philosophers has notably increased in recent years. This has resulted in the reassessment of the classical sources of the doctrine, especially J. S. Mill, as well as new efforts to defend or revise utilitarianism in ways designed to make possible its acceptance as a rationally defensible basis for moral evaluation. This volume brings together basic selections from Bentham and Mill and a selection of studies designed to present a fairly comprehensive survey of utilitarianism and some of the issues involved in its recent discussion. This introduction is intended only to place the following materials in some general context.

Ethical theories traditionally have been classified as either teleological or deontological. Teleological theories maintain that the moral worth of actions is determined solely by their consequences or results. Deontological theories deny this and insist upon the importance of the motive of the agent or the kind of act involved in determining what is morally required. For example, Kant is a deontological theorist for whom the morality of an act is dependent upon the will or motive of the agent in its performance. W. D. Ross, a deontologist to whom frequent reference is made in this volume, argues that certain kinds of acts such as promise-keeping or truth-telling are morally binding quite apart from any consideration of the consequences of their performance. Thus, teleological theories emphasize the results or consequences of the act in moral evaluation, while deontological theories emphasize the act itself and the agent who performs it.

Utilitarianism is a teleological theory which asserts that of the possible acts in a given situation one should perform the one which will bring about the most good for the most number of people; in Bentham's phrase, one should seek "the greatest happiness of the greatest number." By contrast, ethical egoism is a teleological theory according to which the welfare to be maximized is the agent's own. As might be expected, the issues between deontologists and utilitarians are central to the materials in this collection.

Since teleological theories regard the moral worth of acts as determinable by their consequences, such theories must of necessity provide a means of evaluating consequences, of knowing the kinds of consequences which are desirable or undesirable. Questions concerning what kinds of things are good, worthwhile, or desirable are dealt with by the branch of enquiry called the theory of value. More specifically, value theory deals with the question of what kinds of things, if any, can be said to be intrinsically valuable, worth having in and for themselves. Monistic theories of value affirm that only one thing possesses intrinsic worth and that whatever else is worthwhile is so only instrumentally, as a means to the one thing which has intrinsic value. Hedonism is the view that pleasure is the only thing having intrinsic value, and that whatever else is valuable is so because it results in pleasure. Bentham and Mill were hedonists, and thus, in their view the objective of the utilitarian was to perform those actions which would maximize pleasure for as many persons as possible. Pleasure and happiness are sometimes identified as they were by Bentham and Mill, but happiness has traditionally been distinguished from pleasure, eudaemonism as the monistic theory of value which regards happiness as the sole possessor of intrinsic worth. In contrast to monistic theories, pluralistic or ideal value theories hold that more than one thing has value intrinsically: states of character, personal relationships, knowledge, and many other things have been held to be good in and of themselves. Thus utilitarians differ among themselves with regard to theory of value. All utilitarians agree that one should strive to maximize what is intrinsically valuable, but they may differ about what the intrinsically valuable is.

Though there were numerous predecessors, utilitarianism received its classical formulation in the writings of Jeremy Bentham (1784–1832). Bentham was educated for the law but never practiced, having determined at an early age to devote himself entirely to the cause of social reform. He was not primarily interested in the problems of moral philosophy insofar as this concerns the evaluation of individual human acts; rather, utility was devised by Bentham as the principle to be used by the legislator in determining what laws should be enacted, how existing social structures and practices should be changed, and what sorts of new social institutions should be devised. Bentham's writings attracted to him a group of intellectuals who, under his leadership, were active on behalf of many reform causes in Great Britain in the later eighteenth and early nineteenth centuries.

As outlined in the selection from *An Introduction to the Principles of Morals and Legislation* (1789) contained in this volume, Bentham's views are quite straightforward. He regarded pleasures as quantifiable, and thus devised the famous "hedonistic calculus" as a means of measuring the relative values of proposed actions. The use of the calculus was to make possible a science of values so that the moral agent, and more importantly the legislator, could have a precise means of discovering what should be done. Evaluating alternative courses of action was a matter of adding the pleasures and subtracting the pains; given the numerical outcome, one should perform the act which would bring about the most good.

John Stuart Mill (1806–1873) was the son of James Mill, one of the most influential members of the Benthamite circle. The elder Mill personally undertook the education of his son (beginning with Greek at age three) with the aim that he should one day assume leadership in the Benthamite group. Mill's account of his education in his *Autobiography* is a fascinating if not very happy story. The outcome of his unusual preparation, however, was that he reached intellectual maturity as a convinced disciple of Bentham. In his early twenties, Mill experienced what he termed his "mental crisis." Though by this time he had followed his father's precedent by assuming a position in the East India Company and outwardly his life went on as usual, inwardly he was overcome by intense depression. He found himself no longer concerned about the causes to which he had previously been devoted, and he was plagued with doubt regarding the foundations of the Benthamite philosophy. He felt that his education, which lacked appreciable emphasis upon the affections and the imagination, had left him without the capacity to feel, enjoy, and take delight. Gradually the depression passed; among other things, Mill found relief in reading the poetry of Wordsworth. This period had a lasting influence upon Mill's development in that while he remained a Benthamite in the broad sense, he revised his "early narrow creed" in certain important respects.

Utilitarianism (1863) offers the most complete account of Mill's mature moral philosophy. This small book has been the object of numerous scholarly and interpretive disagreements; little of substance can be said about it, in whole or in part, which is not controversial. It is evident, however, that Mill's effort in this volume is almost entirely constructive—to present as convincing a case as possible for his own position—and little effort is spent in argument against rival points of view. This strategy is made plausible by Mill's belief, which was shared by Bentham, that insofar as people do *reason* about moral matters, they do in fact appeal to considerations of general welfare in making and justifying moral judgments. There are, of course, possible theories according to which discursive moral reasoning is unnecessary or even impossible. Adherents of what Bentham calls the "principle of sympathy" believe that moral determinations can be made upon the basis of their own immediate feelings of approval or disapproval and claim that one need be sure only of his own feelings in order to make or justify moral pronouncements. Of more interest to Mill are the various intuitionistic theories which claim immediate knowledge in moral matters on the basis of an inborn faculty of moral discernment. In the most extreme versions of intuitionism, there is no need for the kind of empirical inquiry into the likely consequences of actions required by utilitarianism; by means of the "moral sense" one just "sees" what is right. However, Mill recognizes that such theories are rarely held in forms which eliminate the need for moral enquiry. More commonly the intuitionist claims *a priori* knowledge of moral principles which then must be applied in concrete situations by means of direct investigation into the facts. Mill's response to this position is twofold. First, he believes that an analysis of the moral inquiry actually conducted in such particular situations would reveal that considerations of utility were the most basic if not the sole criterion actually employed in determining what should be done. Second, he attempts to show that the measure of truth contained in these moral principles for which *a priori* knowledge is claimed can be derived from the principle of utility. Mill's problem then is to expose the utilitarianism implicit in both these ways in such a position. The "chief obstacle" to the explicit acknowledgment of the utilitarian point of view is that the principle is not adequately or accurately understood. Furthermore, some of the most serious misunderstandings are precisely the positions of unmodified Benthamism. Mill's task then is to offer a statement of the utilitarian point of view immune from those difficulties which have prevented its acceptance by those persons in whose moral thinking it is implicitly present. This is Mill's basic argument for utilitarianism, but having presented this, he also offers a further proof of the principle in Chapter IV.

It is important to underscore Mill's effort to show that moral principles or beliefs, held on non-utilitarian grounds, are capable of being accounted for within a rightly understood utilitarian framework. Mill characteristically differs from Bentham in the conciliatory attitude he displays towards the moral opinions of others. Thus, he attempts to show the consistency with utility of certain moral emphases of Christianity and Stoicism as well as Epicureanism. The effort to show that certain widely held moral beliefs are consistent or inconsistent with utility will be found to be an issue in the minds of virtually all the authors whose works appear in this volume. Most of the other authors share Mill's assumption that consistency with such widely held beliefs is a criterion of the acceptability of any ethical theory.

Mill's most conspicuous departure from Bentham concerns his effort to broaden the utilitarian understanding of happiness. Critics accused utilitarianism of being a "pig philosophy," and part of the basis for this criticism was the fact that the only distinction among pleasures recognized by Bentham was quantitative. Thus, the pleasures derived from eating and drinking, from reading and writing, or from acting nobly or sacrificially were regarded as qualitatively all the same. This was summarized in Bentham's dictum that if the quantities of pleasure involved were equal, "Pushpin is as good as poetry." Mill, however, introduces distinctions of quality among pleasures so that of two actions which were equivalent in terms of quantity of resulting pleasure, one might still be the more desirable by virtue of its quality. To ascertain which are the "higher" pleasures, Mill believes it sufficient to discover the settled preferences of persons who by experience are competent to judge. With this introduction of qualitative differences among pleasures, Mill implicitly rejects the possibility of a "hedonistic calculus" on which so much of Benthamism was premised, since the possibility of such a device presupposes that pleasures have only quantitative characteristics.

It appears that by the introduction of qualitative distinctions among pleasures Mill departs from a strict hedonism. For the hedonist, the claim that one pleasure is *better than* or *more valuable than* another must mean that it is *more pleasurable than* the other. Mill seems to be denying this and, thus, is accused of inconsistency in this matter. In his defense, some commentators suggest that Mill's qualitative distinction is at bottom only quantitative. The "higher" pleasures, though less intense, are longer lasting and less mixed with pain; this is precisely the position taken by classical Epicureanism as well as by Bentham in defending the belief that the pleasures of the intellect are generally to be preferred to those of the senses. On this interpretation, when Mill asserts that it is "better to be Socrates dissatisfied than a fool satisfied," the reason is that Socrates, even subtracting the pains of his dissatisfactions, has more happiness than the fool whose few desires are fully satisfied. The difficulty for this proposed defense of Mill is to account for the fact that Mill does rather clearly speak as though qualitative considerations offer another and quite different criterion from those of sheer quantity in evaluating the worth of actions.

Another criticism of Bentham to which Mill is reacting is the former's supposed lack of appreciation for the importance of individual achievement and effort. It has been noted that Bentham was primarily concerned with the matter of social improvement from the perspective of the legislator, and in general his proposals for betterment relied primarily upon the functioning legal and social agencies which would reward or punish individual behavior as it conformed to or deviated from the general welfare. Scant attention was given to the importance of individual moral attainment. Furthermore, virtue, nobility, and self-sacrifice were all thought to be of no intrinsic worth, but merely useful means to the end of maximizing the general welfare. Mill is concerned with providing utilitarianism with an important individualistic emphasis and, in addition, with making it clear that the utilitarian of perfected virtue will be one who regards the development of individual character not merely as useful but as an essential part of the good life.

Bentham's supposed lack of regard for the value of individual character was connected more generally with criticism of his psychology. Bentham held a crude form of psychological hedonism, the view that persons are determined by nature to act in accordance with the prospects of maximizing pleasure or minimizing pain for themselves. This creates, of course, a serious inconsistency between Bentham's psychology and his moral theory which requires that everyone seek the general welfare. It seems that people cannot do psychologically what is morally required of them. Bentham sought for a practical resolution of this inconsistency. By social rearrangement the social good could be made to closely correspond to individual welfare. The aims of education, and especially moral education, should be directed to the production of persons who find their own happiness in serving the general good. Mill was also a psychological hedonist, but he held this theory in a revised form which, in his opinion, greatly modified the selfish portrait of human nature which Bentham offered. Indeed, Mill claims that the narrow concern for one's own happiness is a principal cause of unhappiness. Mill maintains that though each person's original desire is only for his own pleasure, through the process of association things other than pleasure could become autonomous objects of desire. Things originally sought because they were conducive to one's own happiness are capable of becoming ingredients in that happiness and, thus, capable of being desired for themselves. Given man's social instincts, Mill holds that any morally educated person can come to desire the happiness of others as an essential element in his own welfare. Mill's associationism does perhaps enable him to alter the selfish portrait of human nature to some degree but, of course, he does not thereby escape the difficulty that psychological hedonism is incompatible with the moral demands of utilitarianism. Even according to Mill, one can seek the general welfare only as long as the desire for the general welfare is part of one's own happiness, and not otherwise. The rejection of this outmoded hedonistic psychology, of course, in no way affects the justification of the principle of utility, despite the fact that Mill may have used psychological hedonism in his proof of the principle in Chapter IV.

Mill's proof of utility has been the subject of intense discussion. The recent controversy regarding the proof has its origins in the work of G. E. Moore, whose influence on the moral philosophy of this century has been enormous. Moore set out to show that the ethical term "good" was indefinable and, in particular, to demonstrate the error of proposals to render "good" in nonethical, natural terms such as "pleasure" or "what people desire." Terms like "pleasure" or "what people desire" are natural in the sense that they refer to qualities or characteristics which are empirically ascertainable, whereas, according to Moore, "good" refers to a non-empirical, nonnatural quality. Thus, to define "good" in non-ethical terms is to commit the *naturalistic fallacy.* In these selections from *Principia Ethica,* Moore explains this fallacy and charges Mill with having committed a paradigm case of it in his proof of utility. However, it should be noted that the subject of Moore's criticism is Mill's hedonism and not utilitarianism as such. Moore himself is a utilitarian, though of the pluralistic sort.

Certain problems of the sort raised by Moore comprise part of what has come to be called *metaethics.* A distinction between *normative ethics* and metaethics is referred to at several points in this volume. Moral philosophy as traditionally conceived is a normative, prescriptive discipline; its purpose is to set forth those principles by which moral choices ought to be made. Metaethics concerns certain questions which may be raised about ethics and about normative theories. In particular, the study of metaethics focuses on two issues. The first is the meaning of moral terms, much as Moore discusses the meaning of "good." Moore contends that "good" refers to a non-natural property; others maintain that "good" is used to express attitudes of approval or to give subtle commands. The second main problem in metaethics concerns the nature of the justification of ethical claims or, as it is sometimes put, the logic of moral reasoning. Metaethicists attempt to display the canons of ethical reasoning in such fashion that one may be able to say when some ethical claim is warranted or justified. Utilitarianism *per se* is not involved in the discussion of the meanings of ethical terms but is quite evidently involved in the question of the justification of ethical claims. Some contemporary philosophers reject the search for true principles of normative ethics but do believe that reasons of a utilitarian sort can be used to justify ethical assertions. Thus, utilitarianism may be discussed from within either a normative or a metaethical framework.

In addition to the naturalistic fallacy, Mill's critics have claimed that his proof in Chapter IV also involves the elementary logical fallacy of composition: assuming that something which is true of the separate parts of a thing is likewise true of the whole.

In this case, Mill allegedly argues from the premise that each person, taken separately, desires his own happiness (psychological hedonism), to the conclusion that everyone desires the general happiness. So stated, the conclusion manifestly does not follow. Professor Hall's paper examines Mill's proof in detail and maintains that it commits neither the naturalistic fallacy nor the fallacy of composition. Professor Hall begins from Mill's repeated assertion that proof in the ordinary sense of the term is not possible for a first principle, since it is by reference to a first principle that everything else is demonstrated. He provides an account of Mill's procedure in the proof—which in the main applies to Bentham also—which in his opinion renders the discussion plausible. Numerous other studies of Mill's proof have been published and the interested reader should consult the bibliography for references. Part of the interest in Mill's proof has been historical, prompted by the conviction that Mill was unjustly criticized about this issue. However, the question of the manner in which one justifies an ethical first principle is at the foundation of moral philosophy, and the nature of such justification is a recurring issue in the following essays.

Criticism of utilitarianism commonly takes the form of attempts to show that its application leads to false conclusions about obligation; more specifically, utilitarianism is held to be incompatible with one or more aspects of the concept of justice. In its simplest and commonest form this criticism points out that it is usually just or right to keep one's promises or to tell the truth even in circumstances in which more net good could be accomplished by doing otherwise. If the utilitarian is concerned only with maximizing utility, then no specific obligation is incurred by the fact that one has, for instance, made a promise. It follows that promises should be kept only if doing so will serve utility but not otherwise, and this seems contrary to common moral opinion.

With regard to legal justice, utilitarianism confronts the classic problem of the punishment of the innocent. There are conceivable circumstances in which the framing and punishing of someone known to be innocent might prevent a great deal of harm, perhaps by pacifying an aroused citizenry and deterring possible offenders in the midst of a crime wave. The utilitarian seems committed to the position that in such circumstances punishment of the innocent would be justified, but this is rather clearly contrary to principles of justice which require the guilt of the offender as a necessary condition of punishment.

In addition, there is the question of the relationship of utility to principles of distributive or social justice. This can best be brought out by indicating a certain ambiguity in the utilitarian formula. The expression "the greatest happiness of the greatest number" can be taken in either of two ways. It might mean considering everyone's interests and doing what will bring about the most net good, the greatest happiness. Alternatively, it may be taken to mean that one should benefit the maximum number of persons. That is, the formula may require that one should do the *most good*, or that one should benefit the *most persons*. Depending on which version of the principle is adopted, different answers are obtained about what is to be done in certain moral situations. Let us consider an idealized case. Imagine that only one of two possible acts can be performed: if one act is done, five people will be greatly benefited, and two will be made extremely unhappy; if the second is performed, ten people will be made only slightly better off, and no one will be harmed. If it be supposed that the quantity of good produced by the first act is greater—even allowing for the unhappiness of two people—then on the first interpretation of the principle the first act should be done. The second act would be dictated by the alternative version of the principle. Utilitarianism has traditionally been interpreted in the first way, i.e., that the most good should be done, and this prompts the charge that the principle is not compatible with the requirements of justice or equity in the distribution of benefits. There do appear to be possible circumstances in which it would be deemed right to do a lesser good if it benefited more persons. Furthermore, maximizing utility by itself does not seem to require that benefits should be distributed according to merit or need, or that persons such as spouses, children, and parents deserve to receive certain benefits even if more good could be done were others to be the recipients.

These criticisms have been stated here in a highly oversimplified fashion, but the apparent force of arguments like these has been the basis of an attempt, which has been of great recent interest, to revise utilitarianism. To this point it has been assumed that the principle of utility is to be applied directly to the moral assessment of particular actions. This form of utilitarianism is now called *act* or *extreme* utilitarianism. The revised form is called *rule* or *restricted* utilitarianism, because the principle of utility is applied to the evaluation of moral rules or kinds of actions. In a pure rule utilitarianism, therefore, particular actions are not justified by their own individual utilities but rather by the worth of the rule under which they fall or the value of the kind of action they exemplify. The rule utilitarian thus sanctions particular actions which do not maximize utility if they are instances of moral rules or types of actions which are generally beneficial. In slightly different terms, the distinction is that the act utilitarian is concerned with the causal effect on the general welfare of the performance of a particular act at a particular time; the rule utilitarian is concerned with the hypothetical question of possible results of the general performance of a certain kind of action which a particular action exemplifies.

The rule utilitarian claims that his position avoids the kind of criticism brought against act utilitarianism. One should keep promises, even if in specific cases it would maximize welfare to do otherwise, because of the great value of the general adherence to the rules regarding promises. Nor should an innocent person be punished, even if it might be useful to do so at a certain time, because of the pernicious consequences which would result if such a practice were to become general. Rules requiring equality in distribution are best in the long run and so should be kept even at the expense of not maximizing utility in certain cases. In addition, the rule utilitarian points out that he has a solution to another long-standing criticism of utilitarianism: since one cannot know the results of his actions, which can be unexpected and long term, one cannot know in any case what he should do. While this is true in the case of particular acts, the rule utilitarian points out that we do certainly know the general consequences which follow upon the doing of certain kinds of actions.

Following Professor Hall's article, the remaining essays deal with the discussion of act and rule utilitarianism. Traditional accounts of Mill have assumed that he was an act utilitarian. Professor Urmson, however, maintains that Mill held a rule utilitarian position. In response, Professor Mabbott distinguishes the two theories somewhat more carefully and raises questions about the accuracy of the interpretation of Mill as a rule utilitarian.

Professor Brandt's discussion deals helpfully with a number of questions, while outlining what he regards as the most plausible form of the utilitarian theory. He proposes an *ideal* rule utilitarianism. The term "ideal" here indicates that the rules by which acts are to be evaluated need not actually exist. He also discusses the different forms which rule utilitarianism may take, as well as the objections which might be raised against these several versions.

Professor Rawls's well-known paper begins by stressing the importance of distinguishing between the justification of social practices, such as legal punishment or promising, and the justification of particular acts falling under these practices. Given this distinction, he points out certain important cases in which arguments of the act-utilitarian variety are inapplicable to the justification of particular acts. Regarding acts which are instances of social practices, it is incompatible with the existence of the practice for individuals to decide particular cases by direct appeal to the general welfare in the manner of act utilitarianism. As he puts it, the whole point of the practice is that one cannot "act in accordance with utilitarian and prudential considerations. . . ." This is by no means a complete rule-utilitarian position, but Professor Rawls has attempted to show the applicability of rule-utilitarian considerations to a range of cases which have historically played an important role in discussions of utilitarianism. His argument implies that rule-utilitarian considerations are relevant in the case of actually existing social practices and is thus distinguished from the position taken by Professor Brandt.

Criticism of rule utilitarianism is offered by Professor McCloskey and Professor Smart. Professor McCloskey argues from a deontological point of view that restricted or rule utilitarianism is no more adequate than act utilitarianism as a theory of obligation. His arguments are developed primarily with reference to Professor Rawls; but Professor Brandt's paper, which being more comprehensive has been placed first in this volume, can be seen as responding to criticisms of the sort Professor McCloskey raises. Professor Smart criticizes rule utilitarianism from the perspective of act utilitarianism. The basic issue he raises concerns adherence to a rule when more good could be done by breaking it. Professor Smart believes such adherence is pointless "rule worship" and, furthermore, he argues that it obscures the role of rules in the moral thinking of enlightened persons. Moral rules, after all, do have justifiable exceptions, and Professor Smart's view is that the act utilitarian presents a more adequate account of the nature and use of moral rules. For the act theory, rules are useful guides in knowing the likely consequences of certain acts, but such guides are only to be trusted when they are in fact pointing accurately.

The issues raised here are far from settled and are subjects of continuing refinement and discussion. There have been further attempts to answer the critics of act utilitarianism. There has been considerable interest in the reducibility of some forms of rule utilitarianism to act, a topic which receives only slight mention in these essays. There is also the suggestion that rule utilitarianism may run afoul of the principle of justice in a quite subtle way. Some goods can be achieved by a general but less than universal adherence to some rule or practice, and in such cases it does not maximize utility to require universal adherence. To take a simple example, suppose the good to be achieved is a beautiful lawn. This does not require that everyone stay off the grass all the time but merely that most people do most of the time. Universal conformity in this case results in a net loss of utility in that some persons could save time and otherwise be convenienced by being permitted to walk on the grass. Suppose that after granting the privilege of walking on the grass to those with handicaps or who have other good reasons, the lawn is still able to tolerate a substantial amount of walking without harm to its appearance. In this case considerations of utility dictate that there be exceptions to the practice, although considerations of justice or fairness would indicate that there be no exceptions. To permit exceptions is to make the privileged group "free loaders," enjoying the benefits of the practice without participating in it.[1] To pursue these and other more technical matters, the reader should consult the bibliography.

[1] David Lyons, *Forms and Limits of Utilitarianism*, Oxford, 1965.

Selections from
An Introduction to
the Principles of
Morals and Legislation

Jeremy Bentham

Chapter I

Of the Principle of Utility

1. Nature has placed mankind under the governance of two sovereign masters, *pain* and *pleasure*. It is for them alone to point out what we ought to do, as well as to determine what we shall do. On the one hand the standard of right and wrong, on the other the chain of causes and effects, are fastened to their throne. They govern us in all we do, in all we say, in all we think: every effort we can make to throw off our subjection, will serve but to demonstrate and confirm it. In words a man may pretend to abjure their empire: but in reality he will remain subject to it all the while. The *principle of utility* [1] recognises this subjection, and assumes it for

From Jeremy Bentham, *An Introduction to the Principles of Morals and Legislation,* London, 1789. Corrected edition, 1823.

[1] Note by the Author, July 1822.

To this denomination has of late been added, or substituted, the *greatest happiness* or *greatest felicity* principle: this for shortness, instead of saying at length *that principle* which states the greatest happiness of all those whose interest is in question, as being the right and proper, and only right and proper and universally desirable, end of human action: of human action in every situation, and in particular in that of a functionary or set of functionaries exercising the powers of Government. The word *utility* does not so clearly point to the ideas of *pleasure* and *pain* as the words *happiness* and *felicity* do: nor does it the foundation of that system, the object of which is to rear the fabric of felicity by the hands of reason and of law. Systems which attempt to question it, deal in sounds instead of senses, in caprice instead of reason, in darkness instead of light.

But enough of metaphor and declamation: it is not by such means that moral science is to be improved.

2. The principle of utility is the foundation of the present work: it will be proper therefore at the outset to give an explicit and determinate account of what is meant by it. By the principle [2] of utility is meant that principle which approves or disapproves of every action whatsoever, according to the tendency which it appears to have to augment or diminish the happiness of the party whose interest is in question: or, what is the same thing in other words, to promote or to oppose that happiness. I say of every action whatsoever; and therefore not only of every action of a private individual, but of every measure of government.

3. By utility is meant that property in any object, whereby it tends to produce benefit, advantage, pleasure, good, or happiness, (all this in the present case comes to the same thing) or (what comes again to the same thing) to prevent the happening of mischief, pain, evil, or unhappiness to the party whose interest is considered: if that party be the community in general, then the happiness of

---

lead us to the consideration of the *number,* of the interests affected; to the *number,* as being the circumstance, which contributes, in the largest proportion, to the formation of the standard here in question; the *standard of right and wrong,* by which alone the propriety of human conduct, in every situation, can with propriety be tried. This want of a sufficiently manifest connexion between the ideas of *happiness* and *pleasure* on the one hand, and the idea of *utility* on the other, I have every now and then found operating, and with but too much efficiency, as a bar to the acceptance, that might otherwise have been given, to this principle.

[2] The word principle is derived from the Latin principium: which seems to be compounded of the two words *primus,* first, or chief, and *cipium,* a termination which seems to be derived from *capio,* to take, as in *mancipium, municipium;* to which are analogous, *aucepts, forceps,* and others. It is a term of very vague and very extensive signification: it is applied to any thing which is conceived to serve as a foundation or beginning to any series of operations: in some cases, of physical operations; but of mental operations in the present case.

The principle here in question may be taken for an act of the mind; a sentiment; a sentiment of approbation; a sentiment which, when applied to an action, approves of its utility, as that quality of it by which the measure of approbation or disapprobation bestowed upon it ought to be governed.

the community: if a particular individual, then the happiness of that individual.

4. The interest of the community is one of the most general expressions that can occur in the phraseology of morals: no wonder that the meaning of it is often lost. When it has a meaning, it is this. The community is a fictitious *body,* composed of the individual persons who are considered as constituting as it were its *members.* The interest of the community then is, what?—the sum of the interests of the several members who compose it.

5. It is in vain to talk of the interest of the community, without understanding what is the interest of the individual.[3] A thing is said to promote the interest, or to be *for* the interest, of an individual, when it tends to add to the sum total of his pleasures: or, what comes to the same thing, to diminish the sum total of his pains.

6. An action then may be said to be conformable to the principle of utility, or, for shortness sake, to utility, (meaning with respect to the community at large) when the tendency it has to augment the happiness of the community is greater than any it has to diminish it.

7. A measure of government (which is but a particular kind of action, performed by a particular person or persons) may be said to be conformable to or dictated by the principle of utility, when in like manner the tendency which it has to augment the happiness of the community is greater than any which it has to diminish it.

8. When an action, or in particular a measure of government, is supposed by a man to be conformable to the principle of utility, it may be convenient, for the purposes of discourse, to imagine a kind of law or dictate, called a law or dictate of utility; and to speak of the action in question, as being conformable to such law or dictate.

9. A man may be said to be a partisan of the principle of utility, when the approbation or disapprobation he annexes to any action, or to any measure, is determined by and proportioned to the tendency which he conceives it to have to augment or to diminish the happiness of the community: or in other words, to its conformity or uncomformity to the laws or dictates of utility.

3 Interest is one of those words, which not having any superior *genus,* cannot in the ordinary way be defined.

10. Of an action that is conformable to the principle of utility one may always say either that it is one that ought to be done, or at least that it is not one that ought not to be done. One may say also, that it is right it should be done; at least that it is not wrong it should be done: that it is a right action; at least that it is not a wrong action. When thus interpreted, the words *ought,* and *right* and *wrong,* and others of that stamp, have a meaning: when otherwise, they have none.

11. Has the rectitude of this principle been ever formally contested? It should seem that it had, by those who have not known what they have been meaning. Is it susceptible of any direct proof? it should seem not: for that which is used to prove every thing else, cannot itself be proved: a chain of proofs must have their commencement somewhere. To give such proof is as impossible as it is needless.

12. Not that there is or ever has been that human creature breathing, however stupid or perverse, who has not on many, perhaps on most occasions of his life, deferred to it. By the natural constitution of the human frame, on most occasions of their lives men in general embrace this principle, without thinking of it: if not for the ordering of their own actions, yet for the trying of their own actions, as well as of those of other men. There have been, at the same time, not many, perhaps, even of the most intelligent, who have been disposed to embrace it purely and without reserve. There are even few who have not taken some occasion or other to quarrel with it, either on account of their not understanding always how to apply it, or on account of some prejudice or other which they were afraid to examine into, or could not bear to part with. For such is the stuff that man is made of: in principle and in practice, in a right track and in a wrong one, the rarest of all human qualities is consistency.

13. When a man attempts to combat the principle of utility, it is with reasons drawn, without his being aware of it, from that very principle itself.[4] His arguments, if they prove any thing, prove not that the principle is *wrong,* but that, according to the applica-

---

4 'The principle of utility, (I have heard it said) is a dangerous principle: it is dangerous on certain occasions to consult it.' This is as much as to say, what? that it is not consonant to utility, to consult utility: in short, that it is *not* consulting it, to consult it.

tions he supposes to be made of it, it is *misapplied*. Is it possible for a man to move the earth? Yes; but he must first find out another earth to stand upon.

14. To disprove the propriety of it by arguments is impossible; but, from the causes that have been mentioned, or from some confused or partial view of it, a man may happen to be disposed not to relish it. Where this is the case, if he thinks the settling of his opinions on such a subject worth the trouble, let him take the following steps and at length, perhaps, he may come to reconcile himself to it.

a.   Let him settle with himself, whether he would wish to discard this principle altogether; if so, let him consider what it is that all his reasonings (in matters of politics especially) can amount to?

b.   If he would, let him settle with himself, whether he would judge and act without any principle, or whether there is any other he would judge and act by?

c.   If there be, let him examine and satisfy himself whether the principle he thinks he has found is really any separate intelligible principle; or whether it be not a mere principle in words, a kind of phrase, which at bottom expresses neither more nor less than the mere averment of his own unfounded sentiments; that is, what in another person he might be apt to call caprice?

d.   If he is inclined to think that his own approbation or disapprobation, annexed to the idea of an act, without any regard to its consequences, is a sufficient foundation for him to judge and act upon, let him ask himself whether his sentiment is to be a standard of right and wrong, with respect to every other man, or whether every man's sentiment has the same privilege of being a standard to itself?

e.   In the first case, let him ask himself whether his principle is not despotical, and hostile to all the rest of human race?

f.   In the second case, whether it is not anarchical, and whether at this rate there are not as many different standards of right and wrong as there are men? and whether even to the sane man, the same thing, which is right today, may not (without the least change in its nature) be wrong tomorrow? and whether the same thing is not right and wrong in the same place at the same time? and in either case, whether all argument is not at an end? and whether, when two men have said, 'I like this,' and 'I don't like it,' they can (upon such a principle) have any thing more to say?

g.   If he should have said to himself, No: for that the sentiment which he proposes as a standard must be grounded on reflection, let him say on what particulars the reflection is to turn? if on particulars having relation to the utility of the act, then let him say whether this is not deserting his own principle, and borrowing assistance from that very one in opposition to which he sets it up: or if not on those particulars, on what other particulars?

h.   If he should be for compounding the matter, and adopting his own principle in part, and the principle of utility in part, let him say how far he will adopt it?

i.   When he has settled with himself where he will stop, then let him ask himself how he justifies to himself the adopting it so far? and why he will not adopt it any farther?

j.   Admitting any other principle than the principle of utility to be a right principle, a principle that it is right for a man to pursue; admitting (what is not true) that the word *right* can have a meaning without reference to utility, let him say whether there is any such thing as a *motive* that a man can have to pursue the dictates of it: if there is, let him say what that motive is, and how it is to be distinguished from those which enforce the dictates of utility: if not, then lastly let him say what it is this other principle can be good for?

Chapter II

Of Principles Adverse to That of Utility

1. If the principle of utility be a right principle to be governed by, and that in all cases, it follows from what has been just observed, that whatever principle differs from it in any case must necessarily be a wrong one. To prove any other principle, therefore, to be a wrong one, there needs no more than just to show it to be what it is, a principle of which the dictates are in some point or other different from those of the principle of utility: to state it is to confute it.

2. A principle may be different from that of utility in two ways: (*a*) By being constantly opposed to it: this is the case with a principle which may be termed the principle of *asceticism*.[1] (*b*) By being sometimes opposed to it, and sometimes not, as it may happen: this is the case with another, which may be termed the principle of *sympathy* and *antipathy*.

3. By the principle of asceticism I mean that principle, which, like the principle of utility, approves or disapproves of any action, according to the tendency which it appears to have to augment or diminish the happiness of the party whose interest is in question; but in the inverse manner: approving of actions in as far as they tend to diminish his happiness; disapproving of them in as far as they tend to augment it.

4. It is evident that any one who reprobates any the least particle of pleasure, as such, from whatever source derived, is *pro tanto* a partisan of the principle of asceticism. It is only upon that principle, and not from the principle of utility, that the most abominable pleasure which the vilest of malefactors ever reaped from his crime would be reprobated, if it stood alone. The case is, that it never does stand alone; but is necessarily followed by such a quantity of pain (or, what comes to the same thing, such a chance for a certain quantity of pain) that the pleasure in comparison of it, is as nothing: and this is the true and sole, but perfectly sufficient, reason for making it a ground for punishment.

---

[1] Ascetic is a term that has been sometimes applied to Monks. It comes from a Greek word which signifies *exercise*. The practices by which Monks sought to distinguish themselves from other men were called their Exercises. These exercises consisted in so many contrivances they had for tormenting themselves. By this they thought to ingratiate themselves with the Deity. For the Deity, said they, is a Being of infinite benevolence: now a Being of the most ordinary benevolence is pleased to see others make themselves as happy as they can: therefore to make ourselves as unhappy as we can is the way to please the Deity. If any body asked them, what motive they could find for doing all this? Oh! said they, you are not to imagine that we are punishing ourselves for nothing: we know very well what we are about. You are to know, that for every grain of pain it costs us now, we are to have a hundred grains of pleasure by and by. The case is, that God loves to see us torment ourselves at present: indeed he has as good as told us so. But this is done only to try us, in order just to see how we should behave: which it is plain he could not know, without making the experiment. Now, then, from the satisfaction it gives him to see us make ourselves as unhappy as we can make ourselves in this present life, we have a sure proof of the satisfaction it will give him to see us as happy as he can make us in a life to come.

5. There are two classes of men of very different complexions, by whom the principle of asceticism appears to have been embraced; the one a set of moralists, the other a set of religionists. Different accordingly have been the motives which appear to have recommended it to the notice of these different parties. Hope, that is the prospect of pleasure, seems to have animated the former: hope, the aliment of philosophic pride: the hope of honour and reputation at the hands of men. Fear, that is the prospect of pain, the latter: fear the offspring of superstitious fancy: the fear of future punishment at the hands of a splenetic and revengeful Deity. I say in this case fear: for of the invisible future, fear is more powerful than hope. These circumstances characterise the two different parties among the partisans of the principle of asceticism; the parties and their motives different, the principle the same.

6. The religious party, however, appear to have carried it farther than the philosophical: they have acted more consistently and less wisely. The philosophical party have scarcely gone farther than to reprobate pleasure: the religious party have frequently gone so far as to make it a matter of merit and of duty to court pain. The philosophical party have hardly gone farther than the making pain a matter of indifference. It is no evil, they have said: they have not said, it is a good. They have not so much as reprobated all pleasure in the lump. They have discarded only what they have called the gross; that is, such as are organical, or of which the origin is easily traced up to such as are organical: they have even cherished and magnified the refined. Yet this, however, not under the name of pleasure: to cleanse itself from the sordes of its impure original, it was necessary it should change its name: the honourable, the glorious, the reputable, the becoming, the *honestum,* the *decorum,* it was to be called: in short, any thing but pleasure.

7. From these two sources have flowed the doctrines from which the sentiments of the bulk of mankind have all along received a tincture of this principle; some from the philosophical, some from the religious, some from both. Men of education more frequently from the philosophical, as more suited to the elevation of their sentiments: the vulgar more frequently from the superstitious, as more suited to the narrowness of their intellect, undilated by knowledge: and to the abjectness of their condition, continually open to the attacks of fear. The tinctures, however, derived from the two

sources, would naturally intermingle, insomuch that a man would not always know by which of them he was most influenced: and they would often serve to corroborate and enliven one another. It was this conformity that made a kind of alliance between parties of a complexion otherwise so dissimilar: and disposed them to unite upon various occasions against the common enemy, the partisan of the principle of utility, whom they joined in branding with the odious name of Epicurean.

8. The principle of asceticism, however, with whatever warmth it may have been embraced by its partisans as a rule of private conduct, seems not to have been carried to any considerable length, when applied to the business of government. In a few instances it has been carried a little way by the philosophical party: witness the Spartan regimen. Though then, perhaps, it may be considered as having been a measure of security: and an application, though a precipitate and perverse application, of the principle of utility. Scarcely in any instances, to any considerable length, by the religious: for the various monastic orders, and the societies of the Quakers, Dumplers, Moravians, and other religionists, have been free societies, whose regimen no man has been astricted to without the intervention of his own consent. Whatever merit a man may have thought there would be in making himself miserable, no such notion seems ever to have occurred to any of them, that it may be a merit, much less a duty, to make others miserable: although it should seem, that if a certain quantity of misery were a thing so desirable, it would not matter much whether it were brought by each man upon himself, or by one man upon another. It is true, that from the same source from whence, among the religionists, the attachment to the principle of asceticism took its rise, flowed other doctrines and practices, from which misery in abundance was produced in one man by the instrumentality of another: witness the holy wars, and the persecutions for religion. But the passion for producing misery in these cases proceeded upon some special ground: the exercise of it was confined to persons of particular descriptions: they were tormented, not as men, but as heretics and infidels. To have inflicted the same miseries on their fellow-believers and fellow-sectaries, would have been as blameable in the eyes even of these religionists, as in those of a partisan of the principle of utility. For a man to give himself a certain number of stripes was indeed meritorious: but to give the

same number of stripes to another man, not consenting, would
have been a sin. We read of saints, who for the good of their souls,
and the mortification of their bodies, have voluntarily yielded themselves a prey to vermin: but though many persons of this class have
wielded the reins of empire, we read of none who have set themselves to work, and made laws on purpose, with a view of stocking
the body politic with the breed of highwaymen, housebreakers, or
incendiaries. If at any time they have suffered the nation to be
preyed upon by swarms of idle pensioners, or useless placemen, it
has rather been from negligence and imbecility, than from any
settled plan for oppressing and plundering of the people. If at any
time they have sapped the sources of national wealth, by cramping
commerce, and driving the inhabitants into emigration, it has been
with other views, and in pursuit of other ends. If they have de-
claimed against the pursuit of pleasure, and the use of wealth, they
have commonly stopped at declamation: they have not, like Lycur-
gus, made express ordinances for the purpose of banishing the
precious metals. If they have established idleness by a law, it has
been not because idleness, the mother of vice and misery, is itself
a virtue, but because idleness (say they) is the road to holiness. If
under the notion of fasting, they have joined in the plan of con-
fining their subjects to a diet, thought by some to be of the most
nourishing and prolific nature, it has been not for the sake of
making them tributaries to the nations by whom that diet was to
be supplied, but for the sake of manifesting their own power, and
exercising the obedience of the people. If they have established,
or suffered to be established, punishments for the breach of celi-
bacy, they have done no more than comply with the petitions of
those deluded rigorists, who, dupes to the ambitious and deep-laid
policy of their rulers, first laid themselves under that idle obligation
by a vow.

9. The principle of asceticism seems originally to have been
the reverie of certain hasty speculators, who having perceived, or
fancied, that certain pleasures, when reaped in certain circumstances, have, at the long run, been attended with pains more than
equivalent to them, took occasion to quarrel with every thing that
offered itself under the name of pleasure. Having then got thus
far, and having forgot the point which they set out from, they
pushed on, and went so much further as to think it meritorious to

fall in love with pain. Even this, we see, is at bottom but the principle of utility misapplied.

10. The principle of utility is capable of being consistently pursued; and it is but tautology to say, that the more consistently it is pursued, the better it must ever be for humankind. The principle of asceticism never was, nor ever can be, consistently pursued by any living creature. Let but one tenth part of the inhabitants of this earth pursue it consistently, and in a day's time they will have turned it into a hell.

11. Among principles adverse to that of utility, that which at this day seems to have most influence in matters of government, is what may be called the principle of sympathy and antipathy. By the principle of sympathy and antipathy, I mean that principle which approves or disapproves of certain actions, not on account of their tending to augment the happiness, nor yet on account of their tending to diminish the happiness of the party whose interest is in question, but merely because a man finds himself disposed to approve or disapprove of them: holding up that approbation or disapprobation as a sufficient reason for itself, and disclaiming the necessity of looking out for any extrinsic ground. Thus far in the general department of morals: and in the particular department of politics, measuring out the quantum (as well as determining the ground) of punishment, by the degree of the disapprobation.

12. It is manifest, that this is rather a principle in name than in reality: it is not a positive principle of itself, so much as a term employed to signify the negation of all principle. What one expects to find in a principle is something that points out some external consideration, as a means of warranting and guiding the internal sentiments of approbation and disapprobation: this expectation is but ill fulfilled by a proposition, which does neither more nor less than hold up each of those sentiments as a ground and standard for itself.

13. In looking over the catalogue of human actions (says a partisan of this principle) in order to determine which of them are to be marked with the seal of disapprobation, you need but to take counsel of your own feelings: whatever you find in yourself a propensity to condemn, is wrong for that very reason. For the same reason it is also meet for punishment: in what proportion it is adverse to utility, or whether it be adverse to utility at all, is a

matter that makes no difference. In that same *proportion* also is
it meet for punishment: if you hate much, punish much: if you
hate little, punish little: punish as you hate. If you hate not at all,
punish not at all: the fine feelings of the soul are not to be over-
borne and tyrannised by the harsh and rugged dictates of political
utility.

14. The various systems that have been formed concerning
the standard of right and wrong, may all be reduced to the principle of sympathy and antipathy. One account may serve for all of
them. They consist all of them in so many contrivances for avoiding the obligation of appealing to any external standard, and for
prevailing upon the reader to accept of the author's sentiment or
opinion as a reason for itself. The phrase is different, but the principle the same.[2]

[2] It is curious enough to observe the variety of inventions men have hit
upon, and the variety of phrases they have brought forward, in order to conceal
from the world, and, if possible, from themselves, this very general and therefore
very pardonable self-sufficiency.

a. One man says, he has a thing made on purpose to tell him what is
right and what is wrong; and that it is called a *moral sense:* and then he goes
to work at his ease, and says, such a thing is right, and such a thing is wrong—
why? 'because my moral sense tells me it is.'

b. Another man comes and alters the phrase: leaving out *moral,* and
putting in *common,* in the room of it. He then tells you, that his common sense
teaches him what is right and wrong, as surely as the other's moral sense did:
meaning by common sense, a sense of some kind or other, which, he says, is
possessed by all mankind: the sense of those, whose sense is not the same as the
author's, being struck out of the account as not worth taking. This contrivance
does better than the other; for a moral sense, being a new thing, a man may
feel about him a good while without being able to find it out: but common
sense is as old as the creation; and there is no man but would be ashamed to be
thought not to have as much of it as his neighbours. It has another great advantage: by appearing to share power, it lessens envy: for when a man gets up
upon this ground, in order to anathematise those who differ from him, it is not
by a *sic volo sic jubeo,* but by a *velitis jubeatis.*

c. Another man comes, and says, that as to a moral sense indeed, he cannot find that he has any such thing: that however he has an *understanding,*
which will do quite as well. This understanding, he says, is the standard of
right and wrong: it tells him so and so. All good and wise men understand as
he does: if other men's understandings differ in any point from his, so much the
worse for them: it is a sure sign they are either defective or corrupt.

d. Another man says, that there is an eternal and immutable Rule of
Right: that the rule of right dictates so and so: and then he begins giving you his
sentiments upon any thing that comes uppermost: and these sentiments (you
are to take for granted) are so many branches of the eternal rule of right.

e. Another man, or perhaps the same man (it's no matter) says, that there

15. It is manifest, that the dictates of this principle will frequently coincide with those of utility, though perhaps without intending any such thing. Probably more frequently than not: and hence it is that the business of penal justice is carried on upon

---

are certain practices conformable, and others repugnant, to the Fitness of Things; and then he tells you, at his leisure, what practices are conformable and what repugnant: just as he happens to like a practice or dislike it.

f. A great multitude of people are continually talking of the Law of Nature; and then they go on giving you their sentiments about what is right and what is wrong: and these sentiments, you are to understand, as so many chapters and sections of the Law of Nature.

g. Instead of the phrase, Law of Nature, you have sometimes, Law of Reason, Right Reason, Natural Justice, Natural Equity, Good Order. Any of them will do equally well. This latter is most used in politics. The three last are much more tolerable than the others, because they do not very explicitly claim to be any thing more than phrases: they insist but feebly upon the being looked upon as so many positive standards of themselves, and seem content to be taken, upon occasion, for phrases expressive of the conformity of the thing in question to the proper standard, whatever that may be. On most occasions, however, it will be better to say *utility: utility* is clearer, as referring more explicitly to pain and pleasure.

h. We have one philosopher, who says, there is no harm in any thing in the world but in telling a lie: and that if, for example, you were to murder your own father, this would only be a particular way of saying, he was not your father. Of course, when this philosopher sees any thing that he does not like, he says, it is a particular way of telling a lie. It is saying, that the act ought to be done, or may be done, when, *in truth,* it ought not to be done.

i. The fairest and openest of them all is that sort of man who speaks out, and says, I am of the number of the Elect: now God himself takes care to inform the Elect what is right: and that with so good effect, and let them strive ever so, they cannot help not only knowing it but practising it. If therefore a man wants to know what is right and what is wrong, he has nothing to do but to come to me.

It is upon the principle of antipathy that such and such acts are often reprobated on the score of their being *unnatural:* the practice of exposing children, established among the Greeks and Romans, was an unnatural practice. Unnatural, when it means any thing, means unfrequent: and there it means something; although nothing to the present purpose. But here it means no such thing: for the frequency of such acts is perhaps the great complaint. It therefore means nothing; nothing, I mean which there is in the act itself. All it can serve to express is, the disposition of the person who is talking of it; the disposition he is in to be angry at the thoughts of it. Does it merit his anger? Very likely it may: but whether it does or no is a question, which, to be answered rightly, can only be answered upon the principle of utility.

Unnatural, is as good a word as moral sense, or common sense; and would be as good a foundation for a system. Such an act is unnatural; that is, repugnant to nature: for I do not like to practise it: and, consequently, do not practise it. It is therefore repugnant to what ought to be the nature of everybody else.

The mischief common to all these ways of thinking and arguing (which,

that tolerable sort of footing upon which we see it carried on in
common at this day. For what more natural or more general ground
of hatred to a practice can there be, than the mischievousness of
such practice? What all men are exposed to suffer by, all men will
be disposed to hate. It is far yet, however, from being a constant

---

in truth, as we have seen, are but one and the same method, couched in different
forms of words) is their serving as a cloke, and pretence, and aliment, to
despotism: if not a despotism in practice, a despotism however in disposition:
which is but too apt, when pretence and power offer, to show itself in practice.
The consequence is, that with intentions very commonly of the purest kind, a
man becomes a torment either to himself or his fellow-creatures. If he be of the
melancholy cast, he sits in silent grief, bewailing their blindness and depravity:
if of the irascible, he declaims with fury and virulence against all who differ
from him; blowing up the coals of fanaticism, and branding with the charge of
corruption and insincerity, every man who does not think, or profess to think,
as he does.

    If such a man happens to possess the advantages of style, his book may do
a considerable deal of mischief before the nothingness of it is understood.

    These principles, if such they can be called, it is more frequent to see
applied to morals than to politics: but their influence extends itself to both. In
politics, as well as morals, a man will be at least equally glad of a pretence for
deciding any question in the manner that best pleases him, without the trouble
of inquiry. If a man is an infallible judge of what is right and wrong in the
actions of private individuals, why not in the measures to be observed by public
men in the direction of those actions? accordingly (not to mention other
chimeras) I have more than once known the pretended law of nature set up in
legislative debates, in opposition to arguments derived from the principle of
utility.

    'But is it never, then, from any other considerations than those of utility,
that we derive our notions of right and wrong?' I do not know: I do not care.
Whether a moral sentiment can be originally conceived from any other source
than a view of utility, is one question: whether upon examination and reflection it can, in point of fact, be actually persisted in and justified on any other
ground, by a person reflecting within himself, is another: whether in point of
right it can properly be justified on any other ground, by a person addressing
himself to the community, is a third. The two first are questions of speculation:
it matters not, comparatively speaking, how they are decided. The last is a question of practice: the decision of it is of as much importance as that of any
can be.

    'I feel in myself,' (say you) 'a disposition to approve of such or such an
action in a moral view: but this is not owing to any notions I have of its being
a useful one to the community. I do not pretend to know whether it be an useful
one or not: it may be, for aught I know, a mischievous one.' 'But is it then,' (say
I) 'a mischievous one? examine; and if you can make yourself sensible that it is
so, then if duty means any thing, that is, moral duty, it is your *duty* at least
to abstain from it: and more than that, if it is what lies in your power, and can
be done without too great a sacrifice, to endeavour to prevent it. It is not your
cherishing the notion of it in your bosom, and giving it the name of virtue, that
will excuse you.'

    'I feel in myself,' (say you again) 'a disposition to detest such or such an
action in a moral view; but this is not owing to any notions I have of its being

ground: for when a man suffers, it is not always that he knows what it is he suffers by. A man may suffer grievously, for instance, by a new tax, without being able to trace up the cause of his sufferings to the injustice of some neighbour, who has eluded the payment of an old one.

16. The principle of sympathy and antipathy is most apt to err on the side of severity. It is for applying punishment in many cases which deserve none: in many cases which deserve some, it is for applying more than they deserve. There is no incident imaginable, be it ever so trivial, and so remote from mischief, from which this principle may not extract a ground of punishment. Any difference in taste: any difference in opinion: upon one subject as well as upon another. No disagreement so trifling which perseverance and altercation will not render serious. Each becomes in the other's eyes an enemy, and if laws permit, a criminal. This is one of the circumstances by which the human race is distinguished (not much indeed to its advantage) from the brute creation.

17. It is not, however, by any means unexampled for this principle to err on the side of lenity. A near and perceptible mischief moves antipathy. A remote and imperceptible mischief, though not less real, has no effect. Instances in proof of this will occur in numbers in the course of the work. It would be breaking in upon the order of it to give them here.

18. It may be wondered, perhaps, that in all this while no mention has been made of the *theological* principle; meaning that principle which professes to recur for the standard of right and

---

a mischievous one to the community. I do not pretend to know whether it be a mischievous one or not: it may be not a mischievous one: it may be, for aught I know, an useful one.'—'May it indeed,' (say I) 'an useful one? but let me tell you then, that unless duty, and right and wrong, be just what you please to make them, if it really be not a mischievous one, and any body has a mind to do it, it is no duty of yours, but, on the contrary, it would be very wrong in you, to take upon you to prevent him: detest it within yourself as much as you please; that it may be a very good reason (unless it be also a useful one) for your not doing it yourself: but if you go about, by word or deed, to do any thing to hinder him, or make him suffer for it, it is you, and not he, that have done wrong; it is not your setting yourself to blame his conduct, or branding it with the name of vice, that will make him culpable, or you blameless. Therefore, if you can make yourself content that he shall be of one mind, and you of another, about this matter, and so continue, it is well: but if nothing will serve you, but that you and he must needs be of the same mind, I'll tell you what you have to do: it is for you to get the better of your antipathy, not for him to truckle to it.'

wrong to the will of God. But the case is, this is not in fact a distinct principle. It is never any thing more or less than one or other of the three before-mentioned principles presenting itself under another shape. The *will* of God here meant cannot be his revealed will, as contained in the sacred writings: for that is a system which nobody ever thinks of recurring to at this time of day, for the details of political administration: and even before it can be applied to the details of private conduct, it is universally allowed, by the most eminent divines of all persuasions, to stand in need of pretty ample interpretations; else to what use are the works of those divines? And for the guidance of these interpretations, it is also allowed, that some other standard must be assumed. The will then which is meant on this occasion, is that which may be called the *presumptive* will: that is to say, that which is presumed to be his will on account of the conformity of its dictates to those of some other principle. What then may be this other principle? it must be one or other of the three mentioned above: for there cannot, as we have seen, be any more. It is plain, therefore, that setting revelation out of the question, no light can ever be thrown upon the standard of right and wrong, by any thing that can be said upon the question, what is God's will. We may be perfectly sure, indeed, that whatever is right is conformable to the will of God: but so far is that from answering the purpose of showing us what is right, that it is necessary to know first whether a thing is right in order to know from thence whether it be conformable to the will of God.[3]

_____ [3] The principle of theology refers every thing to God's pleasure. But what is God's pleasure? God does not, he confessedly does not now, either speak or write to us. How then are we to know what is his pleasure? By observing what is our own pleasure, and pronouncing it to be his. Accordingly what is called the pleasure of God, is and must necessarily be (revelation apart) neither more nor less than the good pleasure of the person, whoever he be, who is pronouncing what he believes, or pretends, to be God's pleasure. How know you it to be God's pleasure that such or such an act should be abstained from? whence come you even to suppose as much? 'Because the engaging in it would, I imagine, be prejudicial upon the whole to the happiness of mankind;' says the partisan of the principle of utility: 'Because the commission of it is attended with a gross and sensual, or at least with a trifling and transient satisfaction;' says the partisan of the principle of asceticism: 'Because I detest the thought of it; and I cannot, neither ought I to be called upon to tell why;' says he who proceeds upon the principle of antipathy. In the words of one or other of these must that person necessarily answer (revelation apart) who professes to take for his standard the will of God.

19. There are two things which are very apt to be con-founded, but which it imports us carefully to distinguish:—the motive or cause, which, by operating on the mind of an individual, is productive of any act: and the ground or reason which warrants a legislator, or other by-stander, in regarding that act with an eye of approbation. When the act happens, in the particular instance in question, to be productive of effects which we approve of, much more if we happen to observe that the same motive may frequently be productive, in other instances, of the like effects, we are apt to transfer our approbation to the motive itself, and to assume, as the just ground for the approbation we bestow on the act, the circumstance of its originating from that motive. It is in this way that the sentiment of antipathy has often been considered as a just ground of action. Antipathy, for instance, in such or such a case, is the cause of an action which is intended with good effects: but this does not make it a right ground of action in that case, any more than in any other. Still farther. Not only the effects are good, but the agent sees beforehand that they will be so. This may make the action indeed a perfectly right action: but it does not make antipathy a right ground of action. For the same sentiment of antipathy, if implicitly deferred to, may be, and very frequently is, productive of the very worst effects. Antipathy, therefore, can never be a right ground of action. No more, therefore, can resentment, which, as will be seen more particularly hereafter, is but a modi-fication of antipathy. The only right ground of action, that can possibly subsist, is, after all, the consideration of utility, which if it is a right principle of action, and of approbation, in any one case, is so in every other. Other principles in abundance, that is, other motives, may be the reasons why such and such an act *has* been done: that is, the reasons or causes of its being done: but it is this alone than can be the reason why it might or ought to have been done. Antipathy or resentment requires always to be regu-lated, to prevent its doing mischief: to be regulated by what? always by the principle of utility. The principle of utility neither requires nor admits of any other regulator than itself.

Chapter III

Of the Four Sanctions or Sources of Pain and Pleasure

1. It has been shown that the happiness of the individuals, of whom a community is composed, that is their pleasures and their security, is the end and the sole end which the legislator ought to have in view: the sole standard, in conformity to which each individual ought, as far as depends upon the legislator, to be *made* to fashion his behaviour. But whether it be this or any thing else that is to be *done,* there is nothing by which a man can ultimately be *made* to do it, but either pain or pleasure. Having taken a general view of these two grand objects (*viz.,* pleasure, and what comes to the same thing, immunity from pain) in the character of *final* causes; it will be necessary to take a view of pleasure and pain itself, in the character of *efficient* causes or means.

2. There are four distinguishable sources from which pleasure and pain are in use to flow: considered separately, they may be termed the *physical,* the *political,* the *moral,* and the *religious:* and inasmuch as the pleasures and pains belonging to each of them are capable of giving a binding force to any law or rule of conduct, they may all of them be termed *sanctions.*[1]

---

[1] Sanctio, in Latin, was used to signify the *act of binding,* and, by a common grammatical transition, *any thing which serves to bind a man:* to wit, to the observance of such or such a mode of conduct. According to a Latin grammarian,[a] the import of the word is derived by rather a far-fetched process (such as those commonly are, and in a great measure indeed must be, by which intellectual ideas are derived from sensible ones) from the word *sanguis,* blood: because, among the Romans, with a view to inculcate into the people a persuasion that such or such a mode of conduct would be rendered obligatory upon a man by the force of which I call the religious sanction (that is, that he would be made to suffer by the extraordinary interposition of some superior being, if he failed to observe the mode of conduct in question) certain ceremonies were contrived by the priests: in the course of which ceremonies the blood of victims was made use of.

A Sanction then is a source of obligatory powers or *motives:* that is, of *pains* and *pleasures;* which, according as they are connected with such or such modes of conduct, operate, and are indeed the only things which can operate, as *motives.*

[a] Servius. See Ainsworth's Dict. ad verbum *Sanctio.*

3. If it be in the present life, and from the ordinary course of nature, not purposely modified by the interposition of the will of any human being, nor by any extraordinary interposition of any superior invisible being, that the pleasure or the pain takes place or is expected, it may be said to issue from or to belong to the *physical sanction.*

4. If at the hands of a *particular* person or set of persons in the community, who under names correspondent to that of *judge,* are chosen for the particular purpose of dispensing it, according to the will of the sovereign or supreme ruling power in the state, it may be said to issue from the *political sanction.*

5. If at the hands of such *chance* persons in the community, as the party in question may happen in the course of his life to have concerns with, according to each man's spontaneous disposition, and not according to any settled or concerted rule, it may be said to issue from the *moral* or *popular sanction.*[2]

6. If from the immediate hand of a superior invisible being, either in the present life, or in a future, it may be said to issue from the *religious sanction.*

7. Pleasures or pains which may be expected to issue from the *physical, political,* or *moral* sanctions, must all of them be expected to be experienced, if ever, in the *present* life: those which may be expected to issue from the *religious* sanction, may be expected to be experienced either in the *present* life or in a *future.*

8. Those which can be experienced in the present life, can of course be no others than such as human nature in the course of the present life is susceptible of: and from each of these sources may flow all the pleasures or pains of which, in the course of the present life, human nature is susceptible. With regard to these then (with which alone we have in this place any concern) those of them which belong to any one of those sanctions, differ not ultimately in kind from those which belong to any one of the other three: the only difference there is among them lies in the circumstances that

[2] Better termed *popular,* as more directly indicative of its constituent cause; as likewise of its relation to the more common phrase *public opinion,* in French *opinion publique,* the name there given to that tutelary power, of which of late so much is said, and by which so much is done. The latter appellation is however unhappy and inexpressive; since if *opinion* is material, it is only in virtue of the influence it exercises over action, through the medium of the affections and the will.

accompany their production. A suffering which befalls a man in the natural and spontaneous course of things, shall be styled, for instance, a *calamity;* in which case, if it be supposed to befall him through any imprudence of his, it may be styled a punishment issuing from the physical sanction. Now this same suffering, if inflicted by the law, will be what is commonly called a *punishment;* if incurred for want of any friendly assistance, which the misconduct, or supposed misconduct, of the sufferer has occasioned to be withholden, a punishment issuing from the *moral* sanction; if through the immediate interposition of a particular providence, a punishment issuing from the religious sanction.

9. A man's goods, or his person, are consumed by fire. If this happened to him by what is called an accident, it was a calamity: if by reason of his own imprudence (for instance, from his neglecting to put his candle out) it may be styled a punishment of the physical sanction: if it happened to him by the sentence of the political magistrate, a punishment belonging to the political sanction; that is, what is commonly called a punishment: if for want of any assistance which his *neighbour* withheld from him out of some dislike to his *moral* character, a punishment of the *moral* sanction: if by an immediate act of *God's* displeasure, manifested on account of some *sin* committed by him, or through any distraction of mind, occasioned by the dread of such displeasure, a punishment of the *religious* sanction.[3]

10. As to such of the pleasures and pains belonging to the religious sanction, as regard a future life, of what kind these may be we cannot know. These lie not open to our observation. During the present life they are matter only of expectation: and, whether that expectation be derived from natural or revealed religion, the particular kind of pleasure or pain, if it be different from all those which lie open to our observation, is what we can have no idea of. The best ideas we can obtain of such pains and pleasures are altogether unliquidated in point of quality. In what other respects our ideas of them *may* be liquidated will be considered in another place.

---

[3] A suffering conceived to befall a man by the immediate act of God, as above, is often, for shortness' sake, called a *judgment:* instead of saying, a suffering inflicted on him in consequence of a special judgment formed, and resolution thereupon taken, by the Deity.

11. Of these four sanctions the physical is altogether, we may observe, the ground-work of the political and the moral: so is it also of the religious, in as far as the latter bears relation to the present life. It is included in each of those other three. This may operate in any case, (that is, any of the pains or pleasures belonging to it may operate) independently of *them:* none of *them* can operate but by means of this. In a word, the powers of nature may operate of themselves; but neither the magistrate, nor men at large, *can* operate, nor is God in the case in question *supposed* to operate, but through the powers of nature.

12. For these four objects, which in their nature have so much in common, it seemed of use to find a common name. It seemed of use, in the first place, for the convenience of giving a name to certain pleasures and pains, for which a name equally characteristic could hardly otherwise have been found: in the second place, for the sake of holding up the efficacy of certain moral forces, the influence of which is apt not to be sufficiently attended to. Does the political sanction exert an influence over the conduct of mankind? The moral, the religious sanctions do so too. In every inch of his career are the operations of the political magistrate liable to be aided or impeded by these two foreign powers: who, one or other of them, or both, are sure to be either his rivals or his allies. Does it happen to him to leave them out of his calculations? he will be sure almost to find himself mistaken in the result. Of all this we shall find abundant proofs in the sequel of this work. It behooves him, therefore, to have them continually before his eyes; and that under such a name as exhibits the relation they bear to his own purposes and designs.

Chapter IV

Value of a Lot of Pleasure or Pain, How to be Measured

1. Pleasures then, and the avoidance of pains, are the *ends* which the legislator has in view: it behoves him therefore to understand their *value*. Pleasures and pains are the *instruments* he has to work with: it behoves him therefore to understand their force, which is again, in other words, their value.

2. To a person considered *by himself,* the value of a pleasure or pain considered *by itself,* will be greater or less, according to the four following circumstances: [1]

a. Its *intensity.*

b. Its *duration.*

c. Its *certainty* or *uncertainty.*

d. Its *propinquity* or *remoteness.*

3. These are the circumstances which are to be considered in estimating a pleasure or a pain considered each of them by itself. But when the value of any pleasure or pain is considered for the purpose of estimating the tendency of any *act* by which it is produced, there are two other circumstances to be taken into account; these are,

e. Its *fecundity,* or the chance it has of being followed by sensations of the *same* kind: that is, pleasures, if it be a pleasure: pains, if it be a pain.

f. Its *purity,* or the chance it has of *not* being followed by sensations of the *opposite* kind: that is, pains, if it be a pleasure: pleasures, if it be a pain.

These two last, however, are in strictness scarcely to be deemed properties of the pleasure or the pain itself; they are not, therefore, in strictness to be taken into the account of the value of that pleasure or that pain. They are in strictness to be deemed properties only of the act, or other event, by which such pleasure or pain has been produced; and accordingly are only to be taken into the account of the tendency of such act or such event.

4. To a *number* of persons, with reference to each of whom the value of a pleasure or a pain is considered, it will be greater or less, according to seven circumstances: to wit, the six preceding ones; *viz.*

[1] These circumstances have since been denominated *elements* or *dimensions* of *value* in a pleasure or a pain.

Not long after the publication of the first edition, the following memoriter verses were framed, in the view of lodging more effectually, in the memory, these points, on which the whole fabric of morals and legislation may be seen to rest.

Intense, long, certain, speedy, fruitful, pure—
Such marks in *pleasures* and in *pains* endure.
Such pleasures seek if *private* be thy end:
If it be *public,* wide let them *extend.*
Such *pains* avoid, whichever be thy view:
If pains *must* come, let them *extend* to few.

a.   Its *intensity.*
b.   Its *duration.*
c.   Its *certainty* or *uncertainty.*
d.   Its *propinquity* or *remoteness.*
e.   Its *fecundity.*
f.   Its *purity.*
        And one other; to wit:
g.   Its *extent;* that is, the number of persons to whom it *extends;* or (in other words) who are affected by it.
        5. To take an exact account then of the general tendency of any act, by which the interests of a community are affected, proceed as follows. Begin with any one person of those whose interests seem most immediately to be affected by it: and take an account,
a.   Of the value of each distinguishable *pleasure* which appears to be produced by it in the *first* instance.
b.   Of the value of each *pain* which appears to be produced by it in the *first* instance.
c.   Of the value of each pleasure which appears to be produced by it *after* the first. This constitutes the *fecundity* of the first *pleasure* and the *impurity* of the first *pain.*
d.   Of the value of each *pain* which appears to be produced by it after the first. This constitutes the *fecundity* of the first *pain,* and the *impurity* of the first pleasure.
e.   Sum up all the values of all the *pleasures* on the one side, and those of all the pains on the other. The balance, if it be on the side of pleasure, will give the *good* tendency of the act upon the whole, with respect to the interests of that *individual* person; if on the side of pain, the *bad* tendency of it upon the whole.
f.   Take an account of the *number* of persons whose interests appear to be concerned; and repeat the above process with respect to each. *Sum up* the numbers expressive of the degrees of *good* tendency, which the act has, with respect to each individual, in regard to whom the tendency of it is *good* upon the whole: do this again with respect to each individual, in regard to whom the tendency of it is *bad* upon the whole. Take the *balance;* which, if on the side of *pleasure,* will give the general *good tendency* of the act, with respect to the total number or community of individuals concerned; if on the

side of pain, the general *evil tendency,* with respect to the same community.

6. It is not to be expected that this process should be strictly pursued previously to every moral judgment, or to every legislative or judicial operation. It may, however, be always kept in view: and as near as the process actually pursued on these occasions approaches to it, so near will such process approach to the character of an exact one.

7. The same process is alike applicable to pleasure and pain, in whatever shape they appear: and by whatever denomination they are distinguished: to pleasure, whether it be called *good* (which is properly the cause or instrument of pleasure) or *profit* (which is distant pleasure, or the cause or instrument of distant pleasure,) or *convenience,* or *advantage, benefit, emolument, happiness,* and so forth: to pain, whether it be called *evil,* (which corresponds to *good*) or *mischief,* or *inconvenience,* or *disadvantage,* or *loss, or unhappiness,* and so forth.

8. Nor is this a novel and unwarranted, any more than it is a useless theory. In all this there is nothing but what the practice of mankind, wheresoever they have a clear view of their own interest, is perfectly conformable to. An article of property, an estate in land, for instance, is valuable, on what account? On account of the pleasures of all kinds which it enables a man to produce, and what comes to the same thing the pains of all kinds which it enables him to avert. But the value of such an article of property is universally understood to rise or fall according to the length or shortness of the time which a man has in it: the certainty or uncertainty of its coming into possession: and the nearness or remoteness of the time at which, if at all, it is to come into possession. As to the *intensity* of the pleasures which a man may derive from it, this is never thought of, because it depends upon the use which each particular person may come to make of it; which cannot be estimated till the particular pleasures he may come to derive from it, or the particular pains he may come to exclude by means of it, are brought to view. For the same reason, neither does he think of the *fecundity* or *purity* of those pleasures.

Thus much for pleasure and pain, happiness and unhappiness, in *general.*

Utilitarianism

J. S. Mill

Chapter I

General Remarks

There are few circumstances among those which make up
the present condition of human knowledge more unlike what
might have been expected, or more significant of the backward
state in which speculation on the most important subjects still
lingers, than the little progress which has been made in the decision
of the controversy respecting the criterion of right and wrong.
From the dawn of philosophy, the question concerning the *summum bonum,* or, what is the same thing, concerning the foundation of morality, has been accounted the main problem in specu-
lative thought, has occupied the most gifted intellects and divided
them into sects and schools carrying on a vigorous warfare against
one another. And after more than two thousand years the same
discussions continue, philosophers are still ranged under the same
contending banners, and neither thinkers nor mankind at large
seem nearer to being unanimous on the subject than when the
youth Socrates listened to the old Protagoras and asserted (if Plato's
dialogue be grounded on a real conversation) the theory of utilitarianism against the popular morality of the so-called sophist.

It is true that similar confusion and uncertainty and, in some
cases, similar discordance exist respecting the first principles of all
the sciences, not excepting that which is deemed the most certain
of them—mathematics, without much impairing, generally indeed
without impairing at all, the trustworthiness of the conclusions of

J. S. Mill, *Utilitarianism,* London, 1863. First published 1861.

those sciences. An apparent anomaly, the explanation of which is that the detailed doctrines of a science are not usually deduced from, nor depend for their evidence upon, what are called its first principles. Were it not so, there would be no science more precarious, or whose conclusions were more insufficiently made out, than algebra, which derives none of its certainty from what are commonly taught to learners as its elements, since these, as laid down by some of its most eminent teachers, are as full of fictions as English law, and of mysteries as theology. The truths which are ultimately accepted as the first principles of a science are really the last results of metaphysical analysis practiced on the elementary notions with which the science is conversant; and their relation to the science is not that of foundations to an edifice, but of roots to a tree, which may perform their office equally well though they be never dug down to and exposed to light. But though in science the particular truths precede the general theory, the contrary might be expected to be the case with a practical art, such as morals or legislation. All action is for the sake of some end, and rules of action, it seems natural to suppose, must take their whole character and color from the end to which they are subservient. When we engage in a pursuit, a clear and precise conception of what we are pursuing would seem to be the first thing we need, instead of the last we are to look forward to. A test of right and wrong must be the means, one would think, of ascertaining what is right or wrong, and not a consequence of having already ascertained it.

The difficulty is not avoided by having recourse to the popular theory of a natural faculty, a sense of instinct, informing us of right and wrong. For—besides that the existence of such a moral instinct is itself one of the matters in dispute—those believers in it who have any pretensions to philosophy have been obliged to abandon the idea that it discerns what is right or wrong in the particular case in hand, as our other senses discern the sight or sound actually present. Our moral faculty, according to all those of its interpreters who are entitled to the name of thinkers, supplies us only with the general principles of moral judgments; it is a branch of our reason, not of our sensitive faculty, and must be looked to for the abstract doctrines of morality, not for perception of it in the concrete. The intuitive, no less than what may be termed the inductive, school of ethics insists on the necessity of general laws. They both agree that the morality of an individual action is not a question of direct perception, but of the application of a law to an individual case. They recognize also, to a great extent, the same moral laws, but differ as to their evidence and the source from which they derive their authority. According to the one opinion, the principles of morals are evident *a priori,* requiring nothing to command assent except that the meaning of the terms be understood. According to the other doctrine, right and wrong, as well as truth and falsehood, are questions of observation and experience. But both hold equally that morality must be deduced from principles, and the intuitive school affirm as strongly as the inductive that there is a science of morals. Yet they seldom attempt to make out a list of the *a priori* principles which are to serve as the premises of the science; still more rarely do they make any effort to reduce those various principles to one first principle or common ground of obligation. They either assume the ordinary precepts of morals as of *a priori* authority, or they lay down as the common groundwork of those maxims some generality much less obviously authoritative than the maxims themselves, and which has never succeeded in gaining popular acceptance. Yet to support their pretensions there ought either to be some one fundamental principle or law at the root of all morality, or, if there be several, there should be a determinate order of precedence among them; and the one principle, or the rule for deciding between the various principles when they conflict, ought to be self-evident.

To inquire how far the bad effects of this deficiency have been mitigated in practice, or to what extent the moral beliefs of mankind have been vitiated or made uncertain by the absence of any distinct recognition of an ultimate standard, would imply a complete survey and criticism of past and present ethical doctrine. It would, however, be easy to show that whatever steadiness or consistency these moral beliefs have attained has been mainly due to the tacit influence of a standard not recognized. Although the nonexistence of an acknowledged first principle has made ethics not so much a guide as a consecration of men's actual sentiments, still, as men's sentiments, both of favor and of aversion, are greatly influenced by what they suppose to be the effects of things upon their happiness, the principle of utility, or, as Bentham latterly called it, the greatest happiness principle, has had a large share in forming the moral doctrines even of those who most scornfully reject its authority. Nor is there any school of thought which refuses to admit that the influence of actions on happiness is a most material and even predominant consideration in many of the details of morals, however unwilling to acknowledge it as the fundamental principle of morality and the source of moral obligation. I might go much further and say that to all those *a priori* moralists who deem it necessary to argue at all, utilitarian arguments are indispensable. It is not my present purpose to criticize these thinkers; but I cannot help referring, for illustration, to a systematic treatise by one of the most illustrious of them, the *Metaphysics of Ethics* by Kant. This remarkable man, whose system of thought will long remain one of the landmarks in the history of philosophical speculation, does, in the treatise in question, lay down a universal first principle as the origin and ground of moral obligation; it is this: "So act that the rule on which thou actest would admit of being adopted as a law by all rational beings." But when he begins to deduce from this precept any of the actual duties of morality, he fails, almost grotesquely, to show that there would be any contradiction, any logical (not to say physical) impossibility, in the adoption by all rational beings of the most outrageously immoral rules of conduct. All he shows is that the *consequences* of their universal adoption would be such as no one would choose to incur.

On the present occasion, I shall, without further discussion of the other theories, attempt to contribute something toward the understanding and appreciation of the "utilitarian" or "happiness" theory, and toward such proof as it is susceptible of. It is evident that this cannot be proof in the ordinary and popular meaning of the term. Questions of ultimate ends are not amenable to direct proof. Whatever can be proved to be good must be so by being shown to be a means to something admitted to be good without proof. The medical art is proved to be good by its conducing to health; but how is it possible to prove that health is good? The art of music is good, for the reason, among others, that it produces pleasure; but what proof is it possible to give that pleasure is good? If, then, it is asserted that there is a comprehensive formula, including all things which are in themselves good, and that whatever else is good is not so as an end but as a means, the formula may be accepted or rejected, but is not a subject of what is commonly understood by proof. We are not, however, to infer that its acceptance or rejection must depend on blind impulse or arbitrary choice. There is a larger meaning of the word "proof," in which this question is as amenable to it as any other of the disputed questions of philosophy. The subject is within the cognizance of the rational faculty; and neither does that faculty deal with it solely in the way of intuition. Considerations may be presented capable of determining the intellect either to give or withhold its assent to the doctrine; and this is equivalent to proof.

We shall examine presently of what nature are these considerations; in what manner they apply to the case, and what rational grounds, therefore, can be given for accepting or rejecting the utilitarian formula. But it is a preliminary condition of rational acceptance or rejection that the formula should be correctly understood. I believe that the very imperfect notion ordinarily formed of its meaning is the chief obstacle which impedes its reception, and that, could it be cleared even from only the grosser misconceptions, the question would be greatly simplified and a large proportion of its difficulties removed. Before, therefore, I attempt to enter into the philosophical grounds which can be given for assenting to the utilitarian standard, I shall offer some illustrations of the doctrine itself, with the view of showing more clearly what it is, distinguishing it from what it is not, and disposing of such of the practical objections to it as either originate in, or are closely connected with, mistaken interpretations of its meaning. Having thus prepared the ground, I shall afterwards endeavor to throw such light as I can call upon the question considered as one of philosophical theory.

Chapter II
What Utilitarianism Is

A passing remark is all that needs be given to the ignorant blunder of supposing that those who stand up for utility as the test of right and wrong use the term in that restricted and merely colloquial sense in which utility is opposed to pleasure. An apology is due to the philosophical opponents of utilitarianism for even the momentary appearance of confounding them with anyone capable of so absurd a misconception; which is the more extraordinary, inasmuch as the contrary accusation, of referring everything to pleasure, and that, too, in its grossest form, is another of the common charges against utilitarianism: and, as has been pointedly remarked by an able writer, the same sort of persons, and often the very same persons, denounce the theory "as impracticably dry when the word 'utility' precedes the word 'pleasure,' and as too practicably voluptuous when the word 'pleasure' precedes the word 'utility.' " Those who know anything about the matter are aware that every writer, from Epicurus to Bentham, who maintained the theory of utility meant by it, not something to be contradistinguished from pleasure, but pleasure itself, together with exemption from pain; and instead of opposing the useful to the agreeable or the ornamental, have always declared that the useful means these, among other things. Yet the common herd, including the herd of writers, not only in newspapers and periodicals, but in books of weight and pretension, are perpetually falling into this shallow mistake. Having caught up the word "utilitarian," while knowing nothing whatever about it but its sound, they habitually express by it the rejection or the neglect of pleasure in some of its forms: of beauty, of ornament, or of amusement. Nor is the term thus ignorantly misapplied solely in disparagement, but occasionally in compliment, as though it implied superiority to frivolity and the mere pleasures of the moment. And this perverted use is the only one in which the word is popularly known, and the one from which the new generation are acquiring their sole notion of its meaning. Those who introduced the word, but who had for many years discontinued it as a distinctive appellation, may well feel themselves called upon to resume it if by doing so they can hope to contribute anything toward rescuing it from this utter degradation.[1]

The creed which accepts as the foundation of morals "utility" or the "greatest happiness principle" holds that actions are right

[1] The author of this essay has reason for believing himself to be the first person who brought the word "utilitarian" into use. He did not invent it, but adopted it from a passing expression in Mr. Galt's *Annals of the Parish*. After using it as a designation for several years, he and others abandoned it from a growing dislike to anything resembling a badge or watchword of sectarian distinction. But as a name for one single opinion, not a set of opinions—to denote the recognition of utility as a standard, not any particular way of applying it—the term supplies a want in the language, and offers, in many cases, a convenient mode of avoiding tiresome circumlocution.

in proportion as they tend to promote happiness; wrong as they tend to produce the reverse of happiness. By happiness is intended pleasure and the absence of pain; by unhappiness, pain and the privation of pleasure. To give a clear view of the moral standard set up by the theory, much more requires to be said; in particular, what things it includes in the ideas of pain and pleasure, and to what extent this is left an open question. But these supplementary explanations do not affect the theory of life on which this theory of morality is grounded—namely, that pleasure and freedom from pain are the only things desirable as ends; and that all desirable things (which are as numerous in the utilitarian as in any other scheme) are desirable either for pleasure inherent in themselves or as means to the promotion of pleasure and the prevention of pain.

Now such a theory of life excites in many minds, and among them in some of the most estimable in feeling and purpose, inveterate dislike. To suppose that life has (as they express it) no higher end than pleasure—no better and nobler object of desire and pursuit—they designate as utterly mean and groveling, as a doctrine worthy only of swine, to whom the followers of Epicurus were, at a very early period, contemptuously likened; and modern holders of the doctrine are occasionally made the subject of equally polite comparisons by its German, French, and English assailants.

When thus attacked, the Epicureans have always answered that it is not they, but their accusers, who represent human nature in a degrading light, since the accusation supposes human beings to be capable of no pleasures except those of which swine are capable. If this supposition were true, the charge could not be gainsaid, but would then be no longer an imputation; for if the sources of pleasure were precisely the same to human beings and to swine, the rule of life which is good enough for the one would be good enough for the other. The comparison of the Epicurean life to that of beasts is felt as degrading, precisely because a beast's pleasures do not satisfy a human being's conceptions of happiness. Human beings have faculties more elevated than the animal appetites and, when once made conscious of them, do not regard anything as happiness which does not include their gratification. I do not, indeed, consider the Epicureans to have been by any means faultless in drawing out their scheme of consequences from the utilitarian principle. To do this in any sufficient manner, many

Stoic, as well as Christian, elements require to be included. But there is no known Epicurean theory of life which does not assign to the pleasures of the intellect, of the feelings and imagination, and of the moral sentiments a much higher value as pleasures than to those of mere sensation. It must be admitted, however, that utilitarian writers in general have placed the superiority of mental over bodily pleasures chiefly in the greater permanency, safety, uncostliness, etc., of the former—that is, in their circumstantial advantages rather than in their intrinsic nature. And on all these points utilitarians have fully proved their case; but they might have taken the other and, as it may be called, higher ground with entire consistency. It is quite compatible with the principle of utility to recognize the fact that some kinds of pleasure are more desirable and more valuable than others. It would be absurd that, while in estimating all other things quality is considered as well as quantity, the estimation of pleasure should be supposed to depend on quantity alone.

If I am asked what I mean by difference of quality in pleasures, or what makes one pleasure more valuable than another, merely as a pleasure, except its being greater in amount, there is but one possible answer. Of two pleasures, if there be one to which all or almost all who have experience of both give a decided preference, irrespective of any feeling of moral obligation to prefer it, that is the more desirable pleasure. If one of the two is, by those who are competently acquainted with both, placed so far above the other that they prefer it, even though knowing it to be attended with a greater amount of discontent, and would not resign it for any quantity of the other pleasure which their nature is capable of, we are justified in ascribing to the preferred enjoyment a superiority in quality so far outweighing quantity as to render it, in comparison, of small account.

Now it is an unquestionable fact that those who are equally acquainted with and equally capable of appreciating and enjoying both do give a most marked preference to the manner of existence which employs their higher faculties. Few human creatures would consent to be changed into any of the lower animals for a promise of the fullest allowance of a beast's pleasures; no intelligent human being would consent to be a fool, no instructed person would be an ignoramus, no person of feeling and conscience would be selfish and base, even though they should be persuaded that the fool, the dunce, or the rascal is better satisfied with his lot than they are with theirs. They would not resign what they possess more than he for the most complete satisfaction of all the desires which they have in common with him. If they ever fancy they would, it is only in cases of unhappiness so extreme that to escape from it they would exchange their lot for almost any other, however undesirable in their own eyes. A being of higher faculties requires more to make him happy, is capable probably of more acute suffering, and certainly accessible to it at more points, than one of an inferior type; but in spite of these liabilities, he can never really wish to sink into what he feels to be a lower grade of existence. We may give what explanation we please of this unwillingness; we may attribute it to pride, a name which is given indiscriminately to some of the most and to some of the least estimable feelings of which mankind are capable; we may refer it to the love of liberty and personal independence, an appeal to which was with the Stoics one of the most effective means for the inculcation of it; to the love of power or to the love of excitement, both of which do really enter into and contribute to it; but its most appropriate appellation is a sense of dignity, which all human beings possess in one form or other, and in some, though by no means in exact, proportion to their higher faculties, and which is so essential a part of the happiness of those in whom it is strong that nothing which conflicts with it could be otherwise than momentarily an object of desire to them. Whoever supposes that this preference takes place at a sacrifice of happiness—that the superior being, in anything like equal circumstances, is not happier than the inferior—confounds the two very different ideas of happiness and content. It is indisputable that the being whose capacities of enjoyment are low has the greatest chance of having them fully satisfied; and a highly endowed being will always feel that any happiness which he can look for, as the world is constituted, is imperfect. But he can learn to bear its imperfections, if they are at all bearable; and they will not make him envy the being who is indeed unconscious of the imperfections, but only because he feels not at all the good which those imperfections qualify. It is better to be a human being dissatisfied than a pig satisfied; better to be Socrates dissatisfied than a fool satisfied. And if the fool, or the pig, are of a different opinion, it is because they only know their own side of the question. The other party to the comparison knows both sides.

It may be objected that many who are capable of the higher pleasures occasionally, under the influence of temptation, postpone them to the lower. But this is quite compatible with a full appreciation of the intrinsic superiority of the higher. Men often, from infirmity of character, make their election for the nearer good, though they know it to be the less valuable; and this no less when the choice is between two bodily pleasures than when it is between bodily and mental. They pursue sensual indulgences to the injury of health, though perfectly aware that health is the greater good. It may be further objected that many who begin with youthful enthusiasm for everything noble, as they advance in years, sink into indolence and selfishness. But I do not believe that those who undergo this very common change voluntarily choose the lower description of pleasures in preference to the higher. I believe that, before they devote themselves exclusively to the one, they have already become incapable of the other. Capacity for the nobler feelings is in most natures a very tender plant, easily killed, not only by hostile influences, but by mere want of sustenance; and in the majority of young persons it speedily dies away if the occupations to which their position in life has devoted them, and the society into which it has thrown them, are not favorable to keeping that higher capacity in exercise. Men lose their high aspirations as they lose their intellectual tastes, because they have not time or opportunity for indulging them; and they addict themselves to inferior pleasures, not because they deliberately prefer them, but because they are either the only ones to which they have access or the only ones which they are any longer capable of enjoying. It may be questioned whether anyone who has remained equally susceptible to both classes of pleasures ever knowingly and calmly preferred the lower, though many, in all ages, have broken down in an ineffectual attempt to combine both.

From this verdict of the only competent judges, I apprehend there can be no appeal. On a question which is the best worth having of two pleasures, or which of two modes of existence is the most grateful to the feelings, apart from its moral attributes and from its consequences, the judgment of those who are qualified by knowledge of both, or, if they differ, that of the majority among them, must be admitted as final. And there needs be the less hesitation to accept this judgment respecting the quality of pleasures, since there is no other tribunal to be referred to even on the question of quantity. What means are there of determining which is the acutest of two pains, or the intensest of two pleasurable sensations, except the general suffrage of those who are familiar with both? Neither pains nor pleasures are homogeneous, and pain is always heterogeneous with pleasure. What is there to decide whether a particular pleasure is worth purchasing at the cost of a particular pain, except the feelings and judgment of the experienced? When, therefore, those feelings and judgment declare the pleasures derived from the higher faculties to be preferable *in kind,* apart from the question of intensity, to those of which the animal nature, disjoined from the higher faculties, is susceptible, they are entitled on this subject to the same regard.

I have dwelt on this point as being a necessary part of a perfectly just conception of utility or happiness considered as the directive rule of human conduct. But it is by no means an indispensable condition to the acceptance of the utilitarian standard; for that standard is not the agent's own greatest happiness, but the greatest amount of happiness altogether; and if it may possibly be doubted whether a noble character is always the happier for its nobleness, there can be no doubt that it makes other people happier, and that the world in general is immensely a gainer by it. Utilitarianism, therefore, could only attain its end by the general cultivation of nobleness of character, even if each individual were only benefited by the nobleness of others, and his own, so far as happiness is concerned, were a sheer deduction from the benefit. But the bare enunciation of such an absurdity as this last renders refutation superfluous.

According to the greatest happiness principle, as above explained, the ultimate end, with reference to and for the sake of which all other things are desirable—whether we are considering our own good or that of other people—is an existence exempt as far as possible from pain, and as rich as possible in enjoyments, both in point of quantity and quality; the test of quality and the rule for measuring it against quantity being the preference felt by those who, in their opportunities of experience, to which must be added their habits of self-consciousness and self-observation, are best furnished with the means of comparison. This, being according to the utilitarian opinion the end of human action, is necessarily also the standard of morality, which may accordingly be defined "the rules and precepts for human conduct," by the observance of which an existence such as has been described might be, to the greatest extent possible, secured to all mankind; and not to them only, but, so far as the nature of things admits, to the whole sentient creation.

Against this doctrine, however, arises another class of objectors who say that happiness, in any form, cannot be the rational purpose of human life and action; because, in the first place, it is unattainable; and they contemptuously ask, What right hast thou to be happy?—a question which Mr. Carlyle clinches by the addition, What right, a short time ago, hadst thou even *to be?* Next they say that men can do *without* happiness; that all noble human beings have felt this, and could not have become noble but by learning the lesson of *Entsagen,* or renunciation; which lesson, thoroughly learned and submitted to, they affirm to be the beginning and necessary condition of all virtue.

The first of these objections would go to the root of the matter were it well founded; for if no happiness is to be had at all by human beings, the attainment of it cannot be the end of morality or of any rational conduct. Though, even in that case, something might still be said for the utilitarian theory, since utility includes not solely the pursuit of happiness, but the prevention or mitigation of unhappiness; and if the former aim be chimerical, there will be all the greater scope and more imperative need for the latter, so long at least as mankind think fit to live and do not take refuge in the simultaneous act of suicide recommended under certain conditions by Novalis. When, however, it is thus positively asserted to be impossible that human life should be happy, the assertion, if not something like a verbal quibble, is at least an exaggeration. If by happiness be meant a continuity of highly pleasurable excitement, it is evident enough that this is impossible. A state of exalted pleasure lasts only moments or in some cases, and with some intermissions, hours or days, and is the occasional brilliant flash of enjoyment, not its permanent and steady flame. Of this the philosophers who have taught that happiness is the end of life were as fully aware as those who taunt them. The happiness which they meant was not a life of rapture, but moments of such, in an existence made up of few and transitory pains, many and various pleasures, with a decided predominance of the active over the passive, and having as the foundation of the whole not to expect more from life than it is capable of bestowing. A life thus composed, to those who have been fortunate enough to obtain it, has always appeared worthy of the name of happiness. And such an existence is even now the lot of many during some considerable portion of their lives. The present wretched education and wretched social arrangements are the only real hindrance to its being attainable by almost all.

The objectors perhaps may doubt whether human beings, if taught to consider happiness as the end of life, would be satisfied with such a moderate share of it. But great numbers of mankind have been satisfied with much less. The main constituents of a satisfied life appear to be two, either of which by itself is often found sufficient for the purpose: tranquillity and excitement. With much tranquillity, many find that they can be content with very little pleasure; with much excitement, many can reconcile themselves to a considerable quantity of pain. There is assuredly no inherent impossibility of enabling even the mass of mankind to unite both, since the two are so far from being incompatible that they are in natural alliance, the prolongation of either being a preparation for, and exciting a wish for, the other. It is only those in whom indolence amounts to a vice that do not desire excitement after an interval of repose; it is only those in whom the need of excitement is a disease that feel the tranquillity which follows excitement dull and insipid, instead of pleasurable in direct proportion to the excitement which preceded it. When people who are tolerably fortunate in their outward lot do not find in life sufficient enjoyment to make it valuable to them, the cause generally is caring for nobody but themselves. To those who have neither public nor private affections, the excitements of life are much curtailed, and in any case dwindle in value as the time approaches when all selfish interests must be terminated by death; while those who leave after them objects of personal affection, and especially those who have also cultivated a fellow-feeling with the collective interests of mankind, retain as lively an interest in life on the eve of death as in the vigor of youth and health. Next to selfishness, the principal cause which makes life unsatisfactory is want of mental cultivation. A cultivated mind—I do not mean that of a philosopher, but any mind to which the fountains of knowledge have been opened, and which has been taught, in any tolerable degree, to exercise its faculties—finds sources of inexhaustible interest in all that surrounds it: in the objects of nature, the achievements of art, the imaginations of poetry, the incidents of history, the ways of mankind, past and present, and their prospects in the future. It is possible, indeed, to become indifferent to all this, and that too without having exhausted a thousandth part of it, but only when one has had from the beginning no moral or human interest in these things and has sought in them only the gratification of curiosity.

Now there is absolutely no reason in the nature of things why an amount of mental culture sufficient to give an intelligent interest in these objects of contemplation should not be the inheritance of everyone born in a civilized country. As little is there an inherent necessity that any human being should be a selfish egotist, devoid of every feeling or care but those which center in his own miserable individuality. Something far superior to this is sufficiently common even now, to give ample earnest of what the human species may be made. Genuine private affections and a sincere interest in the public good are possible, though in unequal degrees, to every rightly brought up human being. In a world in which there is so much to interest, so much to enjoy, and so much also to correct and improve, everyone who has this moderate amount of moral and intellectual requisites is capable of an existence which may be called enviable; and unless such a person, through bad laws or subjection to the will of others, is denied the liberty to use the sources of happiness within his reach, he will not fail to find this enviable existence, if he escape the positive evils of life, the great sources of physical and mental suffering—such as indigence, disease, and the unkindness, worthlessness, or premature loss of objects of affection. The main stress of the problem lies, therefore, in the contest with these calamities from which it is a rare good fortune entirely to escape; which, as things now are, cannot be obviated, and often cannot be in any material degree mitigated. Yet no one whose opinion deserves a moment's consideration can doubt that most of the great positive evils of the world are in themselves removable, and will, if human affairs continue to improve, be in the end reduced within narrow limits. Poverty, in any sense implying suffering, may be completely extinguished by the wisdom of society combined with the good sense and providence of individuals. Even that most intractable of enemies, disease, may be indefinitely reduced in dimensions of good physical and moral education and proper control of noxious influences, while the progress of science holds out a promise for the future of still more direct conquests over this detestable foe. And every advance in that direction relieves us from some, not only of the chances which cut short our own lives, but, what concerns us still more, which deprive us of those in whom our happiness is wrapt up. As for vicissitudes of fortune and other disappointments connected with worldly circumstances, these are principally the effect either of gross imprudence, of ill-regulated desires, or of bad or imperfect social institutions. All the grand sources, in short, of human suffering are in a great degree, many of them almost entirely, conquerable by human care and effort; and though their removal is grievously slow—though a long succession of generations will perish in the breach before the conquest is completed, and this world becomes all that, if will and knowledge were not wanting, it might easily be made—yet every mind sufficiently intelligent and generous to bear a part, however small and inconspicuous, in the endeavor will draw a noble enjoyment from the contest itself, which he would not for any bribe in the form of selfish indulgence consent to be without.

And this leads to the true estimation of what is said by the objectors concerning the possibility and the obligation of learning to do without happiness. Unquestionably it is possible to do without happiness; it is done involuntarily by nineteen-twentieths of mankind, even in those parts of our present world which are least deep in barbarism; and it often has to be done voluntarily by the hero or the martyr, for the sake of something which he prizes more than his individual happiness. But this something, what is it, unless the happiness of others or some of the requisites of happiness? It is noble to be capable of resigning entirely one's own portion of happiness, or chances of it; but, after all, this self-sacrifice must be for some end; it is not its own end; and if we are told that its end is not happiness but virtue, which is better than happiness, I ask, would the sacrifice be made if the hero or martyr did not believe that it would earn for others immunity from similar sacrifices? Would it be made if he thought that his renunciation of happiness for himself would produce no fruit for any of his fellow creatures, but to make their lot like his and place them also in the condition of persons who have renounced happiness? All honor to those who can abnegate for themselves the personal enjoyment of life when by such renunciation they contribute worthily to increase the amount of happiness in the world; but he who does it or professes to do it for any other purpose is no more deserving of admiration than the ascetic mounted on his pillar. He may be an inspiriting proof of what men *can* do, but assuredly not an example of what they *should.*

Though it is only in a very imperfect state of the world's arrangements that anyone can best serve the happiness of others by the absolute sacrifice of his own, yet, so long as the world is in that imperfect state, I fully acknowledge that the readiness to make such a sacrifice is the highest virtue which can be found in man. I will add that in this condition of the world, paradoxical as the assertion may be, the conscious ability to do without happiness gives the best prospect of realizing such happiness as is attainable. For nothing except that consciousness can raise a person above the chances of life by making him feel that, let fate and fortune do their worst, they have not power to subdue him; which, once felt, frees him from excess of anxiety concerning the evils of life and enables him, like many a Stoic in the worst times of the Roman Empire, to cultivate in tranquillity the sources of satisfaction accessible to him, without concerning himself about the uncertainty of their duration any more than about their inevitable end.

Meanwhile, let utilitarians never cease to claim the morality of self-devotion as a possession which belongs by as good a right to them as either to the Stoic or to the Transcendentalist. The utilitarian morality does recognize in human beings the power of sacrificing their own greatest good for the good of others. It only refuses to admit that the sacrifice is itself a good. A sacrifice which does not increase or tend to increase the sum total of happiness, it considers as wasted. The only self-renunciation which it applauds is devotion to the happiness, or to some of the means of happiness, of others, either of mankind collectively or of individuals within the limits imposed by the collective interests of mankind.

I must again repeat what the assailants of utilitarianism seldom have the justice to aknowledge, that the happiness which forms the utilitarian standard of what is right in conduct is not the agent's own happiness but that of all concerned. As between his own happiness and that of others, utilitarianism requires him to be as strictly impartial as a disinterested and benevolent spectator. In the golden rule of Jesus of Nazareth, we read the complete spirit of the ethics of utility. "To do as you would be done by," and "to love your neighbor as yourself," constitute the ideal perfection of utilitarian morality. As the means of making the nearest approach to this ideal, utility would enjoin, first, that laws and social arrangements should place the happiness or (as, speaking practically, it may be called) the interest of every individual as nearly as possible in harmony with the interest of the whole; and, secondly, that education and opinion, which have so vast a power over human character, should so use that power as to establish in the mind of every individual an indissoluble association between his own happiness and the good of the whole, especially between his own happiness and the practice of such modes of conduct, negative and positive, as regard for the universal happiness prescribes; so that not only he may be unable to conceive the possibility of happiness to himself, consistently with conduct opposed to the general good, but also that a direct impulse to promote the general good may be in every individual one of the habitual motives of action, and the sentiments connected therewith may fill a large and prominent place in every human being's sentient existence. If the impugners of the utilitarian morality represented it to their own minds in this its true character, I know not what recommendation possessed by any other morality they could possibly affirm to be wanting to it; what more beautiful or more exalted developments of human nature any other ethical system can be supposed to foster, or what springs of action, not accessible to the utilitarian, such systems rely on for giving effect to their mandates.

The objectors to utilitarianism cannot always be charged with representing it in a discreditable light. On the contrary, those among them who entertain anything like a just idea of its disinterested character sometimes find fault with its standard as being too high for humanity. They say it is exacting too much to require that people shall always act from the inducement of promoting the general interests of society. But this is to mistake the very meaning of a standard of morals and confound the rule of action with the motive of it. It is the business of ethics to tell us what are our duties, or by what test we may know them; but no system of ethics requires that

the sole motive of all we do shall be a feeling of duty; on the contrary, ninety-nine hundredths of all our actions are done from other
motives, and rightly so done if the rule of duty does not condemn
them. It is the more unjust to utilitarianism that this particular
misapprehension should be made a ground of objection to it, inasmuch as utilitarian moralists have gone beyond almost all others
in affirming that the motive has nothing to do with the morality
of the action, though much with the worth of the agent. He who
saves a fellow creature from drowning does what is morally right,
whether his motive be duty or the hope of being paid for his trouble;
he who betrays the friend that trusts him is guilty of a crime, even
if his object be to serve another friend to whom he is under greater
obligations.[2] But to speak only of actions done from the motive of
duty, and in direct obedience to principle: it is a misapprehension
of the utilitarian mode of thought to conceive it as implying that

[2] An opponent, whose intellectual and moral fairness it is a pleasure to
acknowledge (the Rev. J. Llewellyn Davies), has objected to this passage, saying,
"Surely the rightness or wrongness of saving a man from drowning does depend
very much upon the motive with which it is done. Suppose that a tyrant, when
his enemy jumped into the sea to escape from him, saved him from drowning
simply in order that he might inflict upon him more exquisite tortures, would
it tend to clearness to speak of that rescue as 'a morally right action'? Or suppose again, according to one of the stock illustrations of ethical inquiries, that a
man betrayed a trust received from a friend, because the discharge of it would
fatally injure that friend himself or someone belonging to him, would utilitarianism compel one to call the betrayal 'a crime' as much as if it had been done from
the meanest motive?"

I submit that he who saves another from drowning in order to kill him
by torture afterwards does not differ only in motive from him who does the same
thing from duty or benevolence; the act itself is different. The rescue of the man
is, in the case supposed, only the necessary first step of an act far more atrocious
than leaving him to drown would have been. Had Mr. Davies said, "The rightness or wrongness of saving a man from drowning does depend very much"—
not upon the motive, but—"upon the *intention*," no utilitarian would have differed from him. Mr. Davies, by an oversight too common not to be quite venial,
has in this case confounded the very different ideas of Motive and Intention.
There is no point which utilitarian thinkers (and Bentham pre-eminently) have
taken more pains to illustrate than this. The morality of the action depends entirely upon the intention—that is, upon what the agent *wills to do*. But the
motive, that is, the feeling which makes him will so to do, if it makes no difference in the act, makes none in the morality: though it makes a great difference
in our moral estimation of the agent, especially if it indicates a good or a bad
habitual *disposition*—a bent of character from which useful, or from which hurtful actions are likely to arise. [This footnote appeared only in the edition of
1864.]

people should fix their minds upon so wide a generality as the world, or society at large. The great majority of good actions are intended not for the benefit of the world, but for that of individuals, of which the good of the world is made up; and the thoughts of the most virtuous man need not on these occasions travel beyond the particular persons concerned, except so far as is necessary to assure himself that in benefiting them he is not violating the rights, that is, the legitimate and authorized expectations, of anyone else. The multiplication of happiness is, according to the utilitarian ethics, the object of virtue: the occasions on which any person (except one in a thousand) has it in his power to do this on an extended scale—in other words, to be a public benefactor—are but exceptional; and on these occasions alone is he called on to consider public utility; in every other case, private utility, the interest or happiness of some few persons, is all he has to attend to. Those alone the influence of whose actions extends to society in general need concern themselves habitually about so large an object. In the case of abstinences indeed—of things which people forbear to do from moral considerations, though the consequences in the particular case might be beneficial—it would be unworthy of an intelligent agent not to be consciously aware that the action is of a class which, if practiced generally, would be generally injurious, and that this is the ground of the obligation to abstain from it. The amount of regard for the public interest implied in this recognition is no greater than is demanded by every system of morals, for they all enjoin to abstain from whatever is manifestly pernicious to society.

The same considerations dispose of another reproach against the doctrine of utility, founded on a still grosser misconception of the purpose of a standard of morality and of the very meaning of the words "right" and "wrong." It is often affirmed that utilitarianism renders men cold and unsympathizing; that it chills their moral feelings toward individuals; that it makes them regard only the dry and hard consideration of the consequences of actions, not taking into their moral estimate the qualities from which those actions emanate. If the assertion means that they do not allow their judgment respecting the rightness or wrongness of an action to be influenced by their opinion of the qualities of the person who does it, this is a complaint not against utilitarianism, but against any standard of morality at all; for certainly no known ethical standard decides an action to be good or bad because it is done by a good or a bad man, still less because done by an amiable, a brave, or a benevolent man, or the contrary. These considerations are relevant, not to the estimation of actions, but of persons; and there is nothing in the utilitarian theory inconsistent with the fact that there are other things which interest us in persons besides the rightness and wrongness of their actions. The Stoics, indeed, with the paradoxical misuse of language which was part of their system, and by which they strove to raise themselves above all concern about anything but virtue, were fond of saying that he who has that has everything; that he, and only he, is rich, is beautiful, is a king. But no claim of this description is made for the virtuous man by the utilitarian doctrine. Utilitarians are quite aware that there are other desirable possessions and qualities besides virtue, and are perfectly willing to allow to all of them their full worth. They are also aware that a right action does not necessarily indicate a virtuous character, and that actions which are blamable often proceed from qualities entitled to praise. When this is apparent in any particular case, it modifies their estimation, not certainly of the act, but of the agent. I grant that they are, notwithstanding, of opinion that in the long run the best proof of a good character is good actions; and resolutely refuse to consider any mental disposition as good of which the predominant tendency is to produce bad conduct. This makes them unpopular with many people, but it is an unpopularity which they must share with everyone who regards the distinction between right and wrong in a serious light; and the reproach is not one which a conscientious utilitarian need be anxious to repel.

If no more be meant by the objection than that many utilitarians look on the morality of actions, as measured by the utilitarian standards, with too exclusive a regard, and do not lay sufficient stress upon the other beauties of character which go toward making a human being lovable or admirable, this may be admitted. Utilitarians who have cultivated their moral feelings, but not their sympathies, nor their artistic perceptions, do fall into this mistake; and so do all other moralists under the same conditions. What can be said in excuse for other moralists in equally available for them, namely, that, if there is to be any error, it is better that it should be on that side. As a matter of fact, we may affirm that among utilitarians, as among adherents of other systems, there is every imaginable degree of rigidity and of laxity in the application of their standard; some are even puritanically rigorous, while others are as indulgent as can possibly be desired by sinner or by sentimentalist. But on the whole, a doctrine which brings prominently forward the interest that mankind have in the repression and prevention of conduct which violates the moral law is likely to be inferior to no other in turning the sanctions of opinion against such violations. It is true, the question "What does violate the moral law?" is one on which those who recognize different standards of morality are likely now and then to differ. But difference of opinion on moral questions was not first introduced into the world by utilitarianism, while that doctrine does supply, if not always an easy, at all events a tangible and intelligible, mode of deciding such differences.

It may not be superfluous to notice a few more of the common misapprehensions of utilitarian ethics, even those which are so obvious and gross that it might appear impossible for any person of candor and intelligence to fall into them; since persons, even of considerable mental endowment, often give themselves so little trouble to understand the bearings of any opinion against which they entertain a prejudice, and men are in general so little conscious of this voluntary ignorance as a defect that the vulgarest misunderstandings of ethical doctrines are continually met with in the deliberate writings of persons of the greatest pretensions both to high principle and to philosophy. We not uncommonly hear the doctrine of utility inveighed against as a *godless* doctrine. If it be necessary to say anything at all against so mere an assumption, we may say that the question depends upon what idea we have formed of the moral character of the Deity. If it be a true belief that God desires, above all things, the happiness of his creatures, and that this was his purpose in their creation, utility is not only not a godless doctrine, but more profoundly religious than any other. If it be meant that utilitarianism does not recognize the revealed will of God as the supreme law of morals, I answer that a utilitarian who believes in the perfect goodness and wisdom of *God* necessarily believes that whatever God has thought fit to reveal on the subject of morals must fulfill the requirements of utility in a supreme degree. But others besides utilitarians have been of opinion that the Christian revelation was intended, and is fitted, to inform the hearts and minds of mankind with a spirit which should enable them to find for themselves what is right, and incline them to do it when found, rather than to tell them, except in a very general way, what it is; and that we need a doctrine of ethics, carefully followed out, to *interpret* to us the will of God. Whether this opinion is correct or not, it is superfluous here to discuss; since whatever aid religion, either natural or revealed, can afford to ethical investigation is as open to the utilitarian moralist as to any other. He can use it as the testimony of God to the usefulness or hurtfulness of any given course of action by as good a right as others can use it for the indication of a transcendental law having no connection with usefulness or with happiness.

Again, utility is often summarily stigmatized as an immoral doctrine by giving it the name of "expediency," and taking advantage of the popular use of that term to contrast it with principle. But the expedient, in the sense in which it is opposed to the right, generally means that which is expedient for the particular interest of the agent himself; as when a minister sacrifices the interests of his country to keep himself in place. When it means anything better than this, it means that which is expedient for some immediate object, some temporary purpose, but which violates a rule whose observance is expedient in a much higher degree. The expedient, in this sense, instead of being the same thing with the useful, is a branch of the hurtful. Thus it would often be expedient, for the purpose of getting over some momentary embarrassment, or attaining some object immediately useful to ourselves or others, to tell a lie. But inasmuch as the cultivation in ourselves of a sensitive feeling on the subject of veracity is one of the most useful, and the enfeeblement of that feeling one of the most hurtful, things to which our conduct can be instrumental; and inasmuch as any, even unintentional, deviation from truth does that much toward weakening the trustworthiness of human assertion, which is not only the principal support of all present social well-being, but the insufficiency of which does more than any one thing that can be named to keep back civilization, virtue, everything on which human happiness on the largest scale depends—we feel that the violation, for a present advantage, of a rule of such transcendent expediency is not expedient, and that he who, for the sake of convenience to himself or to some other individual, does what depends on him to deprive mankind of the good, and inflict upon them the evil, involved in the greater or less reliance which they can place in each other's word, acts the part of one of their worst enemies. Yet that even this rule, sacred as it is, admits of possible exceptions is acknowledged by all moralists; the chief of which is when the withholding of some fact (as of information from a malefactor, or of bad news from a person dangerously ill) would save an individual (especially an individual other than oneself) from great and unmerited evil, and when the withholding can only be effected by denial. But in order that the exception may not extend itself beyond the need, and may have the least possible effect in weakening reliance on veracity, it ought to be recognized and, if possible, its limits defined; and, if the principle of utility is good for anything, it must be good for weighing these conflicting utilities against one another and marking out the region within which one or the other preponderates.

Again, defenders of utility often find themselves called upon to reply to such objections as this—that there is not time, previous to action, for calculating and weighing the effects of any line of conduct on the general happiness. This is exactly as if anyone were to say that it is impossible to guide our conduct by Christianity because there is not time, on every occasion on which anything has to be done, to read through the Old and New Testaments. The answer to the objection is that there has been ample time, namely, the whole past duration of the human species. During all that time mankind have been learning by experience the tendencies of actions; on which experience all the prudence as well as all the morality of life are dependent. People talk as if the commencement of this course of experience had hitherto been put off, and as if, at the moment when some man feels tempted to meddle with the property or life of another, he had to begin considering for the first time whether murder and theft are injurious to human happiness. Even then I do not think that he would find the question very puzzling; but, at all events, the matter is now done to his hand. It is truly a whimsical supposition that, if mankind were agreed in considering utility to be the test of morality, they would remain without any agreement as to what *is* useful, and would take no measures for having their notions on the subject taught to the young and enforced by law and opinion. There is no difficulty in proving any ethical standard whatever to work ill if we suppose universal idiocy to be conjoined with it; but on any hypothesis short of that, mankind must by this time have acquired positive beliefs as to the effects of some actions on their happiness; and the beliefs which have thus come down are the rules of morality for the multitude, and for the philosopher until he has succeeded in finding better. That philosophers might easily do this, even now, on many subjects; that the received code of ethics is by no means of divine right; and that mankind have still much to learn as to the effects of actions on the general happiness, I admit or rather earnestly maintain. The corollaries from the principle of utility, like the precepts of every practical art, admit of indefinite improvement, and, in a progressive state of the human mind, their improvement is perpetually going on. But to consider the rules of morality as improvable is one thing; to pass over the intermediate generalization entirely and endeavor to test each individual action directly by the first principle is another. It is a strange notion that the acknowledgment of a first principle is inconsistent with the admission of secondary ones. To inform a traveler respecting the place of his ultimate destination is not to forbid the use of landmarks and direction-posts on the way. The proposition that happiness is the end and aim of morality does not mean that no road ought to be laid down to that goal, or that persons going thither should not be advised to take one direction rather than another. Men really ought to leave off talking a kind of nonsense on this subject, which they would neither talk nor listen to on other matters of practical concernment. Nobody argues that the art of navigation is not founded on astronomy because sailors cannot wait to calculate the Nautical Almanac. Being rational creatures, they go to sea with it ready calculated; and all rational creatures go out upon the sea of life with their minds made up on the common questions of right and wrong, as well as on many of the far more difficult questions of wise and foolish. And this, as long as foresight is a human quality, it is to be presumed they will continue to do. Whatever we adopt as the fundamental principle of morality, we require subordinate principles to apply it by; the impossibility of doing without them, being common to all systems, can afford no argument against any one in particular; but gravely to argue as if no such secondary principles could be had, and as if mankind had remained till now, and always must remain, without drawing any general conclusions from the experience of human life is as high a pitch, I think, as absurdity has ever reached in philosophical controversy.

The remainder of the stock arguments against utilitarianism mostly consist in laying to its charge the common infirmities of human nature, and the general difficulties which embarrass conscientious persons in shaping their course through life. We are told that a utilitarian will be apt to make his own particular case an exception to moral rules, and, when under temptation, will see a utility in the breach of a rule, greater than he will see in its observance. But is utility the only creed which is able to furnish us with excuses for evil-doing and means of cheating our own conscience? They are afforded in abundance by all doctrines which recognize as a fact in morals the existence of conflicting considerations, which all doctrines do that have been believed by sane persons. It is not the fault of any creed, but of the complicated nature of human affairs, that rules of conduct cannot be so framed as to require no exceptions, and that hardly any kind of action can safely be laid down as either always obligatory or always condemnable. There is no ethical creed which does not temper the rigidity of its laws by giving a certain latitude, under the moral responsibility of the agent, for accommodation to peculiarities of circumstances; and under every creed, at the opening thus made, self-deception and dishonest casuistry get in. There exists no moral system under which there do not arise unequivocal cases of conflicting obligation. These are the real difficulties, the knotty points both in the theory of ethics and in the conscientious guidance of personal conduct. They are overcome practically, with greater or with less success, according to the intellect and virtue of the individual; but it can hardly be pretended that anyone will be the less qualified for dealing with them, from possessing an ultimate standard to which conflicting rights and duties can be referred. If utility is the ultimate source of moral obligations, utility may be invoked to decide between them when their demands are incompatible. Though the application of the standard may be difficult, it is better than none at all; while in other systems, the moral laws all claiming independent authority, there is no common umpire entitled to interfere between them; their claims to precedence one over another rest on little better than sophistry, and, unless determined, as they generally are, by the unacknowledged influence of consideration of utility, afford a free scope for the action of personal desires and partialities. We must remember that only in these cases of conflict between secondary principles is it requisite that first principles should be appealed to. There is no case of moral obligation in which some secondary principle is not involved; and if only one, there can seldom be any real doubt which one it is, in the mind of any person by whom the principle itself is recognized.

Chapter III

Of the Ultimate Sanction of the Principle of Utility

The question is often asked, and properly so, in regard to any supposed moral standard—What is its sanction? what are the motives to obey? or, more specifically, what is the source of its obligation? whence does it derive its binding force? It is a necessary part of moral philosophy to provide the answer to this question, which, though frequently assuming the shape of an objection to the utilitarian morality, as if it had some special applicability to that above others, really arises in regard to all standards. It arises, in fact, whenever a person is called on to *adopt* a standard, or refer morality to any basis on which he has not been accustomed to rest it. For the customary morality, that which education and opinion have consecrated, is the only one which presents itself to the mind with the feeling of being *in itself* obligatory; and when a person is asked to believe that this morality *derives* its obligation from some general principle round which custom has not thrown the same halo, the assertion is to him a paradox; the supposed corollaries seem to have a more binding force than the original theorem; the super- structure seems to stand better without than with what is repre- sented as its foundation. He says to himself, I feel that I am bound not to rob or murder, betray or deceive; but why am I bound to promote the general happiness? If my own happiness lies in some- thing else, why may I not give that the preference?

If the view adopted by the utilitarian philosophy of the nature of the moral sense be correct, this difficulty will always present itself until the influences which form moral character have taken the same hold of the principle which they have taken of some of the consequences—until, by the improvement of education, the feeling of unity with our fellow creatures shall be (what it cannot be denied that Christ intended it to be) as deeply rooted in our character, and to our own consciousness as completely a part of our nature, as the horror of crime is in an ordinarily well-brought-up young person. In the meantime, however, the difficulty has no peculiar application to the doctrine of utility, but is inherent in every attempt to analyze morality and reduce it to principles; which, unless the principle is already in men's minds invested with as much sacredness as any of its applications, always seems to divest them of a part of their sanctity.

The principle of utility either has, or there is no reason why it might not have, all the sanctions which belong to any other system of morals. Those sanctions are either external or internal. Of the external sanctions it is not necessary to speak at any length. They are the hope of favor and the fear of displeasure from our fellow creatures or from the Ruler of the universe, along with whatever we may have of sympathy or affection for them, or of love and awe of Him, inclining us to do His will independently of selfish consequences. There is evidently no reason why all these motives for observance should not attach themselves to the utilitarian morality as completely and as powerfully as to any other. Indeed, those of them which refer to our fellow creatures are sure to do so, in proportion to the amount of general intelligence; for whether there be any other ground of moral obligation than the general happiness or not, men do desire happiness; and however imperfect may be their own practice, they desire and commend all conduct in others toward themselves by which they think their happiness is promoted. With regard to the religious motive, if men believe, as most profess to do, in the goodness of God, those who think that conduciveness to the general happiness is the essence or even only the criterion of good must necessarily believe that it is also that which God approves. The whole force therefore of external reward and punishment, whether physical or moral, and whether proceeding from God or from our fellow men, together with all that the capacities of human nature admit of disinterested devotion to either, become available to enforce the utilitarian morality, in proportion as that morality is recognized; and the more powerfully, the more the appliances of education and general cultivation are bent to the purpose.

So far as to external sanctions. The internal sanction of duty, whatever our standard of duty may be, is one and the same—a feeling in our own mind; a pain, more or less intense, attendant on violation of duty, which in properly cultivated moral natures rises, in the more serious cases, into shrinking from it as an impossibility. This feeling, when disinterested and connecting itself with the pure idea of duty, and not with some particular form of it, or with any of the merely accessory circumstances, is the essence of conscience; though in that complex phenomenon as it actually exists, the simple fact is in general all encrusted over with collateral associations derived from sympathy, from love, and still more from fear; from all the forms of religious feeling; from the recollections of childhood and of all our past life; from self-esteem, desire of the esteem of others, and occasionally even self-abasement. This extreme complication is, I apprehend, the origin of the sort of mystical character which, by a tendency of the human mind of which there are many other examples, is apt to be attributed to the idea of moral obligation, and which leads people to believe that the idea cannot possibly attach itself to any other objects than those which, by a supposed mysterious law, are found in our present experience to excite it. Its binding force, however, consists in the existence of a mass of feeling which must be broken through in order to do what violates our standard of right, and which, if we do nevertheless violate that standard, will probably have to be encountered afterwards in the form of remorse. Whatever theory we have of the nature or origin of conscience, this is what essentially constitutes it.

The ultimate sanction, therefore, of all morality (external motives apart) being a subjective feeling in our own minds, I see nothing embarrassing to those whose standard is utility in the question, What is the sanction of that particular standard? We may answer, the same as of all other moral standards—the conscientious feelings of mankind. Undoubtedly this sanction has no binding efficacy on those who do not possess the feelings it appeals to; but neither will these persons be more obedient to any other moral principle than to the utilitarian one. On them morality of any kind has no hold but through the external sanctions. Meanwhile the feelings exist, a fact in human nature, the reality of which, and the great power with which they are capable of acting on those in whom they have been duly cultivated, are proved by experience. No reason has ever been shown why they may not be cultivated to as great intensity in connection with the utilitarian as with any other rule of morals.

There is, I am aware, a disposition to believe that a person who sees in moral obligation a transcendental fact, an objective reality belonging to the province of "things in themselves," is likely to be more obedient to it than one who believes it to be entirely subjective, having its seat in human consciousness only. But whatever a person's opinion may be on this point of ontology, the force he is really urged by is his own subjective feeling, and is exactly measured by its strength. No one's belief that duty is an objective reality is stronger than the belief that God is so; yet the belief in God, apart from the expectation of actual reward and punishment, only operates on conduct through, and in proportion to, the subjective religious feeling. The sanction, so far as it is disinterested, is always in the mind itself; and the notion, therefore, of the transcendental moralists must be that this sanction will not exist *in* the mind unless it is believed to have its root out of the mind; and that if a person is able to say to himself, "That which is restraining me and which is called my conscience is only a feeling in my own mind," he may possibly draw the conclusion that when the feeling ceases the obligation ceases, and that if he find the feeling inconvenient, he may disregard it and endeavor to get rid of it. But is this danger confined to the utilitarian morality? Does the belief that moral obligation has its seat outside the mind make the feeling of it too strong to be got rid of? The fact is so far otherwise that all moralists admit and lament the ease with which, in the generality of minds, conscience can be silenced or stifled. The question, "Need I obey my conscience?" is quite as often put to themselves by persons who never heard of the principle of utility as by its adherents. Those whose conscientious feelings are so weak as to allow of their asking this question, if they answer it affirmatively, will not do so because they believe in the transcendental theory, but because of the external sanctions.

It is not necessary, for the present purpose, to decide whether the feeling of duty is innate or implanted. Assuming it to be innate, it is an open question to what objects it naturally attaches itself;

for the philosophic supporters of that theory are now agreed that the intuitive perception is of principles of morality and not of the details. If there be anything innate in the matter, I see no reason why the feeling which is innate should not be that of regard to the pleasures and pains of others. If there is any principle of morals which is intuitively obligatory, I should say it must be that. If so, the intuitive ethics would coincide with the utilitarian, and there would be no further quarrel between them. Even as it is, the intuitive moralists, though they believe that there are other intuitive moral obligations, do already believe this to be one; for they unanimously hold that a large *portion* of morality turns upon the consideration due to the interests of our fellow creatures. Therefore, if the belief in the transcendental origin of moral obligation gives any additional efficacy to the internal sanction, it appears to me that the utilitarian principle has already the benefit of it.

On the other hand, if, as is my own belief, the moral feelings are not innate but acquired, they are not for that reason the less natural. It is natural to man to speak, to reason, to build cities, to cultivate the ground, though these are acquired faculties. The moral feelings are not indeed a part of our nature in the sense of being in any perceptible degree present in all of us; but this, unhappily, is a fact admitted by those who believe the most strenuously in their transcendental origin. Like the other acquired capacities above referred to, the moral faculty, if not a part of our nature, is a natural outgrowth from it; capable, like them, in a certain small degree, of springing up spontaneously; and susceptible of being brought by cultivation to a high degree of development. Unhappily it is also susceptible, by a sufficient use of the external sanctions and of the force of early impressions, of being cultivated in almost any direction, so that there is hardly anything so absurd or so mischievous that it may not, by means of these influences, be made to act on the human mind with all the authority of conscience. To doubt that the same potency might be given by the same means to the principle of utility, even if it had no foundation in human nature, would be flying in the face of all experience.

But moral associations which are wholly of artificial creation, when the intellectual culture goes on, yield by degrees to the dissolving force of analysis; and if the feeling of duty, when associated with utility, would appear equally arbitrary; if there were no leading department of our nature, no powerful class of sentiments, with which that association would harmonize, which would make us feel it congenial and incline us not only to foster it in others (for which we have abundant interested motives), but also to cherish it in ourselves—if there were not, in short, a natural basis of sentiment for utilitarian morality, it might well happen that this association also, even after it had been implanted by education, might be analyzed away.

But there *is* this basis of powerful natural sentiment; and this it is which, when once the general happiness is recognized as the ethical standard, will constitute the strength of the utilitarian morality. This firm foundation is that of the social feelings of mankind—the desire to be in unity with our fellow creatures, which is already a powerful principle in human nature, and happily one of those which tend to become stronger, even without express inculcation, from the influences of advancing civilization. The social state is at once so natural, so necessary, and so habitual to man, that, except in some unusual circumstances or by an effort of voluntary abstraction, he never conceives himself otherwise than as a member of a body; and this association is riveted more and more, as mankind are further removed from the state of savage independence. Any condition, therefore, which is essential to a state of society becomes more and more an inseparable part of every person's conception of the state of things which he is born into, and which is the destiny of a human being. Now society between human beings, except in the relation of master and slave, is manifestly impossible on any other footing than that the interests of all are to be consulted. Society between equals can only exist on the understanding that the interests of all are to be regarded equally. And since in all states of civilization, every person, except an absolute monarch, has equals, everyone is obliged to live on these terms with somebody; and in every age some advance is made toward a state in which it will be impossible to live permanently on other terms with anybody. In this way people grow up unable to conceive as possible to them a state of total disregard of other people's interests. They are under a necessity of conceiving themselves as at least abstaining from all the grosser injuries, and (if only for their own protection) living in a state of constant protest against them. They are also familiar with the fact of cooperating with others and proposing to themselves a collective, not an individual, interest as the aim (at least for the time being) of their actions. So long as they are co-operating, their ends are identified with those of others; there is at least a temporary feeling that the interests of others are their own interests. Not only does all strengthening of social ties, and all healthy growth of society, give to each individual a stronger personal interest in practically consulting the welfare of others, it also leads him to identify his *feelings* more and more with their good, or at least with an even greater degree of practical consideration for it. He comes, as though instinctively, to be conscious of himself as a being who *of course* pays regard to others. The good of others becomes to him a thing naturally and necessarily to be attended to, like any of the physical conditions of our existence. Now, whatever amount of this feeling a person has, he is urged by the strongest motives both of interest and of sympathy to demonstrate it, and to the utmost of his power encourage it in others; and even if he has none of it himself, he is as greatly interested as anyone else that others should have it. Consequently, the smallest germs of the feeling are laid hold of and nourished by the contagion of sympathy and the influences of education; and a complete web of corroborative association is woven round it by the powerful agency of the external sanctions. This mode of conceiving ourselves and human life, as civilization goes on, is felt to be more and more natural. Every step in political improvement renders it more so, by removing the sources of opposition of interest and leveling those inequalities of legal privilege between individuals or classes, owing to which there are large portions of mankind whose happiness it is still practicable to disregard. In an improving state of the human mind, the influences are constantly on the increase which tend to generate in each individual a feeling of unity with all the rest; which, if perfect, would make him never think of, or desire, any beneficial condition for himself in the benefits of which they are not included. If we now suppose this feeling of unity to be taught as a religion, and the whole force of education, of institutions, and of opinion directed, as it once was in the case of religion, to make every person grow up from infancy surrounded on all sides both by the profession and the practice of it, I think that no one who can realize this conception will feel any misgiving about the sufficiency of the ultimate sanction for the happiness morality. To any ethical student who finds the realization difficult, I recommend, as a means of facilitating it, the second of M. Comte's two principal works, the *Traité de politique positive*. I entertain the strongest objections to the system of politics and morals set forth in that treatise, but I think it has superabundantly shown the possibility of giving to the service of humanity, even without the aid of belief in a Providence, both the psychological power and the social efficacy of a religion, making it take hold of human life, and color all thought, feeling, and action in a manner of which the greatest ascendancy ever exercised by any religion may be but a type and foretaste; and of which the danger is, not that it should be insufficient, but that it should be so excessive as to interfere unduly with human freedom and individuality.

Neither is it necessary to the feeling which constitutes the binding force of the utilitarian morality on those who recognize it to wait for those social influences which would make its obligation felt by mankind at large. In the comparatively early state of human advancement in which we now live, a person cannot, indeed, feel that entireness of sympathy with all others which would make any real discordance in the general direction of their conduct in life impossible, but already a person in whom the social feeling is at all developed cannot bring himself to think of the rest of his fellow creatures as struggling rivals with him for the means of happiness, whom he must desire to see defeated in their object in order that he may succeed in his. The deeply rooted conception which every individual even now has of himself as a social being tends to make him feel it one of his natural wants that there should be harmony between his feelings and aims and those of his fellow creatures. If differences of opinion and of mental culture make it impossible for him to share many of their actual feelings—perhaps make him denounce and defy those feelings—he still needs to be conscious that his real aim and theirs do not conflict; that he is not opposing himself to what they really wish for, namely, their own good, but is, on the contrary, promoting it. This feeling in most individuals is much inferior in strength to their selfish feelings, and is often wanting altogether. But to those who have it, it possesses all the characters of a natural feeling. It does not present itself to their minds as a superstition of education or a law despotically imposed by the power of society, but as an attribute which it would not be well for them to be without. This conviction is the ultimate sanction

of the greatest happiness morality. This it is which makes any mind
of well-developed feelings work with, and not against, the outward
motives to care for others, afforded by what I have called the external
sanctions; and, when those sanctions are wanting or act in an opposite direction, constitutes in itself a powerful internal binding
force, in proportion to the sensitiveness and thoughtfulness of the
character, since few but those whose mind is a moral blank could
bear to lay out their course of life on the plan of paying no regard
to others except so far as their own private interest compels.

Chapter IV

Of What Sort of Proof the Principle of Utility Is Susceptible

It has already been remarked that questions of ultimate ends
do not admit of proof, in the ordinary acceptation of the term. To
be incapable of proof by reasoning is common to all first principles,
to the first premises of our knowledge, as well as to those of our
conduct. But the former, being matters of fact, may be the subject
of a direct appeal to the faculties which judge of fact—namely, our
senses and our internal consciousness. Can an appeal be made to
the same faculties on questions of practical ends? Or by what other
faculty is cognizance taken of them?

Questions about ends are, in other words, questions what
things are desirable. The utilitarian doctrine is that happiness is
desirable, and the only thing desirable, as an end; all other things
beings only desirable as means to that end. What ought to be required of this doctrine, what conditions is it requisite that the doctrine should fulfill—to make good its claim to be believed?

The only proof capable of being given that an object is visible
is that people actually see it. The only proof that a sound is audible
is that people hear it; and so of the other sources of our experience.
In like manner, I apprehend, the sole evidence it is possible to
produce that anything is desirable is that people do actually desire
it. If the end which the utilitarian doctrine proposes to itself were
not, in theory and in practice, acknowledged to be an end, nothing
could ever convince any person that it was so. No reason can be

given why the general happiness is desirable, except that each person, so far as he believes it to be attainable, desires his own happiness. This, however, being a fact, we have not only all the proof which the case admits of, but all which it is possible to require, that happiness is a good, that each person's happiness is a good to that person, and the general happiness, therefore, a good to the aggregate of all persons. Happiness has made out its title as *one* of the ends of conduct and, consequently, one of the criteria of morality.

But it has not, by this alone, proved itself to be the sole criterion. To do that, it would seem, by the same rule, necessary to show, not only that people desire happiness, but that they never desire anything else. Now it is palpable that they do desire things which, in common language, are decidedly distinguished from happiness. They desire, for example, virtue and the absence of vice no less really than pleasure and the absence of pain. The desire of virtue is not as universal, but it is as authentic a fact as the desire of happiness. And hence the opponents of the utilitarian standard deem that they have a right to infer that there are other ends of human action besides happiness, and that happiness is not the standard of approbation and disapprobation.

But does the utilitarian doctrine deny that people desire virtue, or maintain that virtue is not a thing to be desired? The very reverse. It maintains not only that virtue is to be desired, but that it is to be desired disinterestedly, for itself. Whatever may be the opinion of utilitarian moralists as to the original conditions by which virtue is made virtue, however they may believe (as they do) that actions and dispositions are only virtuous because they promote another end than virtue, yet this being granted, and it having been decided, from considerations of this description, what *is* virtuous, they not only place virtue at the very head of the things which are good as means to the ultimate end, but they also recognize as a psychological fact the possibility of its being, to the individual, a good in itself, without looking to any end beyond it; and hold that the mind is not in a right state, not in a state conformable to utility, not in the state most conducive to the general happiness, unless it does love virtue in this manner—as a thing desirable in itself, even although, in the individual instance, it should not produce those other desirable consequences which it tends to produce, and on account of which it is held to be virtue. This opinion is not, in the smallest degree, a departure from the happiness principle. The ingredients of happiness are very various, and each of them is desirable in itself, and not merely when considered as swelling an aggregate. The principle of utility does not mean that any given pleasure, as music, for instance, or any given exemption from pain, as for example health, is to be looked upon as means to a collective something termed happiness, and to be desired on that account. They are desired and desirable in and for themselves; besides being means, they are a part of the end. Virtue, according to the utilitarian doctrine, is not naturally and originally part of the end, but it is capable of becoming so; and in those who live it disinterestedly it has become so, and is desired and cherished, not as a means to happiness, but as a part of their happiness.

To illustrate this further, we may remember that virtue is not the only thing originally a means, and which if it were not a means to anything else would be and remain indifferent, but which by association with what it is a means to comes to be desired for itself, and that too with the utmost intensity. What, for example, shall we say of the love of money? There is nothing originally more desirable about the money than about any heap of glittering pebbles. Its worth is solely that of the things which it will buy; the desires for other things than itself, which it is a means of gratifying. Yet the love of money is not only one of the strongest moving forces of human life, but money is, in many cases, desired in and for itself; the desire to possess it is often stronger than the desire to use it, and goes on increasing when all the desires which point to ends beyond it, to be compassed by it, are falling off. It may, then, be said truly that money is desired not for the sake of an end, but as part of the end. From being a means to happiness, it has come to be itself a principal ingredient of the individual's conception of happiness. The same may be said of the majority of the great objects of human life: power, for example, or fame, except that to each of these there is a certain amount of immediate pleasure annexed, which has at least the semblance of being naturally inherent in them—a thing which cannot be said of money. Still, however, the strongest natural attraction, both of power and of fame, is the immense aid they give to the attainment of our other wishes; and it is the strong association thus generated between them and all our objects of desire which gives to the direct desire of them the intensity it often assumes, so as in some characters to surpass in strength all other desires. In these cases the means have become a part of the end, and a more important part of it than any of the things which they are means to. What was once desired as an instrument for the attainment of happiness has come to be desired for its own sake. In being desired for its own sake it is, however, desired as *part* of happiness. The person is made, or thinks he would be made, happy by its mere possession; and is made unhappy by failure to obtain it. The desire of it is not a different thing from the desire of happiness any more than the love of music or the desire of health. They are included in happiness. They are some of the elements of which the desire of happiness is made up. Happiness is not an abstract idea but a concrete whole; and these are some of its parts. And the utilitarian standard sanctions and approves their being so. Life would be a poor thing, very ill provided with sources of happiness if there were not this provision of nature by which things originally indifferent, but conducive to, or otherwise associated with, the satisfaction of our primitive desires, become in themselves sources of pleasure more valuable than the primitive pleasures, both in permanency, in the space of human existence that they are capable of covering, and even in intensity.

Virtue, according to the utilitarian conception, is a good of this description. There was no original desire of it, or motive to it, save its conduciveness to pleasure, and especially to protection from pain. But through the association thus formed it may be felt a good in itself, and desired as such with as great intensity as any other good; and with this difference between it and the love of money, of power, or of fame—that all of these may, and often do, render the individual noxious to the other members of the society to which he belongs, whereas there is nothing which makes him so much a blessing to them as the cultivation of the disinterested love of virtue. And consequently, the utilitarian standard, while it tolerates and approves those other acquired desires, up to the point beyond which they would be more injurious to the general happiness than promotive of it, enjoins and requires the cultivation of the love of virtue up to the greatest strength possible, as being above all things important to the general happiness.

It results from the preceding considerations that there is in reality nothing desired except happiness. Whatever is desired otherwise than as a means to some end beyond itself, and ultimately to happiness, is desired as itself a part of happiness, and is not desired for itself until it has become so. Those who desire virtue for its own sake desire it either because the consciousness of it is a pleasure, or because the consciousness of being without it is a pain, or for both reasons united; as in truth the pleasure and pain seldom exist separately, but almost always together—the same person feeling pleasure in the degree of virtue attained, and pain in not having attained more. If one of these gave him no pleasure, and the other no pain, he would not love or desire virtue, or would desire it only for the other benefits which it might produce to himself or to persons whom he cared for.

We have now, then, an answer to the question, of what sort of proof the principle of utility is susceptible. If the opinion which I have now stated is psychologically true—if human nature is so constituted as to desire nothing which is not either a part of happiness or a means of happiness—we can have no other proof, and we require no other, that these are the only things desirable. If so, happiness is the sole end of human action, and the promotion of it the test by which to judge of all human conduct; from whence it necessarily follows that it must be the criterion of morality, since a part is included in the whole.

And now to decide whether this is really so, whether mankind do desire nothing for itself but that which is a pleasure to them, or of which the absence is a pain, we have evidently arrived at a question of fact and experience, dependent, like all similar questions, upon evidence. It can only be determined by practiced self-consciousness and self-observation, assisted by observation of others. I believe that these sources of evidence, impartially consulted, will declare that desiring a thing and finding it pleasant, aversion to it and thinking of it as painful, are phenomena entirely inseparable or, rather, two parts of the same phenomenon—in strictness of language, two different modes of naming the same psychological fact; that to think of an object as desirable (unless for the sake of its consequences) and to think of it as pleasant are one and the same thing; and that to desire anything except in proportion as the idea of it is pleasant is a physical and metaphysical impossibility.

So obvious does this appear to me that I expect it will hardly be disputed; and the objection made will be, not that desire can possibly be directed to anything ultimately except pleasure and exemption from pain, but that the will is a different thing from desire; that a person of confirmed virtue or any other person whose purposes are fixed carries out his purposes without any thought of the pleasure he has in contemplating them or expects to derive from their fulfillment, and persists in acting on them, even though these pleasures are much diminished by changes in his character or decay of his passive sensibilities, or are outweighed by the pains which the pursuit of the purposes may bring upon him. All this I fully admit and have stated it elsewhere as positively and emphatically as anyone. Will, the active phenomenon, is a different thing from desire, the state of passive sensibility, and, though originally an offshoot from it, may in time take root and detach itself from the parent stock, so much so that in the case of a habitual purpose, instead of willing the thing because we desire it, we often desire it only because we will it. This, however, is but an instance of that familiar fact, the power of habit, and is nowise confined to the case of virtuous actions. Many indifferent things which men originally did from a motive of some sort they continue to do from habit. Sometimes this is done unconsciously, the consciousness coming only after the action; at other times with conscious volition, but volition which has become habitual and is put in operation by the force of habit, in opposition perhaps to the deliberate preference, as often happens with those who have contracted habits of vicious or hurtful indulgence. Third and last comes the case in which the habitual act of will in the individual instance is not in contradiction to the general intention prevailing at other times, but in fulfillment of it, as in the case of the person of confirmed virtue and of all who pursue deliberately and consistently any determinate end. The distinction between will and desire thus understood is an authentic and highly important psychological fact; but the fact consists solely in this—that will, like all other parts of our constitution, is amenable to habit, and that we may will from habit what we no longer desire for itself, or desire only because we will it. It is not the less true that will, in the beginning, is entirely produced by desire, including in that term the repelling influence of pain as well as the attractive one of pleasure. Let us take into consideration no longer the person who has a confirmed will to do right, but him in whom that virtuous will is still feeble, conquerable by temptation, and not to be fully relied on; by what means can it be strengthened? How can the will to be virtuous, where it does not exist in sufficient force, be implanted or awakened? Only by making the person *desire* virtue—by making him think of it in a pleasurable light, or of its absence in a painful one. It is by associating the doing right with pleasure, or the wrong with pain, or by eliciting and impressing and bringing home to the person's experience the pleasure naturally involved in the one or the pain in the other, that it is possible to call forth that will to be virtuous which, when confirmed, acts without any thought of either pleasure or pain. Will is the child of desire, and passes out of the dominion of its parent only to come under that of habit. That which is the result of habit affords no presumption of being intrinsically good; and there would be no reason for wishing that the purpose of virtue should become independent of pleasure and pain were it not that the influence of the pleasurable and painful associations which prompt to virtue is not sufficiently to be depended on for unerring constancy of action until it has acquired the support of habit. Both in feeling and in conduct, habit is the only thing which imparts certainty; and it is because of the importance to others of being able to rely absolutely on one's feelings and conduct, and to oneself of being able to rely on one's own, that the will to do right ought to be cultivated into this habitual independence. In other words, this state of the will is a means to good, not intrinsically a good; and does not contradict the doctrine that nothing is a good to human beings but in so far as it is either itself pleasurable or a means of attaining pleasure or averting pain.

But if this doctrine be true, the principle of utility is proved. Whether it is so or not must now be left to the consideration of the thoughtful reader.

Chapter V

On the Connection Between Justice and Utility

In all ages of speculation one of the strongest obstacles to the reception of the doctrine that utility or happiness is the criterion of right and wrong has been drawn from the idea of justice. The powerful sentiment and apparently clear perception which that word recalls with a rapidity and certainty resembling an instinct have seemed to the majority of thinkers to point to an inherent quality in things; to show that the just must have an existence in nature as something absolute, generically distinct from every variety of the expedient and, in idea, opposed to it, though (as is commonly acknowledged) never, in the long run, disjoined from it in fact.

In the case of this, as of our other moral sentiments, there is no necessary connection between the question of its origin and that of its binding force. That a feeling is bestowed on us by nature does not necessarily legitimate all its promptings. The feeling of justice might be a peculiar instinct, and might yet require, like our other instincts, to be controlled and enlightened by a higher reason. If we have intellectual instincts leading us to judge in a particular way, as well as animal instincts that prompt us to act in a particular way, there is no necessity that the former should be more infallible in their sphere than the latter in theirs; it may as well happen that wrong judgments are occasionally suggested by those, as wrong actions by these. But though it is one thing to believe that we have natural feelings of justice, and another to acknowledge them as an ultimate criterion of conduct, these two opinions are very closely connected in point of fact. Mankind are always predisposed to believe that any subjective feeling, not otherwise accounted for, is a revelation of some objective reality. Our present object is to determine whether the reality to which the feeling of justice corresponds is one which needs any such special revelation, whether the justice or injustice of an action is a thing intrinsically peculiar and distinct from all its other qualities or only a combination of certain of those qualities presented under a peculiar aspect. For the purpose of this inquiry it is practically important to consider whether the feeling itself, of justice and injustice, is *sui generis* like our sensations of color and taste or a derivative feeling formed by a combination of others. And this it is the more essential to examine, as people are in general willing enough to allow that objectively the dictates of justice coincide with a part of the field of general expediency; but inasmuch as the subjective mental feeling of justice is different from that which commonly attaches to simple expediency, and, except in the extreme cases of the latter, is far more imperative in its demands, people find it difficult to see in justice only a particular kind or branch of general utility, and think that its superior binding force requires a totally different origin.

To throw light upon this question, it is necessary to attempt to ascertain what is the distinguishing character of justice, or of injustice; what is the quality, or whether there is any quality, attributed in common to all modes of conduct designated as unjust (for justice, like many other moral attributes, is best defined by its opposite), and distinguishing them from such modes of conduct as are disapproved, but without having that particular epithet of disapprobation applied to them. If in everything which men are accustomed to characterize as just or unjust some one common attribute or collection of attributes is always present, we may judge whether this particular attribute or combination of attributes would be capable of gathering round it a sentiment of that peculiar character and intensity by virtue of the general laws of our emotional constitution, or whether the sentiment is inexplicable and requires to be regarded as a special provision of nature. If we find the former to be the case, we shall, in resolving this question, have resolved also the main problem; if the latter, we shall have to seek for some other mode of investigating it.

To find the common attributes of a variety of objects, it is necessary to begin by surveying the objects themselves in the concrete. Let us therefore advert successively to the various modes of action and arrangements of human affairs which are classed, by universal or widely spread opinion, as just or as unjust. The things well known to excite the sentiments associated with those names are of a very multifarious character. I shall pass them rapidly in review, without studying any particular arrangement.

In the first place, it is mostly considered unjust to deprive anyone of his personal liberty, his property, or any other thing which belongs to him by law. Here, therefore, is one instance of the application of the terms "just" and "unjust" in a perfectly definite sense, namely, that it is just to respect, unjust to violate, the *legal rights* of anyone. But this judgment admits of several exceptions, arising from the other forms in which the notions of justice and injustice present themselves. For example, the person who suffers the deprivation may (as the phrase is) have *forfeited* the rights

which he is so deprived of—a case to which we shall return presently.
But also—

Secondly, the legal rights of which he is deprived may be
rights which *ought* not to have belonged to him; in other words,
the law which confers on him these rights may be a bad law. When
it is so or when (which is the same thing for our purpose) it is
supposed to be so, opinions will differ as to the justice or injustice
of infringing it. Some maintain that no law, however bad, ought to
be disobeyed by an individual citizen; that his opposition to it, if
shown at all, should only be shown in endeavoring to get it altered
by competent authority. This opinion (which condemns many of
the most illustrious benefactors of mankind, and would often protect pernicious institutions against the only weapons which, in the
state of things existing at the time, have any chance of succeeding
against them) is defended by those who hold it on grounds of
expediency, principally on that of the importance to the common
interest of mankind, of maintaining inviolate the sentiment of sub-
mission to law. Other persons, again, hold the directly contrary
opinion that any law, judged to be bad, may blamelessly be disobeyed, even though it be not judged to be unjust but only inexpedient, while others would confine the license of disobedience to
the case of unjust laws; but, again, some say that all laws which
are inexpedient are unjust, since every law imposes some restriction
on the natural liberty of mankind, which restriction is an injustice
unless legitimated by tending to their good. Among these diversities
of opinion it seems to be universally admitted that there may be
unjust laws, and that law, consequently, is not the ultimate criterion
of justice, but may give to one person a benefit, or impose on another an evil, which justice condemns. When, however, a law is
thought to be unjust, it seems always to be regarded as being so
in the same way in which a breach of law is unjust, namely, by infringing somebody's right, which, as it cannot in this case be a legal
right, receives a different appellation and is called a moral right.
We may say, therefore, that a second case of injustice consists in
taking or withholding from any person that to which he has a
moral right.

Thirdly, it is universally considered just that each person
should obtain that (whether good or evil) which he *deserves*, and

unjust that he should obtain a good or be made to undergo an evil which he does not deserve. This is, perhaps, the clearest and most emphatic form in which the idea of justice is conceived by the general mind. As it involves the notion of desert, the question arises what constitutes desert? Speaking in a general way, a person is understood to deserve good if he does right, evil if he does wrong; and in a more particular sense, to deserve good from those to whom he does or has done good, and evil from those to whom he does or has done evil. The precept of returning good for evil has never been regarded as a case of the fulfillment of justice, but as one in which the claims of justice are waived, in obedience to other considerations.

Fourthly, it is confessedly unjust to *break faith* with anyone: to violate an engagement, either express or implied, or disappoint expectations raised by our own conduct, at least if we have raised those expectations knowingly and voluntarily. Like the other obligations of justice already spoken of, this one is not regarded as absolute, but as capable of being overruled by a stronger obligation of justice on the other side, or by such conduct on the part of the person concerned as is deemed to absolve us from our obligation to him and to constitute a *forfeiture* of the benefit which he has been led to expect.

Fifthly, it is, by universal admission, inconsistent with justice to be *partial*—to show favor or preference to one person over another in matters to which favor and preference do not properly apply. Impartiality, however, does not seem to be regarded as a duty in itself, but rather as instrumental to some other duty; for it is admitted that favor and preference are not always censurable, and, indeed, the cases in which they are condemned are rather the exception than the rule. A person would be more likely to be blamed than applauded for giving his family or friends no superiority in good offices over strangers when he could do so without violating any other duty; and no one thinks it unjust to seek one person in preference to another as a friend, connection, or companion. Impartiality where rights are concerned is of course obligatory, but this is involved in the more general obligation of giving to everyone his right. A tribunal, for example, must be impartial because it is bound to award, without regard to any other consideration, a disputed object to the one of two parties who has the right to it. There are other cases in which impartiality means being solely influenced by desert, as with those who, in the capacity of judges, preceptors, or parents, administer reward and punishment as such. There are cases, again, in which it means being solely influenced by consideration for the public interest, as in making a selection among candidates for a government employment. Impartiality, in short, as an obligation of justice, may be said to mean being exclusively influenced by the considerations which it is supposed ought to influence the particular case in hand, and resisting solicitation of any motives which prompt to conduct different from what those considerations would dictate.

Nearly allied to the idea of impartiality is that of *equality*, which often enters as a component part both into the conception of justice and into the practice of it, and, in the eyes of many persons, constitutes its essence. But in this, still more than in any other case, the notion of justice varies in different persons, and always conforms in its variations to their notion of utility. Each person maintains that equality is the dictate of justice, except where he thinks that expediency requires inequality. The justice of giving equal protection to the rights of all is maintained by those who support the most outrageous inequality in the rights themselves. Even in slave countries it is theoretically admitted that the rights of the slave, such as they are, ought to be as sacred as those of the master, and that a tribunal which fails to enforce them with equal strictness is wanting in justice; while, at the same time, institutions which leave to the slave scarcely any rights to enforce are not deemed unjust because they are not deemed inexpedient. Those who think that utility requires distinctions of rank do not consider it unjust that riches and social privileges should be unequally dispensed; but those who think this inequality inexpedient think it unjust also. Whoever thinks that government is necessary sees no injustice in as much inequality as is constituted by giving to the magistrate powers not granted to other people. Even among those who hold leveling doctrines, there are differences of opinion about expediency. Some communists consider it unjust that the produce of the labor of the community should be shared on any other principle than that of exact equality; others think it just that those should receive most whose wants are greatest; while others hold that those who work harder, or who produce more, or whose services are more valuable to the community, may justly claim a larger quota in the division of the produce. And the sense of natural justice may be plausibly appealed to in behalf of every one of these opinions.

Among so many diverse applications of the term "justice," which yet is not regarded as ambiguous, it is a matter of some difficulty to seize the mental link which holds them together, and on which the moral sentiment adhering to the term essentially depends. Perhaps, in this embarrassment, some help may be derived from the history of the word, as indicated by its etymology.

In most if not in all languages, the etymology of the word which corresponds to "just" points distinctly to an origin connected with the ordinances of law. *Justum* is a form of *jussum,* that which has been ordered. *Dikaion* comes directly from *dike,* a suit at law. *Recht,* from which came *right* and *righteous,* is synonymous with law. The courts of justice, the administration of justice, are the courts and the administration of law. *La justice,* in French, is the established term for judicature. I am not committing the fallacy, imputed with some show of truth to Horne Tooke, of assuming that a word must still continue to mean what it originally meant. Etymology is slight evidence of what the idea now signified is, but the very best evidence of how it sprang up. There can, I think, be no doubt that the *idée mère,* the primitive element, in the formation of the notion of justice was conformity to law. It constituted the entire idea among the Hebrews, up to the birth of Christianity; as might be expected in the case of a people whose laws attempted to embrace all subjects on which precepts were required, and who believed those laws to be a direct emanation from the Supreme Being. But other nations, and in particular the Greeks and Romans, who knew that their laws had been made originally, and still continued to be made, by men, were not afraid to admit that those men might make bad laws; might do, by law, the same things, and from the same motives, which if done by individuals without the sanction of law would be called unjust. And hence the sentiment of injustice came to be attached, not to all violations of law, but only to violations of such laws as *ought* to exist, including such as ought to exist but do not, and to laws themselves if supposed to be contrary to what ought to be law. In this manner the idea of law and of its injunctions was still predominant in the notion of justice, even when the laws actually in force ceased to be accepted as the standard of it.

It is true that mankind consider the idea of justice and its obligations as applicable to many things which neither are, nor is it desired that they should be, regulated by law. Nobody desires that laws should interfere with the whole detail of private life; yet everyone allows that in all daily conduct a person may and does show himself to be either just or unjust. But even here, the idea of the breach of what ought to be law still lingers in a modified shape. It would always give us pleasure, and chime in with our feelings of fitness, that acts which we deem unjust should be punished, though we do not always think it expedient that this should be done by the tribunals. We forego that gratification on account of incidental inconveniences. We should be glad to see just conduct enforced and injustice repressed, even in the minutest details, if we were not, with reason, afraid of trusting the magistrate with so unlimited an amount of power over individuals. When we think that a person is bound in justice to do a thing, it is an ordinary form of language to say that he ought to be compelled to do it. We should be gratified to see the obligation enforced by anybody who had the power. If we see that its enforcement by law would be inexpedient, we lament the impossibility, we consider the impunity given to injustice as an evil, and strive to make amends for it by bringing a strong expression of our own and the public disapprobation to bear upon the offender. Thus the idea of legal constraint is still the generating idea of the notion of justice, though undergoing several transformations before that notion as it exists in an advanced state of society becomes complete.

The above is, I think, a true account, as far as it goes, of the origin and progressive growth of the idea of justice. But we must observe that it contains as yet nothing to distinguish that obligation from moral obligation in general. For the truth is that the idea of penal sanction, which is the essence of law, enters not only into the conception of injustice, but into that of any kind of wrong. We do not call anything wrong unless we mean to imply that a person ought to be punished in some way or other for doing it—if not by law, by the opinion of his fellow creatures; if not by opinion, by the reproaches of his own conscience. This seems the real turning point of the distinction between morality and simple expediency. It is a part of the notion of duty in every one of its forms that a person may rightfully be compelled to fulfill it. Duty is a thing which may be *exacted* from a person, as one exacts a debt. Unless we think that it may be exacted from him, we do not call it his duty. Reasons of prudence, or the interest of other people, may militate against actually exacting it, but the person himself, it is clearly understood, would not be entitled to complain. There are other things, on the contrary, which we wish that people should do, which we like or admire them for doing, perhaps dislike or despise them for not doing, but yet admit that they are not bound to do; it is not a case of moral obligation; we do not blame them, that is, we do not think that they are proper objects of punishment. How we come by these ideas of deserving and not deserving punishment will appear, perhaps, in the sequel; but I think there is no doubt that this distinction lies at the bottom of the notions of right and wrong; that we call any conduct wrong, or employ, instead, some other term of dislike or disparagement, according as we think that the person ought, or ought not, to be punished for it; and we say it would be right to do so and so, or merely that it would be desirable or laudable, according as we would wish to see the person whom it concerns compelled, or only persuaded and exhorted, to act in that manner.[3]

This, therefore, being the characteristic difference which marks off, not justice, but morality in general from the remaining provinces of expediency and worthiness, the character is still to be sought which distinguishes justice from other branches of morality. Now it is known that ethical writers divide moral duties into two classes, denoted by the ill-chosen expressions, duties of perfect and of imperfect obligation; the latter being those in which, though the act is obligatory, the particular occasions of performing it are left to our choice, as in the case of charity or beneficence, which we are indeed bound to practice but not toward any definite person, nor at any prescribed time. In the more precise language of philosophic jurists, duties of perfect obligation are those duties in virtue of which a correlative *right* resides in some person or persons; duties of im-

---

[3] See this point enforced and illustrated by Professor Bain, in an admirable chapter (entitled "The Ethical Emotions, or the Moral Sense"), of the second of the two treatises composing his elaborate and profound work on the Mind.

perfect obligation are those moral obligations which do not give birth to any right. I think it will be found that this distinction exactly coincides with that which exists between justice and the other obligations of morality. In our survey of the various popular acceptations of justice, the term appeared generally to involve the idea of a personal right—a claim on the part of one or more individuals, like that which the law gives when it confers a proprietary or other legal right. Whether the injustice consists in depriving a person of a possession, or in breaking faith with him, or in treating him worse than he deserves, or worse than other people who have no greater claims—in each case the supposition implies two things: a wrong done, and some assignable person who is wronged. Injustice may also be done by treating a person better than others; but the wrong in this case is to his competitors, who are also assignable persons. It seems to me that this feature in the case—a right in some person, correlative to the moral obligation—constitutes the specific difference between justice and generosity or beneficence. Justice implies something which it is not only right to do, and wrong not to do, but which some individual person can claim from us as his moral right. No one has a moral right to our generosity or beneficence because we are not morally bound to practice those virtues toward any given individual. And it will be found with respect to this as to every correct definition that the instances which seem to conflict with it are those which most confirm it. For if a moralist attempts, as some have done, to make out that mankind generally, though not any given individual, have a right to all the good we can do them, he at once, by that thesis, includes generosity and beneficence within the category of justice. He is obliged to say that our utmost exertions are *due* to our fellow creatures, thus assimilating them to a debt; or that nothing less can be a sufficient *return* for what society does for us, thus classing the case as one of gratitude; both of which are acknowledged cases of justice, and not of the virtue of beneficence; and whoever does not place the distinction between justice and morality in general, where we have now placed it, will be found to make no distinction between them at all, but to merge all morality in justice.

Having thus endeavored to determine the distinctive elements which enter into the composition of the idea of justice, we are ready to enter on the inquiry whether the feeling which accompanies the idea is attached to it by a special dispensation of nature, or whether it could have grown up, by any known laws, out of the idea itself; and, in particular, whether it can have originated in considerations of general expediency.

I conceive that the sentiment itself does not arise from anything which would commonly or correctly be termed an idea of expediency, but that, though the sentiment does not, whatever is moral in it does.

We have seen that the two essential ingredients in the sentiment of justice are the desire to punish a person who has done harm and the knowledge or belief that there is some definite individual or individuals to whom harm has been done.

Now it appears to me that the desire to punish a person who has done harm to some individual is a spontaneous outgrowth from two sentiments, both in the highest degree natural and which either are or resemble instincts: the impulse of self-defense and the feeling of sympathy.

It is natural to resent and to repel or retaliate any harm done or attempted against ourselves or against those with whom we sympathize. The origin of this sentiment it is not necessary here to discuss. Whether it be an instinct or a result of intelligence, it is, we know, common to all animal nature; for every animal tries to hurt those who have hurt, or who it thinks are about to hurt, itself or its young. Human beings, on this point, only differ from other animals in two particulars. First, in being capable of sympathizing, not solely with their offspring, or, like some of the more noble animals, with some superior animal who is kind to them, but with all human, and even with all sentient, beings; secondly, in having a more developed intelligence, which gives a wider range to the whole of their sentiments, whether self-regarding or sympathetic. By virtue of his superior intelligence, even apart from his superior range of sympathy, a human being is capable of apprehending a community of interest between himself and the human society of which he forms a part, such that any conduct which threatens the security of the society generally is threatening to his own, and calls forth his instinct (if instinct it be) of self-defense. The same superiority of intelligence, joined to the power of sympathizing with human beings generally, enables him to attach himself to the collective idea of his tribe, his country, or mankind in such a manner that any act hurtful to them raises his instinct of sympathy and urges him to resistance.

The sentiment of justice, in that one of its elements which consists of the desire to punish, is thus, I conceive, the natural feeling of retaliation or vengeance, rendered by intellect and sympathy applicable to those injuries, that is, to those hurts, which wound us through, or in common with, society at large. This sentiment, in itself, has nothing moral in it; what is moral is the exclusive subordination of it to the social sympathies, so as to wait on and obey their call. For the natural feeling would make us resent indiscriminately whatever anyone does that is disagreeable to us; but, when moralized by the social feeling, it only acts in the directions conformable to the general good: just persons resenting a hurt to society, though not otherwise a hurt to themselves, and not resenting a hurt to themselves, however painful, unless it be of the kind which society has a common interest with them in the repression of.

It is no objection against this doctrine to say that, when we feel our sentiment of justice outraged, we are not thinking of society at large or of any collective interest, but only of the individual case. It is common enough, certainly, though the reverse of commendable, to feel resentment merely because we have suffered pain; but a person whose resentment is really a moral feeling, that is, who considers whether an act is blamable before he allows himself to resent it—such a person, though he may not say expressly to himself that he is standing up for the interest of society, certainly does feel that he is asserting a rule which is for the benefit of others as well as for his own. If he is not feeling this, if he is regarding the act solely as it affects him individually, he is not consciously just; he is not concerning himself about the justice of his actions. This is admitted even by anti-utilitarian moralists. When Kant (as before remarked) propounds as the fundamental principle of morals, "So act that thy rule of conduct might be adopted as a law by all rational beings," he virtually acknowledges that the interest of mankind collectively, or at least of mankind indiscriminately, must be in the mind of the agent when conscientiously deciding on the morality of the act. Otherwise he uses words without a meaning; for that a rule even of utter selfishness could not *possibly* be adopted by all rational beings—that there is any insuperable obstacle in the nature of things to its adoption—cannot be even plausibly main-

tained. To give any meaning to Kant's principle, the sense put upon
it must be that we ought to shape our conduct by a rule which all
rational beings might adopt *with benefit to their collective interest.*

To recapitulate: the idea of justice supposes two things—a
rule of conduct and a sentiment which sanctions the rule. The first
must be supposed common to all mankind and intended for their
good. The other (the sentiment) is a desire that punishment may be
suffered by those who infringe the rule. There is involved, in addition, the conception of some definite person who suffers by the
infringement, whose rights (to use the expression appropriated to
the case) are violated by it. And the sentiment of justice appears to
me to be the animal desire to repel or retaliate a hurt or damage
to oneself or to those with whom one sympathizes, widened so as to
include all persons, by the human capacity of enlarged sympathy
and the human conception of intelligent self-interest. From the latter elements the feeling derives its morality; from the former, its
peculiar impressiveness and energy of self-assertion.

I have, throughout, treated the idea of a *right* residing in the
injured person and violated by the injury, not as a separate element in the composition of the idea and sentiment, but as one of
the forms in which the other two elements clothe themselves. These
elements are a hurt to some assignable person or persons, on the one
hand, and a demand for punishment, on the other. An examination
of our own minds, I think, will show that these two things include
all that we mean when we speak of violation of a right. When we
call anything a person's right, we mean that he has a valid claim
on society to protect him in the possession of it, either by the force
of law or by that of education and opinion. If he has what we
consider a sufficient claim, on whatever account, to have something
guaranteed to him by society, we say that he a right to it. If we
desire to prove that anything does not belong to him by right, we
think this done as soon as it is admitted that society ought not to
take measures for securing it to him, but should leave him to
chance or to his own exertions. Thus a person is said to have a
right to what he can earn in fair professional competition, because
society ought not to allow any other person to hinder him from
endeavoring to earn in that manner as much as he can. But he has
not a right to three hundred a year, though he may happen to be

earning it; because society is not called on to provide that he shall earn that sum. On the contrary, if he owns ten thousand pounds three-percent stock, he *has* a right to three hundred a year because society has come under an obligation to provide him with an income of that amount.

To have a right, then, is, I conceive, to have something which society ought to defend me in the possession of. If the objector goes on to ask why it ought, I can give him no other reason than general utility. If that expression does not seem to convey a sufficient feeling of the strength of the obligation, nor to account for the peculiar energy of the feeling, it is because there goes to the composition of the sentiment, not a rational only but also an animal element— the thirst for retaliation; and this thirst derives its intensity, as well as its moral justification, from the extraordinarily important and impressive kind of utility which is concerned. The interest involved is that of security, to everyone's feelings the most vital of all interests. All other earthly benefits are needed by one person, not needed by another; and many of them can, if necessary, be cheerfully foregone or replaced by something else; but security no human being can possibly do without; on it we depend for all our immunity from evil and for the whole value of all and every good, beyond the passing moment, since nothing but the gratification of the instant could be of any worth to us if we could be deprived of everything the next instant by whoever was momentarily stronger than ourselves. Now this most indispensable of all necessaries, after physical nutriment, cannot be had unless the machinery for providing it is kept unintermittedly in active play. Our notion, therefore, of the claim we have on our fellow creatures to join in making safe for us the very groundwork of our existence gathers feelings around it so much more intense than those concerned in any of the more common cases of utility that the difference in degree (as is often the case in psychology) becomes a real difference in kind. The claim assumes that character of absoluteness, that apparent infinity and incommensurability with all other considerations which constitute the distinction between the feeling of right and wrong and that of ordinary expediency and inexpediency. The feelings concerned are so powerful, and we count so positively on finding a responsive feeling in others (all being alike interested) that *ought* and *should* grow into *must,* and recognized indispensability becomes a moral necessity, analogous to physical, and often not inferior to it in binding force.

If the preceding analysis, or something resembling it, be not the correct account of the notion of justice—if justice be totally independent of utility, and be a standard *per se,* which the mind can recognize by simple introspection of itself—it is hard to understand why that internal oracle is so ambiguous, and why so many things appear either just or unjust, according to the light in which they are regarded.

We are continually informed that utility is an uncertain standard, which every different person interprets differently, and that there is no safety but in the immutable, ineffaceable, and unmistakable dictates of justice, which carry their evidence in themselves and are independent of the fluctuations of opinion. One would suppose from this that on questions of justice there could be no controversy; that, if we take that for our rule, its application to any given case could leave us in as little doubt as a mathematical demonstration. So far is this from being the fact that there is as much difference of opinion, and as much discussion, about what is just as about what is useful to society. Not only have different nations and individuals different notions of justice, but in the mind of one and the same individual, justice is not some one rule, principle, or maxim, but many which do not always coincide in their dictates, and, in choosing between which, he is guided either by some extraneous standard or by his own personal predilections.

For instance, there are some who say that it is unjust to punish anyone for the sake of example to others, that punishment is just only when intended for the good of the sufferer himself. Others maintain the extreme reverse, contending that to punish persons who have attained years of discretion, for their own benefit, is despotism and injustice, since, if the matter at issue is solely their own good, no one has a right to control their own judgment of it; but that they may justly be punished to prevent evil to others, this being the exercise of the legitimate right of self-defense. Mr. Owen, again, affirms that it is unjust to punish at all, for the criminal did not make his own character; his education and the circumstances which surrounded him have made him a criminal, and for these he is not responsible. All these opinions are extremely plausible;

and so long as the question is argued as one of justice simply, without going down to the principles which lie under justice and are the source of its authority, I am unable to see how any of these reasoners can be refuted. For in truth every one of the three builds upon rules of justice confessedly true. The first appeals to the acknowledged injustice of singling out an individual and making him a sacrifice, without his consent, for other people's benefit. The second relies on the acknowledged justice of self-defense and the admitted injustice of forcing one person to conform to another's notions of what constitutes his good. The Owenite invokes the admitted principle that it is unjust to punish anyone for what he cannot help. Each is triumphant so long as he is not compelled to take into consideration any other maxims of justice than the one he has selected; but as soon as their several maxims are brought face to face, each disputant seems to have exactly as much to say for himself as the others. No one of them can carry out his own notion of justice without trampling upon another equally binding. These are difficulties; they have always been felt to be such; and many devices have been invented to turn rather than to overcome them. As a refuge from the last of the three, men imagined what they called the freedom of the will—fancying that they could not justify punishing a man whose will is in a thoroughly hateful state unless it be supposed to have come into that state through no influence of anterior circumstances. To escape from the other difficulties, a favorite contrivance has been the fiction of a contract whereby at some unknown period all the members of society engaged to obey the laws and consented to be punished for any disobedience to them, thereby giving to their legislators the right, which it is assumed they would not otherwise have had, of punishing them, either for their own good or for that of society. This happy thought was considered to get rid of the whole difficulty and to legitimate the infliction of punishment, in virtue of another received maxim of justice, *volenti non fit injuria*—that is not unjust which is done with the consent of the person who is supposed to be hurt by it. I need hardly remark that, even if the consent were not a mere fiction, this maxim is not superior in authority to the others which it is brought in to supersede. It is, on the contrary, an instructive specimen of the loose and irregular manner in which supposed principles of justice grow up. This particular one evidently came into use as a help to the coarse exigencies of courts of law, which are sometimes obliged to be content with very uncertain presumptions, on account of the greater evils which would often arise from any attempt on their part to cut finer. But even courts of law are not able to adhere consistently to the maxim, for they allow voluntary engagements to be set aside on the ground of fraud, and sometimes on that of mere mistake or misinformation.

Again, when the legitimacy of inflicting punishment is admitted, how many conflicting conceptions of justice come to light in discussing the proper apportionment of punishments to offenses. No rule on the subject recommends itself so strongly to the primitive and spontaneous sentiment of justice as the *lex talionis*, an eye for an eye and a tooth for a tooth. Though this principle of the Jewish and of the Mohammedan law has been generally abandoned in Europe as a practical maxim, there is, I suspect, in most minds, a secret hankering after it; and when retribution accidentally falls on an offender in that precise shape, the general feeling of satisfaction evinced bears witness how natural is the sentiment to which this repayment in kind is acceptable. With many, the test of justice in penal infliction is that the punishment should be proportioned to the offense, meaning that it should be exactly measured by the moral guilt of the culprit (whatever be their standard for measuring moral guilt), the consideration what amount of punishment is necessary to deter from the offense having nothing to do with the question of justice, in their estimation; while there are others to whom that consideration is all in all, who maintain that it is not just, at least for man, to inflict on a fellow creature, whatever may be his offenses, any amount of suffering beyond the least that will suffice to prevent him from repeating, and others from imitating, his misconduct.

To take another example from a subject already once referred to. In cooperative industrial association, is it just or not that talent or skill should give a title to superior remuneration? On the negative side of the question it is argued that whoever does the best he can deserves equally well, and ought not in justice to be put in a position of inferiority for no fault of his own; that superior abilities have already advantages more than enough, in the admiration they excite, the personal influence they command, and the internal sources of satisfaction attending them, without adding to these a superior share of the world's goods; and that society is bound in justice rather to make compensation to the less favored for this unmerited inequality of advantages than to aggravate it. On the contrary side it is contended that society receives more from the more efficient laborer; that, his services being more useful, society owes him a larger return for them; that a greater share of the joint result is actually his work, and not to allow his claim to it is a kind of robbery; that, if he is only to receive as much as others, he can only be justly required to produce as much, and to give a smaller amount of time and exertion, proportioned to his superior efficiency. Who shall decide between these appeals to conflicting principles of justice? Justice has in this case two sides to it, which it is impossible to bring into harmony, and the two disputants have chosen opposite sides; the one looks to what it is just that the individual should receive, the other to what it is just that the community should give. Each, from his own point of view, is unanswerable; and any choice between them, on grounds of justice, must be perfectly arbitrary. Social utility alone can decide the preference.

How many, again, and how irreconcilable are the standards of justice to which reference is made in discussing the repartition of taxation. One opinion is that payment to the state should be in numerical proportion to pecuniary means. Others think that justice dictates what they term graduated taxation—taking a higher percentage from those who have more to spare. In point of natural justice a strong case might be made for disregarding means altogether, and taking the same absolute sum (whenever it could be got) from everyone; as the subscribers to a mess or to a club all pay the same sum for the same privileges, whether they can all equally afford it or not. Since the protection (it might be said) of law and government is afforded to and is equally required by all, there is no injustice in making all buy it at the same price. It is reckoned justice, not injustice, that a dealer should charge to all customers the same price for the same article, not a price varying according to their means of payment. This doctrine, as applied to taxation, finds no advocates because it conflicts so strongly with man's feelings of humanity and of social expediency; but the principle of justice which it invokes is as true and as binding as those which can be appealed to against it. Accordingly it exerts a tacit influence on the line of defense employed for other modes of assessing taxation.

People feel obliged to argue that the state does more for the rich man than for the poor, as a justification for its taking more from them, though this is in reality not true, for the rich would be far better able to protect themselves, in the absence of law or government, than the poor, and indeed would probably be successful in converting the poor into their slaves. Others, again, so far defer to the same conception of justice as to maintain that all should pay an equal capitation tax for the protection of their persons (these being of equal value to all), and an unequal tax for the protection of their property, which is unequal. To this others reply that the all of one man is as valuable to him as the all of another. From these confusions there is no other mode of extrication than the utilitarian.

Is, then, the difference between the just and the expedient a merely imaginary distinction? Have mankind been under a delusion in thinking that justice is a more sacred thing than policy, and that the latter ought only to be listened to after the former has been satisfied? By no means. The exposition we have given of the nature and origin of the sentiment recognizes a real distinction; and no one of those who profess the most sublime contempt for the consequences of actions as an element in their morality attaches more importance to the distinction than I do. While I dispute the pretensions of any theory which sets up an imaginary standard of justice not grounded on utility, I account the justice which is grounded on utility to be the chief part, and incomparably the most sacred and binding part, of all morality. Justice is a name for certain classes of moral rules which concern the essentials of human well-being more nearly, and are therefore of more absolute obligation, than any other rules for the guidance of life; and the notion which we have found to be of the essence of the idea of justice—that of a right residing in an individual—implies and testifies to this more binding obligation.

The moral rules which forbid mankind to hurt one another (in which we must never forget to include wrongful interference with each other's freedom) are more vital to human well-being than any maxims, however important, which only point out the best mode of managing some department of human affairs. They have also the peculiarity that they are the main element in determining the whole of the social feelings of mankind. It is their observance which alone preserves peace among human beings; if obedience to them were not the rule, and disobedience the exception, everyone would see in everyone else an enemy against whom he must be perpetually guarding himself. What is hardly less important, these are the precepts which mankind have the strongest and the most direct inducements for impressing upon one another. By merely giving to each other prudential instruction or exhortation, they may gain, or think they gain, nothing; in inculcating on each other the duty of positive beneficence, they have an unmistakable interest, but far less in degree; a person may possibly not need the benefits of others, but he always needs that they should not do him hurt. Thus the moralities which protect every individual from being harmed by others, either directly or by being hindered in his freedom of pursuing his own good, are at once those which he himself has most at heart and those which he has the strongest interest in publishing and enforcing by word and deed. It is by a person's observance of these that his fitness to exist as one of the fellowship of human beings is tested and decided; for on that depends his being a nuisance or not to those with whom he is in contact. Now it is these moralities primarily which compose the obligations of justice. The most marked cases of injustice, and those which give the tone to the feeling of repugnance which characterizes the sentiment, are acts of wrongful aggression or wrongful exercise of power over someone; the next are those which consist in wrongfully withholding from him something which is his due—in both cases inflicting on him a positive hurt, either in the form of direct suffering or of the privation of some good which he had reasonable ground, either of a physical or of a social kind, for counting upon.

The same powerful motives which command the observance of these primary moralities enjoin the punishment of those who violate them; and as the impulses of self-defense, of defense of others, and of vengeance are all called forth against such persons, retribution, or evil for evil, becomes closely connected with the sentiment of justice, and is universally included in the idea. Good for good is also one of the dictates of justice; and this, though its social utility is evident, and though it carries with it a natural human feeling, has not at first sight that obvious connection with hurt or injury which, existing in the most elementary cases of just and unjust, is the source of the characteristic intensity of the sentiment. But the connection, though less obvious, is not less real. He who accepts benefits and denies a return of them when needed inflicts a real hurt by disappointing one of the most natural and reasonable of expectations, and one which he must at least tacitly have encouraged, otherwise the benefits would seldom have been conferred. The important rank, among human evils and wrongs, of the disappointment of expectation is shown in the fact that it constitutes the principal criminality of two such highly immoral acts as a breach of friendship and a breach of promise. Few hurts which human beings can sustain are greater, and none wound more, than when that on which they habitually and with full assurance relied fails them in the hour of need; and few wrongs are greater than this mere withholding of good; none excite more resentment, either in the person suffering or in a sympathizing spectator. The principle, therefore, of giving to each what they deserve, that is, good for good as well as evil for evil, is not only included within the idea of justice as we have defined it, but is a proper object of that intensity of sentiment which places the just in human estimation above the simply expedient.

Most of the maxims of justice current in the world, and commonly appealed to in its transactions, are simply instrumental to carrying into effect the principles of justice which we have now spoken of. That a person is only responsible for what he has done voluntarily, or could voluntarily have avoided, that it is unjust to condemn any person unheard; that the punishment ought to be proportioned to the offense, and the like, are maxims intended to prevent the just principle of evil for evil from being perverted to the infliction of evil without that justification. The greater part of these common maxims have come into use from the practice of courts of justice, which have been naturally led to a more complete recognition and elaboration than was likely to suggest itself to others, of the rules necessary to enable them to fulfill their double function—of inflicting punishment when due, and of awarding to each person his right.

That first of judicial virtues, impartiality, is an obligation of justice, partly for the reason last mentioned, as being a necessary condition of the fulfillment of other obligations of justice. But this is not the only source of the exalted rank, among human obligations, of those maxims of equality and impartiality, which, both in popular estimation and in that of the most enlightened, are included among the precepts of justice. In one point of view, they may be considered as corollaries from the principles already laid down. If it is a duty to do to each according to his deserts, returning good for good, as well as repressing evil by evil, it necessarily follows that we should treat all equally well (when no higher duty forbids) who have deserved equally well of *us,* and that society should treat all equally well who have deserved equally well of *it,* that is, who have deserved equally well absolutely. This is the highest abstract standard of social and distributive justice, toward which all institutions and the efforts of all virtuous citizens should be made in the utmost possible degree to converge. But this great moral duty rests upon a still deeper foundation, being a direct emanation from the first principle of morals, and not a mere logical corollary from secondary or derivative doctrines. It is involved in the very meaning of utility, or the greatest happiness principle. That principle is a mere form of words without rational signification unless one person's happiness, supposed equal in degree (with the proper allowance made for kind), is counted for exactly as much as another's. Those conditions being supplied, Bentham's dictum, "everybody to count for one, nobody for more than one," might be written under the principle of utility as an explanatory commentary.[4] The equal claim of everybody to

4 This implication, in the first principle of the utilitarian scheme, of perfect impartiality between persons is regarded by Mr. Herbert Spencer (in his *Social Statics*) as a disproof of the pretensions of utility to be a sufficient guide to right; since (he says) the principle of utility presupposes the anterior principle that everybody has an equal right to happiness. It may be more correctly described as supposing that equal amounts of happiness are equally desirable, whether felt by the same or different persons. This, however, is not a *pre*supposition, not a premise needful to support the principle of utility, but the very principle itself; for what is the principle of utility if it be not that "happiness" and "desirable" are synonymous terms? If there is any anterior principle implied, it can be no other than this, that the truths of arithmetic are applicable to the valuation of happiness, as of all other measurable quantities.

(Mr. Herbert Spencer, in a private communication on the subject of the preceding note, objects to being considered an opponent of utilitarianism and states that he regards happiness as the ultimate end of morality; but deems that end only partially attainable by empirical generalizations from the observed results of conduct, and completely attainable only by deducing, from the laws of life and the conditions of existence, what kinds of action necessarily tend to produce happiness, and what kinds to produce unhappiness. With the exception of the word "necessarily," I have no dissent to express from this doctrine; and (omitting that word) I am not aware that any modern advocate of utilitarianism is of a different opinion. Bentham, certainly, to whom in the *Social Statics* Mr.

happiness, in the estimation of the moralist and of the legislator, involves an equal claim to all the means of happiness except in so far as the inevitable conditions of human life and the general interest in which that of every individual is included set limits to the maxim; and those limits ought to be strictly construed. As every other maxim of justice, so this is by no means applied or held applicable universally; on the contrary, as I have already remarked, it bends to every person's ideas of social expediency. But in whatever case it is deemed applicable at all, it is held to be the dictate of justice. All persons are deemed to have a *right* to equality of treatment, except when some recognized social expediency requires the reverse. And hence all social inequalities which have ceased to be considered expedient assume the character, not of simple inexpendiency, but of injustice, and appear so tyrannical that people are apt to wonder how they ever could have been tolerated—forgetful that they themselves, perhaps, tolerate other inequalities under an equally mistaken notion of expediency, the correction of which would make that which they approve seem quite as monstrous as what they have at least learned to condemn. The entire history of social improvement has been a series of transitions by which one custom or institution after another, from being a supposed primary necessity of social existence, has passed into the rank of a universally stigmatized injustice and tyranny. So it has been with the distinctions of slaves and freemen, nobles and serfs, patricians and plebeians; and so it will be, and in part already is, with the aristocracies of color, race, and sex.

It appears from what has been said that justice is a name for certain moral requirements which, regarded collectively, stand higher in the scale of social utility, and are therefore of more paramount obligation, than any others, though particular cases

Spencer particularly referred, is, least of all writers, chargeable with unwillingness to deduce the effect of actions on happiness from the laws of human nature and the universal conditions of human life. The common charge against him is of relying too exclusively upon such deductions and declining altogether to be bound by the generalizations from specific experience which Mr. Spencer thinks that utilitarians generally confine themselves to. My own opinion (and, as I collect, Mr. Spencer's) is that in ethics, as in all other branches of scientific study, the consilience of the results of both these processes, each corroborating and verifying the other, is requisite to give to any general proposition the kind and degree of evidence which constitutes scientific proof.)

may occur in which some other social duty is so important as to overrule any one of the general maxims of justice. Thus, to save a life, it may not only be allowable, but a duty, to steal or take by force the necessary food or medicine, or to kidnap and compel to officiate the only qualified medical practitioner. In such cases, as we do not call anything justice which is not a virtue, we usually say, not that justice must give way to some other moral principle, but that what is just in ordinary cases is, by reason of that other principle, not just in the particular case. By this useful accommodation of language, the character of indefeasibility attributed to justice is kept up, and we are saved from the necessity of maintaining that there can be laudable injustice.

The considerations which have now been adduced resolve, I conceive, the only real difficulty in the utilitarian theory of morals. It has always been evident that all cases of justice are also cases of expediency; the difference is in the peculiar sentiment which attaches to the former, as contradistinguished from the latter. If this characteristic sentiment has been sufficiently accounted for; if there is no necessity to assume for it any peculiarity of origin; if it is simply the natural feeling of resentment, moralized by being made coextensive with the demands of social good; and if this feeling not only does but ought to exist in all the classes of cases to which the idea of justice corresponds—that idea no longer presents itself as a stumbling block to the utilitarian ethics. Justice remains the appropriate name for certain social utilities which are vastly more important, and therefore more absolute and imperative, than any others are as a class (though not more so than others may be in particular cases); and which, therefore, ought to be, as well as naturally are, guarded by a sentiment, not only different in degree, but also in kind; distinguished from the milder feeling which attaches to the mere idea of promoting human pleasure or convenience at once by the more definite nature of its commands and by the sterner character of its sanctions.

Selections from
Principia Ethica

G. E. Moore

Preface

It appears to me that in Ethics, as in all other philosophical studies, the difficulties and disagreements, of which its history is full, are mainly due to a very simple cause: namely to the attempt to answer questions, without first discovering precisely *what* question it is which you desire to answer. I do know how far this source of error would be done away, if philosophers would *try* to discover what question they were asking, before they set about to answer it; for the work of analysis and distinction is often very difficult: we may often fail to make the necessary discovery, even though we make a definite attempt to do so. But I am inclined to think that in many cases a resolute attempt would be sufficient to ensure success; so that, if only this attempt were made, many of the most glaring difficulties and disagreements in philosophy would disappear. At all events, philosophers seem, in general, not to make the attempt; and, whether in consequence of this omission or not, they are constantly endeavouring to prove that 'Yes' or 'No' will answer questions, to which *neither* answer is correct, owing to the fact that what they have before their minds is not one question, but several, to some of which the true answer is 'No,' to others 'Yes.'

I have tried in this book to distinguish clearly two kinds of question, which moral philosophers have always professed to answer, but which, as I have tried to shew, they have almost always con-

From G. E. Moore, *Principia Ethica*, 1903, Cambridge University Press. Reprinted by permission of the publisher.

fused both with one another and with other questions. These two questions may be expressed, the first in the form: What kind of things ought to exist for their own sakes? the second in the form: What kind of actions ought we to perform? I have tried to shew exactly what it is that we ask about a thing, when we ask whether it ought to exist for its own sake, is good in itself or has intrinsic value; and exactly what it is that we ask about an action, when we ask whether we ought to do it, whether it is a right action or a duty.

But from a clear insight into the nature of these two questions, there appears to me to follow a second most important result: namely, what is the nature of the evidence, by which alone any ethical proposition can be proved or disproved, confirmed or rendered doubtful. Once we recognise the exact meaning of the two questions, I think it also becomes plain exactly what kind of reasons are relevant as arguments for or against any particular answer to them. It becomes plain that, for answers to the *first* question, no relevant evidence whatever can be adduced: from no other truth, except themselves alone, can it be inferred that they are either true or false. We can guard against error only by taking care, that, when we try to answer a question of this kind, we have before our minds that question only, and not some other or others; but that there is great danger of such errors of confusion I have tried to shew, and also what are the chief precautions by the use of which we may guard against them. As for the *second* question, it becomes equally plain, that any answer to it *is* capable of proof or disproof—that, indeed, so many different considerations are relevant to its truth or falsehood, as to make the attainment of probability very difficult, and the attainment of certainty impossible. Nevertheless the *kind* of evidence, which is both necessary and alone relevant to such proof and disproof, is capable of exact definition. Such evidence must contain propositions of two kinds and of two kinds only: it must consist, in the first place, of truths with regard to the results of the action in question—of *causal* truths—but it must *also* contain ethical truths of our first or self-evident class. Many truths of both kinds are necessary to the proof that any action ought to be done; and any other kind of evidence is wholly irrelevant. It follows that, if any ethical philosopher offers for propositions of the first kind any evidence whatever, or if, for propositions of the second kind, he either fails to adduce both causal and ethical truths, or adduces truths that are neither, his reasoning has not the least tendency to establish his conclusions. But not only are his conclusions totally devoid of weight: we have, moreover, reason to suspect him of the error of confusion; since the offering of irrelevant evidence generally indicates that the philosopher who offers it has had before his mind, not the question which he professes to answer, but some other entirely different one. Ethical discussion, hitherto, has perhaps consisted chiefly in reasoning of this totally irrelevant kind. . . .

In order to express the fact that ethical propositions of my *first* class are incapable of proof or disproof, I have sometimes followed Sidgwick's usage in calling them 'Intuitions.' But I beg it may be noticed that I am not an 'Intuitionist,' in the ordinary sense of the term. Sidgwick himself seems never to have been clearly aware of the immense importance of the difference which distinguishes his Intuitionism from the common doctrine, which has generally been called by that name. The Intuitionist proper is distinguished by maintaining that propositions of my *second* class—propositions which assert that a certain action is *right* or a *duty*—are incapable of proof or disproof by any enquiry into the results of such actions. I, on the contrary, am no less anxious to maintain that propositions of *this* kind are *not* 'Intuitions,' than to maintain that propositions of my *first* class *are* Intuitions.

Again, I would wish it observed that, when I call such propositions 'Intuitions,' I mean *merely* to assert that they are incapable of proof; I imply nothing whatever as to the manner or origin of our cognition of them. Still less do I imply (as most Intuitionists have done) that any proposition whatever is true, *because* we cognise it in a particular way or by the exercise of any particular faculty: I hold, on the contrary, that in every way in which it is possible to cognise a true proposition, it is also possible to cognise a false one. . . .

Chapter I

The Subject-Matter of Ethics

6. What, then, is good? How is good to be defined? Now, it may be thought that this is a verbal question. A definition does

indeed often mean the expressing of one word's meaning in other words. But this is not the sort of definition I am asking for. Such a definition can never be of ultimate importance in any study except lexicography. If I wanted that kind of definition I should have to consider in the first place how people generally used the word 'good'; but my business is not with its proper usage, as established by custom. I should, indeed, be foolish, if I tried to use it for something which it did not usually denote: if, for instance, I were to announce that, whenever I used the word 'good,' I must be understood to be thinking of that object which is usually denoted by the word 'table.' I shall, therefore, use the word in the sense in which I think it is ordinarily used; but at the same time I am not anxious to discuss whether I am right in thinking that it is so used. My business is solely with that object or idea, which I hold, rightly or wrongly, that the word is generally used to stand for. What I want to discover is the nature of that object or idea, and about this I am extremely anxious to arrive at an agreement.

But, if we understand the question in this sense, my answer to it may seem a very disappointing one. If I am asked 'What is good?' my answer is that good is good, and that is the end of the matter. Or if I am asked 'How is good to be defined?' my answer is that it cannot be defined, and that is all I have to say about it. But disappointing as these answers may appear, they are of the very last importance. To readers who are familiar with philosophic terminology, I can express their importance by saying that they amount to this: That propositions about the good are all of them synthetic and never analytic; and that is plainly no trivial matter. And the same thing may be expressed more popularly, by saying that, if I am right, then nobody can foist upon us such an axiom as that 'Pleasure is the only good' or that 'The good is the desired' on the pretence that this is 'the very meaning of the word.'

7. Let us, then, consider this position. My point is that 'good' is a simple notion, just as 'yellow' is a simple notion; that, just as you cannot, by any manner of means, explain to any one who does not already know it, what yellow is, so you cannot explain what good is. Definitions of the kind that I was asking for, definitions which describe the real nature of the object or notion denoted by a word, and which do not merely tell us what the word is used to mean, are only possible when the object or notion in question is

something complex. You can give a definition of a horse, because a horse has many different properties and qualities, all of which you can enumerate. But when you have enumerated them all, when you have reduced a horse to his simplest terms, then you can no longer define those terms. They are simply something which you think of or perceive, and to any one who cannot think of or perceive them, you can never, by any definition, make their nature known. It may perhaps be objected to this that we are able to describe to others, objects which they have never seen or thought of. We can, for instance, make a man understand what a chimaera is, although he has never heard of one or seen one. You can tell him that it is an animal with a lioness's head and body, with a goat's head growing from the middle of its back, and with a snake in place of a tail. But here the object which you are describing is a complex object; it is entirely composed of parts, with which we are all perfectly familiar—a snake, a goat, a lioness; and we know, too, the manner in which those parts are to be put together, because we know what is meant by the middle of a lioness's back, and where her tail is wont to grow. And so it is with all objects, not previously known, which we are able to define: they are all complex; all composed of parts, which may themselves, in the first instance, be capable of similar definition, but which must in the end be reducible to simplest parts, which can no longer be defined. But yellow and good, we say, are not complex: they are notions of that simple kind, out of which definitions are composed and with which the power of further defining ceases.

8. When we say, as Webster says, 'The definition of horse is "A hoofed quadruped of the genus Equus," ' we may, in fact, mean three different things. (1) We may mean merely: 'When I say "horse," you are to understand that I am talking about a hoofed quadruped of the genus Equus.' This might be called the arbitrary verbal definition: and I do not mean that good is indefinable in that sense. (2) We may mean, as Webster ought to mean: 'When most English people say "horse," they mean a hoofed quadruped of the genus Equus.' This may be called the verbal definition proper, and I do not say that good is indefinable in this sense either; for it is certainly possible to discover how people use a word: otherwise, we could never have known that 'good' may be translated by 'gut' in German and by 'bon' in French. But (3) we may, when we

define horse, mean something much more important. We may mean
that a certain object, which we all of us know, is composed in a
certain manner: that it has four legs, a head, a heart, a liver, etc.,
etc., all of them arranged in definite relations to one another. It is
in this sense that I deny good to be definable. I say that it is not
composed of any parts, which we can substitute for it in our minds
when we are thinking of it. We might think just as clearly and correctly about a horse, if we thought of all its parts and their arrangement instead of thinking of the whole: we could, I say, think how
a horse differed from a donkey just as well, just as truly, in this
way, as now we do, only not so easily; but there is nothing whatsoever which we could so substitute for good; and that is what I
mean, when I say that good is indefinable.

9. But I am afraid I have still not removed the chief difficulty
which may prevent acceptance of the proposition that good is indefinable. I do not mean to say that *the* good, that which is good,
is thus indefinable; if I did think so, I should not be writing on
Ethics, for my main object is to help towards discovering that definition. It is just because I think there will be less risk of error in our
search for a definition of 'the good,' that I am now insisting that
good is indefinable. I must try to explain the difference between
these two. I suppose it may be granted that 'good' is an adjective.
Well 'the good,' 'that which is good,' must therefore be the sub-
stantive to which the adjective 'good' will apply: it must be the whole
of that to which the adjective will apply, and the adjective must
always truly apply to it. But if it is that to which the adjective will
apply, it must be something different from that adjective itself; and
the whole of that something different, whatever it is, will be our
definition of *the* good. Now it may be that this something will have
other adjectives, beside 'good,' that will apply to it. It may be full of
pleasure, for example; it may be intelligent: and if these two adjectives are really part of its definition, then it will certainly be true,
that pleasure and intelligence are good. And many people appear
to think that, if we say 'Pleasure and intelligence are good,' or if
we say 'Only pleasure and intelligence are good,' we are defining
'good.' Well, I cannot deny that propositions of this nature may
sometimes be called definitions; I do not know well enough how
the word is generally used to decide upon this point. I only wish
it to be understood that that is not what I mean when I say there

is no possible definition of good, and that I shall not mean this if I use the word again. I do most fully believe that some true proposition of the form 'Intelligence is good and intelligence alone is good' can be found; if none could be found, our definition of *the* good would be impossible. As it is, I believe *the* good to be definable; and yet I still say that good itself is indefinable.

10. 'Good,' then, if we mean by it that quality which we assert to belong to a thing, when we say that the thing is good, is incapable of any definition, in the most important sense of that word. The most important sense of 'definition' is that in which a definition states what are the parts which invariably compose a certain whole; and in this sense 'good' has no definition because it is simple and has no parts. It is one of those innumerable objects of thought which are themselves incapable of definition, because they are the ultimate terms by reference to which whatever *is* capable of definition must be defined. That there must be an indefinite number of such terms is obvious, on reflection; since we cannot define anything except by an analysis, which, when carried as far as it will go, refers us to something, which is simply different from anything else, and which by that ultimate difference explains the peculiarity of the whole which we are defining: for every whole contains some parts which are common to other wholes also. There is, therefore, no intrinsic difficulty in the contention that 'good' denotes a simple and indefinable quality. There are many other instances of such qualities.

Consider yellow, for example. We may try to define it, by describing its physical equivalent; we may state what kind of light-vibrations must stimulate the normal eye, in order that we may perceive it. But a moment's reflection is sufficient to shew that those light-vibrations are not themselves what we mean by yellow. *They* are not what we perceive. Indeed we should never have been able to discover their existence, unless we had first been struck by the patent difference of quality between the different colours. The most we can be entitled to say of those vibrations is that they are what corresponds in space to the yellow which we actually perceive.

Yet a mistake of this simple kind has commonly been made about 'good.' It may be true that all things which are good are *also* something else, just as it is true that all things which are yellow produce a certain kind of vibration in the light. And it is a fact, that Ethics aims at discovering what are those other properties belonging to all things which are good. But far too many philosophers have thought that when they named those other properties they were actually defining good; that these properties, in fact, were simply not 'other,' but absolutely and entirely the same with goodness. This view I propose to call the 'naturalistic fallacy' and of it I shall now endeavour to dispose.

11. Let us consider what it is such philosophers say. And first it is to be noticed that they do not agree among themselves. They not only say that they are right as to what good is, but they endeavour to prove that other people who say that it is something else, are wrong. One, for instance, will affirm that good is pleasure, another, perhaps, that good is that which is desired; and each of these will argue eagerly to prove that the other is wrong. But how is that possible? One of them says that good is nothing but the object of desire, and at the same time tries to prove that it is not pleasure. But from his first assertion, that good just means the object of desire, one of two things must follow as regards his proof:

(1) He may be trying to prove that the object of desire is not pleasure. But, if this be all, where is his Ethics? The position he is maintaining is merely a psychological one. Desire is something which occurs in our minds, and pleasure is something else which so occurs; and our would-be ethical philosopher is merely holding that the latter is not the object of the former. But what has that to do with the question in dispute? His opponent held the ethical proposition that pleasure was the good, and although he should prove a million times over the psychological proposition that pleasure is not the object of desire, he is no nearer proving his opponent to be wrong. The position is like this. One man says a triangle is a circle: another replies 'A triangle is a straight line, and I will prove to you that I am right: *for*' (this is the only argument) 'a straight line is not a circle.' 'That is quite true,' the other may reply; 'but nevertheless a triangle is a circle, and you have said nothing whatever to prove the contrary. What is proved is that one of us is wrong, for we agree that a triangle cannot be both a straight line and a circle: but which is wrong, there can be no earthly means of proving, since you define triangle as straight line and I define it as circle.'—Well, that is one alternative which any naturalistic Ethics has to face; if good is *defined* as something else, it is then impossible

either to prove that any other definition is wrong or even to deny such definition.

(2) The other alternative will scarcely be more welcome. It is that the discussion is after all a verbal one. When A says 'Good means pleasant' and B says 'Good means desired,' they may merely wish to assert that most people have used the word for what is pleasant and for what is desired respectively. And this is quite an interesting subject for discussion: only it is not a whit more an ethical discussion than the last was. Nor do I think that any exponent of naturalistic Ethics would be willing to allow that this was all he meant. They are all so anxious to persuade us that what they call the good is what we really ought to do. 'Do, pray, act so, because the word "good" is generally used to denote actions of this nature': such, on this view, would be the substance of their teaching. And in so far as they tell us how we ought to act, their teaching is truly ethical, as they mean it to be. But how perfectly absurd is the reason they would give for it! 'You are to do this, because most people use a certain word to denote conduct such as this.' 'You are to say the thing which is not, because most people call it lying.' That is an argument just as good!—My dear sirs, what we want to know from you as ethical teachers, is not how people use a word; it is not even, what kind of actions they approve, which the use of this word 'good' may certainly imply: what we want to know is simply what *is* good. We may indeed agree that what most people do think good, is actually so; we shall at all events be glad to know their opinions: but when we say their opinions about what *is* good, we do mean what we say; we do not care whether they call that thing which they mean 'horse' or 'table' or 'chair,' 'gut' or 'bon' or 'agathos'; we want to know what it is that they so call. When they say 'Pleasure is good,' we cannot believe that they merely mean 'Pleasure is pleasure' and nothing more than that.

12. Suppose a man says 'I am pleased'; and suppose that is not a lie or a mistake but the truth. Well, if it is true, what does that mean? It means that his mind, a certain definite mind, distinguished by certain definite marks from all others, has at this moment a certain definite feeling called pleasure. 'Pleased' *means* nothing but having pleasure, and though we may be more pleased or less pleased, and even, we may admit for the present, have one or another kind of pleasure; yet in so far as it is pleasure we have, whether there be more or less of it, and whether it be of one kind or another, what we have is one definite thing, absolutely indefinable, some one thing that is the same in all the various degrees and in all the various kinds of it that there may be. We may be able to say how it is related to other things: that, for example, it is in the mind, that it causes desire, that we are conscious of it, etc., etc. We can, I say, describe its relations to other things, but define it we can *not*. And if anybody tried to define pleasure for us as being any other natural object; if anybody were to say, for instance, that pleasure *means* the sensation of red, and were to proceed to deduce from that that pleasure is a colour, we should be entitled to laugh at him and to distrust his future statements about pleasure. Well, that would be the same fallacy which I have called the naturalistic fallacy. That 'pleased' does not mean 'having the sensation of red,' or anything else whatever, does not prevent us from understanding what it does mean. It is enough for us to know that 'pleased' does mean 'having the sensation of pleasure,' and though pleasure is absolutely indefinable, though pleasure is pleasure and nothing else whatever, yet we feel no difficulty in saying that we are pleased. The reason is, of course, that when I say 'I am pleased,' I do *not* mean that 'I' am the same thing as 'having pleasure.' And similarly no difficulty need be found in my saying that 'pleasure is good' and yet not meaning that 'pleasure' is the same thing as 'good,' that pleasure *means* good, and that good *means* pleasure. If I were to imagine that when I said 'I am pleased,' I meant that I was exactly the same thing as 'pleased,' I should not indeed call that a naturalistic fallacy, although it would be the same fallacy as I have called naturalistic with reference to Ethics. The reason of this is obvious enough. When a man confuses two natural objects with one another, defining the one by the other, if for instance, he confuses himself, who is one natural object, with 'pleased' or with 'pleasure' which are others, then there is no reason to call the fallacy naturalistic. But if he confuses 'good,' which is not in the same sense a natural object, with any natural object whatever, then there is a reason for calling that a naturalistic fallacy; its being made with regard to 'good' marks it as something quite specific, and this specific mistake deserves a name because it is so common. As for the reasons why good is not to be considered a natural object, they may be reserved for discussion in another place. But, for the present, it is sufficient to notice this: Even if it were a natural object, that would not alter the nature of the fallacy nor diminish its importance one whit. All that I have said about it would remain quite equally true: only the name which I have called it would not be so appropriate as I think it is. And I do not care about the name: what I do care about is the fallacy. It does not matter what we call it, provided we recognise it when we meet with it. It is to be met with in almost every book on Ethics; and yet it is not recognised: and that is why it is necessary to multiply illustrations of it, and convenient to give it a name. It is a very simple fallacy indeed. When we say that an orange is yellow, we do not think our statement binds us to hold that 'orange' means nothing else than 'yellow,' or that nothing can be yellow but an orange. Supposing the orange is also sweet! Does that bind us to say that 'sweet' is exactly the same thing as 'yellow,' that 'sweet' must be defined as 'yellow'? And supposing it be recognised that 'yellow' just means 'yellow' and nothing else whatever, does that make it any more difficult to hold that oranges are yellow? Most certainly it does not: on the contrary, it would be absolutely meaningless to say that oranges were yellow, unless yellow did in the end mean just 'yellow' and nothing else whatever—unless it was absolutely indefinable. We should not get any very clear notion about things, which are yellow—we should not get very far with our science, if we were bound to hold that everything which was yellow, *meant* exactly the same thing as yellow. We should find we had to hold that an orange was exactly the same thing as a stool, a piece of paper, a lemon, anything you like. We could prove any number of absurdities; but should we be the nearer to the truth? Why, then, should it be different with 'good'? Why, if good is good and indefinable, should I be held to deny that pleasure is good? Is there any difficulty in holding both to be true at once? On the contrary, there is no meaning in saying that pleasure is good, unless good is something different from pleasure. It is absolutely useless, so far as Ethics is concerned, to prove, as Mr Spencer tries to do, that increase of pleasure coincides with increase of life, unless good *means* something different from either life or pleasure. He might just as well try to prove that an orange is yellow by shewing that it always is wrapped up in paper.

13. In fact, if it is not the case that 'good' denotes something simple and indefinable, only two alternatives are possible: either

it is a complex, a given whole, about the correct analysis of which
there may be disagreement; or else it means nothing at all, and
there is no such subject as Ethics. In general, however, ethical
philosophers have attempted to define good, without recognising
what such an attempt must mean. They actually use arguments
which involve one or both of the absurdities considered in § 11.
We are, therefore, justified in concluding that the attempt to define
good is chiefly due to want of clearness as to the possible nature of
definition. There are, in fact, only two serious alternatives to be
considered, in order to establish the conclusion that 'good' does
denote a simple and indefinable notion. It might possibly denote a
complex, as 'horse' does; or it might have no meaning at all. Neither
of these possibilities has, however, been clearly conceived and seriously maintained, as such, by those who presume to define good;
and both may be dismissed by a simple appeal to facts.

a.   The hypothesis that disagreement about the meaning of good
     is disagreement with regard to the correct analysis of a given
     whole, may be most plainly seen to be incorrect by considera-
     tion of the fact that, whatever definition be offered, it may be
     always asked, with significance, of the complex so defined,
     whether it is itself good. To take, for instance, one of the
     more plausible, because one of the more complicated, of such
     proposed definitions, it may easily be thought, at first sight,
     that to be good may mean to be that which we desire to desire.
     Thus if we apply this definition to a particular instance and
     say 'When we think that A is good, we are thinking that A is
     one of the things which we desire to desire,' our proposition
     may seem quite plausible. But, if we carry the investigation
     further, and ask ourselves 'Is it good to desire to desire A?' it
     is apparent, on a little reflection, that this question is itself as
     intelligible, as the original question 'Is A good?'—that we are,
     in fact, now asking for exactly the same information about
     the desire to desire A, for which we formerly asked with re-
     gard to A itself. But it is also apparent that the meaning of
     this second question cannot be correctly analysed into 'Is the
     desire to desire A one of the things which we desire to desire'?:
     we have not before our minds anything so complicated as the
     question 'Do we desire to desire to desire to desire A?' More-
     over any one can easily convince himself by inspection that

the predicate of this proposition—'good'—is positively different from the notion of 'desiring to desire' which enters into its subject: 'That we should desire to desire A is good' is *not* merely equivalent to 'That A should be good is good.' It may indeed be true that what we desire to desire is always also good; perhaps, even the converse may be true: but it is very doubtful whether this is the case, and the mere fact that we understand very well what is meant by doubting it, shews clearly that we have two different notions before our minds.

b. And the same consideration is sufficient to dismiss the hypothesis that 'good' has no meaning whatsoever. It is very natural to make the mistake of supposing that what is universally true is of such a nature that its negation would be self-contradictory: the importance which has been assigned to analytic propositions in the history of philosophy shews how easy such a mistake is. And thus it is very easy to conclude that what seems to be a universal ethical principle is in fact an identical proposition; that, if, for example, whatever is called 'good' seems to be pleasant, the proposition 'Pleasure is the good' does not assert a connection between two different notions, but involves only one, that of pleasure, which is easily recognised as a distinct entity. But whoever will attentively consider with himself what is actually before his mind when he asks the question 'Is pleasure (or whatever it may be) after all good?' can easily satisfy himself that he is not merely wondering whether pleasure is pleasant. And if he will try this experiment with each suggested definition in succession, he may become expert enough to recognise that in every case he has before his mind a unique object, with regard to the connection of which with any other object, a distinct question may be asked. Every one does in fact understand the question 'Is this good?' When he thinks of it, his state of mind is different from what it would be, were he asked 'Is this pleasant, or desired, or approved?' It has a distinct meaning for him, even though he may not recognise in what respect it is distinct. Whenever he thinks of 'intrinsic value,' or 'intrinsic worth,' or says that a thing 'ought to exist,' he has before his mind the unique object—the unique property of things—which I mean by 'good.' Everybody is constantly aware of this notion, although he may never become aware at all that it is different from other notions of which he is also aware. But, for correct ethical reasoning, it is extremely important that he should become aware of this fact; and, as soon as the nature of the problem is clearly understood, there should be little difficulty in advancing so far in analysis.

14. 'Good,' then, is indefinable; and yet, so far as I know, there is only one ethical writer, Prof. Henry Sidgwick, who has clearly recognised and stated this fact. We shall see, indeed, how far many of the most reputed ethical systems fall short of drawing the conclusions which follow from such a recognition. At present I will only quote one instance, which will serve to illustrate the meaning and importance of this principle that 'good' is indefinable, or, as Prof. Sidgwick says, an 'unanalysable notion.' It is an instance to which Prof. Sidgwick himself refers in a note on the passage, in which he argues that 'ought' is unanalysable.[1]

'Bentham,' says Sidgwick, 'explains that his fundamental principle "states the greatest happiness of all those whose interest is in question as being the right and proper end of human action" '; and yet 'his language in other passages of the same chapter would seem to imply' that he *means* by the word "right" "conducive to the general happiness." Prof. Sidgwick sees that, if you take these two statements together, you get the absurd result that 'greatest happiness is the end of human action, which is conducive to the general happiness'; and so absurd does it seem to him to call this result, as Bentham calls it, 'the fundamental principle of a moral system,' that he suggests that Bentham cannot have meant it. Yet Prof. Sidgwick himself states elsewhere [2] that Psychological Hedonism is 'not seldom confounded with Egoistic Hedonism'; and that confusion, as we shall see, rests chiefly on that same fallacy, the naturalistic fallacy, which is implied in Bentham's statements. Prof. Sidgwick admits therefore that this fallacy is sometimes committed, absurd as it is; and I am inclined to think that Bentham may really have been one of those who committed it. Mill, as we shall see, certainly did commit it. In any case, whether Bentham committed it or not, his doctrine, as above quoted, will serve as a very good illustration of

[1] *Methods of Ethics,* Bk. I, Chap. iii, § 1 (6th edition).
[2] *Methods of Ethics,* Bk. I, Chap. iv, § 1.

this fallacy, and of the importance of the contrary proposition that good is indefinable.

Let us consider this doctrine. Bentham seems to imply, so Prof. Sidgwick says, that the word 'right' *means* 'conducive to general happiness.' Now this, by itself, need not necessarily involve the naturalistic fallacy. For the word 'right' is very commonly appropriated to actions which lead to the attainment of what is good; which are regarded as *means* to the ideal and not as ends-in-themselves. This use of 'right,' as denoting what is good as a means, whether or not it be also good as an end, is indeed the use to which I shall confine the word. Had Bentham been using 'right' in this sense, it might be perfectly consistent for him to *define* right as 'conducive to the general happiness,' *provided only* (and notice this proviso) he had already proved, or laid down as an axiom, that general happiness was *the* good, or (what is equivalent to this) that general happiness alone was good. For in that case he would have already defined *the* good as general happiness (a position perfectly consistent, as we have seen, with the contention that 'good' is indefinable), and, since right was to be defined as 'conducive to *the* good,' it would actually *mean* 'conducive to general happiness.' But this method of escape from the charge of having committed the naturalistic fallacy has been closed by Bentham himself. For his fundamental principle is, we see, that the greatest happiness of all concerned is the *right* and proper *end* of human action. He applies the word 'right,' therefore, to the end, as such, not only to the means which are conducive to it; and, that being so, right can no longer be defined as 'conducive to the general happiness,' without involving the fallacy in question. For now it is obvious that the definition of right as conducive to general happiness can be used by him in support of the fundamental principle that general happiness is the right end; instead of being itself derived from that principle. If right, by definition, means conducive to general happiness, then it is obvious that general happiness is the right end. It is not necessary now first to prove or assert that general happiness is the right end, before right is defined as conducive to general happiness—a perfectly valid procedure; but on the contrary the definition of right as conducive to general happiness proves general happiness to be the right end—a perfectly invalid procedure, since in this case the statement that 'general happiness is the right end of human

action' is not an ethical principle at all, but either, as we have seen,
a proposition about the meaning of words, or else a proposition
about the *nature* of general happiness, not about its rightness or
goodness.

Now, I do not wish the importance I assign to this fallacy to
be misunderstood. The discovery of it does not at all refute Bentham's contention that greatest happiness is the proper end of
human action, if that be understood as an ethical proposition, as he
undoubtedly intended it. That principle may be true all the same;
we shall consider whether it is so in succeeding chapters. Bentham
might have maintained it, as Prof. Sidgwick does, even if the fallacy
had been pointed out to him. What I am maintaining is that the
reasons which he actually gives for his ethical proposition are fallacious ones so far as they consist in a definition of right. What I suggest is that he did not perceive them to be fallacious; that, if he had
done so, he would have been led to seek for other reasons in support
of his Utilitarianism; and that, had he sought for other reasons, he
might have found none which he thought to be sufficient. In that
case he would have changed his whole system—a most important
consequence. It is undoubtedly also possible that he would have
thought other reasons to be sufficient, and in that case his ethical
system, in its main results, would still have stood. But, even in this
latter case, his use of the fallacy would be a serious objection to him
as an ethical philosopher. For it is the business of Ethics, I must
insist, not only to obtain true results, but also to find valid reasons
for them. The direct object of Ethics is knowledge and not practice;
and any one who uses the naturalistic fallacy has certainly not fulfilled this first object, however correct his practical principles may be.

My objections to Naturalism are then, in the first place, that
it offers no reason at all, far less any valid reason, for any ethical
principle whatever; and in this it already fails to satisfy the requirements of Ethics, as a scientific study. But in the second place I contend that, though it gives a reason for no ethical principle, it is a
cause of the acceptance of false principles—it deludes the mind into
accepting ethical principles, which are false; and in this it is contrary to every aim of Ethics. It is easy to see that if we start with
a definition of right conduct as conduct conducive to general happiness; then, knowing that right conduct is universally conduct conducive to the good, we very easily arrive at the result that the good

is general happiness. If, on the other hand, we once recognise that we must start our Ethics without a definition, we shall be much more apt to look about us, before we adopt any ethical principle whatever; and the more we look about us, the less likely are we to adopt a false one. It may be replied to this: Yes, but we shall look about us just as much, before we settle on our definition, and are therefore just as likely to be right. But I will try to shew that this is not the case. If we start with the conviction that a definition of good can be found, we start with the conviction that good *can mean* nothing else than some one property of things; and our only business will then be to discover what that property is. But if we recognise that, so far as the meaning of good goes, anything whatever may be good, we start with a much more open mind. Moreover, apart from the fact that, when we think we have a definition, we cannot logically defend our ethical principles in any way whatever, we shall also be much less apt to defend them well, even if illogically. For we shall start with the conviction that good must mean so and so, and shall therefore be inclined either to misunderstand our opponent's arguments or to cut them short with the reply, 'This is not an open question: the very meaning of the word decides it; no one can think otherwise except through confusion.' . . .

Chapter III

Hedonism

36. In this chapter we have to deal with what is perhaps the most famous and the most widely held of all ethical principles—the principle that nothing is good but pleasure. My chief reason for treating of this principle in this place is, as I said, that Hedonism appears in the main to be a form of Naturalistic Ethics: in other words, that pleasure has been so generally held to be the sole good, is almost entirely due to the fact that it has seemed to be somehow involved in the *definition* of 'good'—to be pointed out by the very meaning of the word. If this is so, then the prevalence of Hedonism has been mainly due to what I have called the naturalistic fallacy—the failure to distinguish clearly that unique and indefinable quality which we mean by good. . . .

39. I propose, then, to begin by an examination of Mill's *Utilitarianism.* That is a book which contains an admirably clear and fair discussion of many ethical principles and methods. Mill exposes not a few simple mistakes which are very likely to be made by those who approach ethical problems without much previous reflection. But what I am concerned with is the mistakes which Mill himself appears to have made, and these only so far as they concern the Hedonistic principle. Let me repeat what that principle is. It is, I said, that pleasure is the only thing at which we ought to aim, the only thing that is good as an end and for its own sake. And now let us turn to Mill and see whether he accepts this description of the question at issue. 'Pleasure,' he says at the outset, 'and freedom from pain, are the only things desirable as ends' (p. 10 [3] [p. 45]); and again, at the end of his argument, 'To think of an object as desirable (unless for the sake of its consequences) and to think of it as pleasant are one and the same thing' (p. 58 [p. 76]). These statements, taken together, and apart from certain confusions which are obvious in them, seem to imply the principle I have stated; and if I succeed in shewing that Mill's reasons for them do not prove them, it must at least be admitted that I have not been fighting with shadows or demolishing a man of straw.

It will be observed that Mill adds 'absence of pain' to 'pleasure' in his first statement, though not in his second. There is, in this, a confusion, with which, however, we need not deal. I shall talk of 'pleasure' alone, for the sake of conciseness; but all my arguments will apply *à fortiori* to 'absence of pain': it is easy to make the necessary substitutions.

Mill holds, then, that 'happiness is desirable, and *the only thing desirable,*[4] as an end; all other things being only desirable as means to that end' (p. 52 [p. 72]). Happiness he has already defined as 'pleasure, and the absence of pain' (p. 10 [p. 45]); he does not pretend that this is more than an arbitrary verbal definition; and, as *such,* I have not a word to say against it. His principle, then, is 'pleasure is the only thing desirable,' if I may be allowed, when I say 'pleasure,' to include in that word (so far as necessary) absence of pain. And now what are his reasons for holding that principle to be true? He has already told us (p. 6 [p. 42]) that 'Questions of ultimate ends are not amenable to direct proof. Whatever can be proved

[3] My references are to the 13th edition, 1897.
[4] My italics.

to be good, must be so by being shewn to be a means to something *admitted to be good without proof.*' With this, I perfectly agree: indeed the chief object of my first chapter was to shew that this is so. Anything which is good as an end must be admitted to be good without proof. We are agreed so far. Mill even uses the same examples which I used in my second chapter. 'How,' he says, 'is it possible to prove that health is good?' 'What proof is it possible to give that pleasure is good?' Well, in Chapter IV, in which he deals with the proof of his Utilitarian principle, Mill repeats the above statement in these words: 'It has already,' he says, 'been remarked, that questions of ultimate ends do not admit of proof, in the ordinary acceptation of the term' (p. 52 [p. 72]). 'Questions about ends,' he goes on in this same passage, 'are, in other words, questions what things are desirable.' I am quoting these repetitions, because they make it plain what otherwise might have been doubted, that Mill is using the words 'desirable' or 'desirable as an end' as absolutely and precisely equivalent to the words 'good as an end.' We are, then, now to hear, what reasons he advances for this doctrine that pleasure alone is good as an end.

40. 'Questions about ends,' he says (pp. 52–3 [pp. 72–73]), 'are, in other words, questions what things are desirable. The utilitarian doctrine is, that happiness is desirable, and the only thing desirable, as an end; all other things being only desirable as means to that end. What ought to be required of this doctrine—what conditions is it requisite that the doctrine should fulfil—to make good its claim to be believed?

'The only proof capable of being given that a thing is visible, is that people actually see it. The only proof that a sound is audible, is that people hear it; and so of the other sources of our experience. In like manner, I apprehend, the sole evidence it is possible to produce that anything is desirable, is that people do actually desire it. If the end which the utilitarian doctrine proposes to itself were not, in theory and in practice, acknowledged to be an end, nothing could ever convince any person that it was so. No reason can be given why the general happiness is desirable, except that each person, so far as he believes it to be attainable, desires his own happiness. This, however, being the fact, we have not only all the proof which the case admits of, but all which it is possible to require, that happiness is a good: that each person's happiness is a good to that person, and the general happiness, therefore, a good to the aggregate of all persons. Happiness has made out its title as *one* of the ends of conduct, and consequently one of the criteria of morality.'

There, that is enough. That is my first point. Mill has made as naïve and artless a use of the naturalistic fallacy as anybody could desire. 'Good,' he tells us, means 'desirable,' and you can only find out what is desirable by seeking to find out what is actually desired. This is, of course, only one step towards the proof of Hedonism; for it may be, as Mill goes on to say, that other things beside pleasure are desired. Whether or not pleasure is the only thing desired is, as Mill himself admits (p. 58 [p. 76]), a psychological question, to which we shall presently proceed. The important step for Ethics is this one just taken, the step which pretends to prove that 'good' means 'desired.'

Well, the fallacy in this step is so obvious, that it is quite wonderful how Mill failed to see it. The fact is that 'desirable' does not mean 'able to be desired' as 'visible' means 'able to be seen.' The desirable means simply what *ought* to be desired or *deserves* to be desired; just as the detestable means not what can be but what ought to be detested and the damnable what deserves to be damned. Mill has, then, smuggled in, under cover of the word 'desirable,' the very notion about which he ought to be quite clear. 'Desirable' does indeed mean 'what it is good to desire'; but when this is understood, it is no longer plausible to say that our only test of *that*, is what is actually desired. Is it merely a tautology when the Prayer Book talks of *good* desires? Are not *bad* desires also possible? Nay, we find Mill himself talking of a 'better and nobler object of desire' (p. 10 [p. 45]), as if, after all, what is desired were not *ipso facto* good, and good in proportion to the amount it is desired. Moreover, if the desired is *ipso facto* the good; then the good is *ipso facto* the motive of our actions, and there can be no question of finding motives for doing it, as Mill is at such pains to do. If Mill's explanation of 'desirable' be *true,* then his statement (p. 26 [p. 55]) that the rule of action may be *confounded* with the motive of it is untrue: for the motive of action will then be according to him *ipso facto* its rule; there can be no distinction between the two, and therefore no confusion, and thus he has contradicted himself flatly. These are specimens of the contradictions, which, as I have tried to shew, must always follow from the use of the naturalistic fallacy; and I hope I need now say no more about the matter.

The "Proof" of Utility in Bentham and Mill

Everett W. Hall

The ostensible object of the present paper is to correct an interpretation that, in the author's estimation, involves a grave historical injustice. Frankly, however, this would never have been undertaken had there not been a supporting motivation—the desire to bring to the attention of contemporary ethicists a basic, yet simple, methodological distinction, a distinction imbedded, so it will be contended, in the writings of Bentham and Mill but almost completely neglected up to the present.

One need not be a worshiper at the shrine of one's intellectual ancestors to feel a slight sense of distaste at the sight of every author of an elementary textbook in logic or ethics scurrying to chapter iv of Mill's *Utilitarianism*, "Of What Sort of Proof the Principle of Utility Is Susceptible," for examples of fallacies sufficiently blatant to be grasped at a glance by the untrained mind. It is just too obvious that the relation of "desirable" to "desired" is only suffixally similar to the relation of "audible" to "heard" ("audited"). And who cannot spot the error of deriving "everyone desires the general happiness" from "each desires his own happiness"? And so we might go down through the traditional list. But were we to try to understand Mill's argument as a whole and in the simple and obvious sense in which, when viewed as a whole, it seems only fair to take it, we might find a core worth serious consideration.

We must charge this tendency to force Mill's proof of the principle of utility into a set of the most patent fallacies to really first-

Reprinted from *Ethics*, Vol. LX (1949), pp. 1–18, by permission of The University of Chicago Press.

line philosophers. For example, F. H. Bradley, in *Ethical Studies*,[1] excuses himself for taking time to point out the tissue of inconsistencies that, so he claims, is Mill's argument. "I am ashamed," he writes, "to have to examine such reasoning, but it is necessary to do so, since it is common enough." [2] I shall, however, be mainly concerned to scrutinize the criticisms of another first-line philosopher, partly because I think he is probably the most influential source of the traditional disparagement of Mill's argument and partly because he has stated the supposed case against Mill's proof most clearly and cogently. I refer to G. E. Moore, and specifically to chapter iii of *Principia Ethica*. Moore here admits, candidly enough, that his analysis derives from Sidgwick. This is entirely true, but the tone is quite different, for Sidgwick believed he was simply explicating certain hidden, but necessary, intuitionistic assumptions in utilitarianism, whereas Moore is an avowed, even an aggressive, opponent of that position.

Let us see what Moore's criticism is. For purposes of analysis it is well to have Mill's argument before us, familiar as that argument is. For the moment we shall note only what Moore calls the "first step" and, in fact, only the first half of the first step, which I shall designate "1*A*":

1*A*. "The only proof capable of being given that a thing is visible, is that people actually see it. The only proof that a sound is audible, is that people hear it; and so of the other sources of our experience. In like manner, I apprehend, the sole evidence it is possible to produce that anything is desirable, is that people do actually desire it. If the end which the utilitarian doctrine proposes to itself were not, in theory and in practice, acknowledged to be an end, nothing could ever convince any person that it was so." [3]

Of this, Moore says: "Well, the fallacy in this step is so obvious, that it is quite wonderful how Mill failed to see it." [4] What fallacy? A fallacy Moore calls "the naturalistic fallacy." "Mill has made as naïve and artless a use of the naturalistic fallacy as anybody could desire. 'Good,' he tells us, means 'desirable,' and you can only find

1 (2d ed.; Oxford, 1927), pp. 113–24.
2 *Ibid.*, p. 115 n.
3 Quoted by Moore, *Principia Ethica*, p. 66 [p. 121].
4 *Ibid.*, p. 67 [p. 122].

out what is desirable by seeking to find out what is actually desired.
. . . The important step for Ethics is this one just taken, the step
which pretends to prove that 'good' means 'desired.' " [5]

And just what is this naturalistic fallacy that Mill committed
so naïvely and artlessly? Let me quote one or two passages, as I fear
I cannot find a single straightforward answer:

It may be true that all things which are good are *also* something
else, just as it is true that all things which are yellow produce a certain
kind of vibration in the light. And it is a fact, that Ethics aims at discovering what are those other properties belonging to all things which
are good. But far too many philosophers have thought that when they
named those other properties they were actually defining good; that these
properties, in fact, were simply not "other," but absolutely and entirely
the same with goodness. This view I propose to call the "naturalistic
fallacy" and of it I shall now endeavour to dispose.[6]

If I were to imagine that when I said "I am pleased," I meant that
I was exactly the same thing as "pleased," I should not indeed call that
a naturalistic fallacy, although it would be the same fallacy as I have
called naturalistic with reference to Ethics.[7]

It is a very simple fallacy indeed. When we say that an orange is
yellow, we do not think our statement binds us to hold that "orange"
means nothing else than "yellow," or that nothing can be yellow but an
orange. Supposing the orange is also sweet. Does that bind us to say
that "sweet" is exactly the same thing as "yellow," that "sweet" must be
defined as "yellow"? [8]

. . . There is no meaning in saying that pleasure is good, unless
good is something different from pleasure.[9]

Professor Frankena, in an article on "The Naturalistic Fallacy," [10] has taken these and similar passages in *Principia Ethica* to
mean that the naturalistic fallacy is a species of the definist fallacy,
which "is the process of confusing or identifying two properties." [11]

[5] *Ibid.*, p. 66 [p. 122].
[6] *Ibid.*, p. 10 [pp. 109–10].
[7] *Ibid.*, p. 13 [p. 112].
[8] *Ibid.*, p. 14 [p. 113].
[9] *Ibid.*, p. 14 [p. 113].
[10] *Mind,* XLVIII (new ser., 1939), 464–77.
[11] *Ibid.*, p. 471.

Mr. Frankena rightly points out that this fallacy can occur only within a system that distinguishes the properties said (by him who claims a commission of the naturalistic fallacy) to be confused or identified. Thus a naturalist who denies any property of goodness or desirableness as different from desiredness has not committed the definist fallacy in saying, "The desirable just is the desired." This seems so obviously correct that one wonders how Moore could have failed to see it or how he could have made the equivalent error, "that 'good is indefinable,' and that to deny this involves a fallacy, is a point capable of strict proof: for to deny it involves contradictions." [12]

I think the truth is that Moore had in mind, as well as the definist fallacy, and confused therewith, two others, which *are* strictly fallacies and which, if committed, would involve one in the commission of the definist fallacy or would easily lead to it. The passages already quoted seem to bear this out. First, there is the confusion of the predicative with the identity "is." Let us call this the "predicative fallacy." To go from "the orange is yellow" to "the orange is nothing but yellow," or from "I am pleased" to "I am identical with having pleasure" would be to commit the predicative fallacy. Second, there is what, for lack of a recognized name, I might call the "extensionalist fallacy." This goes from the extensional equivalence of two predicate terms (whenever either is truly predicated of a particular, the other is also) to their identity (they designate the same property). Of course, an extensional language could be set up such that this implication holds. But it does not hold in ordinary language. Moore makes frequent appeal to its invalidity. To go from "Properties A and B always accompany goodness" to "Goodness just is A and B" would be to commit the extensionalist fallacy.

Now to return to the issue. When Moore says that Mill, in step 1*A*, has committed the naturalistic fallacy, what does he accuse him of? I think it is the definist fallacy. In any case, he does nothing to show that Mill committed the extensionalist fallacy. For example, he does not accuse Mill of going from "Whatever is desirable is desired and *vice versa*" to " 'Desirableness' and 'desiredness' designate the same property." And, were he to do so, Mill's actual statement

[12] Moore, *op. cit.*, p. 77.

would not bear him out; for that statement simply is that the *sole evidence* that anything is desirable is that it is desired. This does not claim extensional equivalence of "*x* is desirable" and "*x* is desired," nor does it go from this to an identification of the two predicates. Nor does Moore show that Mill has committed the predicative fallacy, that, for example, he has gone from "Desirableness is desired" to "Desirableness just is desiredness." So I think that Moore simply means to accuse Mill of identifying two properties that are different, viz., desirableness and desiredness, and this, perhaps, as a step toward identifying goodness with pleasure.

Now we have seen that the definist fallacy is no fallacy unless the predicates definitionally identified are also taken to refer to different properties. So here, if Mill is saying that there is no property of desirableness or goodness different from the property of desiredness, that it is consonant with common usage to suppose that the word "desirableness" just refers to desiredness, he has committed no fallacy whatsoever. I happen to believe, however, that Mill does mean to accept desirableness and desiredness as different properties and that his argument makes this clear and that he does not commit the definist fallacy.

Turning back to step 1*A*, we find Mill saying: "The sole evidence it is possible to produce that anything is desirable is that people actually do desire it." Moore himself correctly paraphrases this in one place: ". . . you can only find out what is desirable by seeking to find out what is actually desired." But then, later, he makes the astounding assertion, without any foundation, that Mill has pretended "to prove that 'good' means 'desired' "! I can only account for this flagrant reading into Mill of the definist fallacy by supposing Moore could not grasp any other sense to Mill's argument and so thought that Mill *must* have committed this fallacy. But *there is* another and an obvious sense to any interpreter not debauched with verbal casuistry, as I hope to show.

To proceed: Moore continues his attack as follows:

The fact is that "desirable" does not mean "able to be desired" as "visible" means "able to be seen." The desirable means simply what *ought* to be desired or *deserves* to be desired; just as the detestable means not what can be but what ought to be detested and the damnable what deserves to be damned. Mill has, then, smuggled in, under cover of the word "desirable," the very notion about which he ought to be quite clear. "Desirable" does indeed mean "what it is good to desire"; but when this is understood, it is no longer plausible to say that our only test of *that,* is what is actually desired.[13]

This passage is a classic. Does it not show the complete bankruptcy of Mill's proof of utility? But there is one small question. What reason is there to suppose that Mill was not perfectly aware that "desirable" does not mean "able to be desired" and so, in *this* respect, was not at all analogous to "visible"? Could there be no other way in which the evidence for desirability must be like the evidence for visibility than in the suffixes of the adjectival designations? I think a glance at the whole argument shows that there is. And on what grounds does Moore so peremptorily continue: " 'Desirable' does indeed mean 'what it is good to desire'; but when this is understood, it is no longer plausible to say that our only test of *that* is what is actually desired"? Does he mean to make the astounding assertion which he seems to make, that anyone who says that the only test of the occurrence of A is the occurrence of B must be identifying A with B? This would force everyone who admits the extensional equivalence of two properties into a commission of the extensionalist fallacy!

Let us continue with Moore's criticism:

> Is it merely a tautology when the Prayer Book talks of *good* desires? Are not *bad* desires also possible? Nay, we find Mill himself talking of a "better and nobler object of desire," . . . as if, after all, what is desired were not *ipso facto* good, and good in proportion to the amount it is desired.[14]

Heaven forbid that any English philosopher should espouse a position that makes anything in the prayer-book a trivial tautology! I shall not undertake to defend Mill in general against such a serious charge, but on the particular point at issue I think I can clear his name. Apparently Moore's argument (which is here mostly suppressed, which perhaps accounts for its mounting vehemence) is that, since the desirable just is the desired for Mill, every desire must be good (desirable). Note, first, that this again assumes that Mill has

13 *Ibid.,* p. 67 [p. 122].
14 *Ibid.* [p. 122].

committed the definist fallacy. Now, even supposing that he had, Moore's argument breaks down; for this fallacy would identify the desirable with the desired, not with desire. A desirable desire would be a desired desire, and not every desire is desired (in fact, even if it were, to state this would require a synthetic sentence). And, still on the assumption that the definist fallacy has been committed, it would be appropriate to define "bad" as "being the object of an aversion," so that it could be plausibly held that there are bad desires. However, all this is out of the whole utilitarian framework of ideas. That framework requires that a motive be judged good or bad not by the goodness or badness of its object but by the goodness or badness of its tendency, that is, of its total probable consequences if its object be realized. It is true that Mill rejects the hedonic calculus of Bentham (if that means that the morally good man must calculate the probable effects of every alternative in every choice-situation) in favor of living by traditional moral rules in most situations, but this is only a concession as to a tool for ascertaining probable consequences and does not entail giving up the position that desires can be judged good or bad only by the test of their total probable consequences.

This leads immediately into a consideration of Moore's next thrust:

> Moreover, if the desired is *ipso facto* the good; then the good is *ipso facto* the motive of our actions, and there can be no question of finding motives for doing it, as Mill is at such pains to do. If Mill's explanation of "desirable" be *true,* then his statement . . . that the rule of action may be *confounded* with the motive of it is untrue: for the motive of action will then be according to him *ipso facto* its rule; there can be no distinction between the two, and therefore no confusion, and thus he has contradicted himself flatly.[15]

The reference here is to the following passage from chapter ii of *Utilitarianism:* Some objectors to utilitarianism

. . . say it is exacting too much to require that people shall always act from the inducement of promoting the general interests of society. But this is to mistake the very meaning of a standard of morals, and con-

---

[15] *Ibid.* [p. 122].

found the rule of action with the motive of it. It is the business of ethics to tell us what are our duties, or by what test we may know them; but no system of ethics requires that the sole motive of all we do shall be a feeling of duty; on the contrary, ninety-nine hundredths of all our actions are done from other motives, and rightly so done, if the rule of duty does not condemn them.[16]

This is in manifest contradiction with the definist fallacy of identifying good with desired (on the assumption, probably correct, that "motive of action" refers to the object desired)—so much so, in fact, that it should have at least raised the suspicion that Mill's argument for the principle of utility does not reduce to a commission of that fallacy.

Finally, Moore formulates his criticism of Mill's step 1*A* in the form of an accusation that Mill has committed the fallacy of ambiguous middle:

> Well, then, the first step by which Mill has attempted to establish his Hedonism is simply fallacious. He has attempted to establish the identity of the good with the desired, by confusing the proper sense of "desirable," in which it denotes that which it is good to desire, with the sense which it would bear if it were analogous to such words as "visible." If "desirable" is to be identical with "good," then it must bear one sense; and if it is to be identical with "desired," then it must bear quite another sense. And yet to Mill's contention that the desired is necessarily good, it is quite essential that these two senses of "desirable" should be the same.[17]

I take it Moore is saying that Mill's argument can be formulated as a syllogism in *Barbara:*

> The good is identical with the desirable.
> The desirable is identical with the desired.
> Therefore, the good is identical with the desired.

And in this syllogism, says Moore, the middle term, "desirable," is ambiguous. Here the definist fallacy would appear as the conclusion

---

[16] *Utilitarianism* (Everyman's ed.), p. 17 [pp. 55–56].
[17] Moore, *op. cit.*, pp. 67–68.

of a fallacious line of proof. But what evidence is there that Mill meant to use such a syllogism? I find none. Of the whole syllogism, it is clear only that Mill would accept the minor premise, that the desirable and the good are identical.

It is now time to turn to the second half of Mill's first step, which I shall name "1*B*":

1*B*. "No reason can be given why the general happiness is desirable, except that each person, so far as he believes it to be attainable, desires his own happiness. This, however, being the fact, we have not only all the proof which the case admits of, but all which it is possible to require, that happiness is a good: that each person's happiness is a good to that person, and the general happiness, therefore, a good to the aggregate of all persons. Happiness has made out its title as *one* of the ends of conduct, and consequently one of the criteria of morality." [18]

Moore does not specifically criticize this passage, though it is easy to guess how he would criticize it by reference to his method of dealing with step 1*A* and his discussion (without special reference to this passage) of egoistic hedonism.[19] But there is no need to construct a hypothetical criticism; we can fill in the lacuna in Moore by turning to Bradley, who, in this particular conflict, is clearly an ally. Referring to step 1*B*, Bradley writes:

Whether our "great modern logician" thought that by this he had proved that the happiness of all was desirable for each, I will not undertake to say. He either meant to prove this, or has proved what he started with, viz. that each desires his own pleasure. And yet there is a certain plausibility about it. If many pigs are fed at one trough, each desires his own food, and somehow as a consequence does seem to desire the food of all; and by parity of reasoning it should follow that each pig, desiring his own pleasure, desires also the pleasure of all.[20]

And in a footnote he adds:

Either Mill meant to argue, "*Because* everybody desires his own pleasure, *therefore* everybody desires his own pleasure"; or "Because every-

---

[18] Quoted by Moore (*ibid.,* p. 66 [pp. 121–22]).
[19] Cf. *ibid.,* pp. 96, 105. His object of condemnation here is Sidgwick.
[20] *Ethical Studies* (2d ed., 1927), p. 113.

body desires his own pleasure, *therefore* everybody desires the pleasure of everybody else." Disciples may take their choice.[21]

Somehow the warning that Mill put right into step 1B—"all the proof that the case admits of"—did not make any impression. Bradley, like Moore, is assuming that our "great modern logician," as he derisively characterizes Mill, *must* be presenting in his "proof" of the principle of utility a strict logical deduction. It is high time that this whole interpretation be fundamentally and decisively challenged.

If we turn back to chapter i of *Utilitarianism,* we find Mill unequivocally rejecting any such interpretation:

> On the present occasion, I shall, without further discussion of the other theories, attempt to contribute something towards the understanding and appreciation of the Utilitarian or Happiness theory, and towards such proof as it is susceptible of. It is evident that this cannot be proof in the ordinary and popular meaning of the term. Questions of ultimate ends are not amenable to direct proof. Whatever can be proved to be good, must be so by being shown to be a means to something admitted to be good without proof. . . . If, then, it is asserted that there is a comprehensive formula, including all things which are in themselves good, and that whatever else is good, is not so as an end, but as a mean, the formula may be accepted or rejected, but is not a subject of what is commonly understood by proof.[22]

And the very first sentence of chapter iv reverts to this disavowal of any strict proof of the principle of utility: "It has already been remarked, that questions of ultimate ends do not admit of strict proof, in the ordinary acceptation of the term." [23] Not only does Mill thus explicitly disavow any attempt to give a strict proof of the principle of utility, but he makes it clear that the "proof" which he offers is quite another sort of thing. Returning to chapter i, we find him continuing:

> We are not, however, to infer that its acceptance or rejection must depend on blind impulse, or arbitrary choice. There is a larger meaning

---

21 *Ibid.,* pp. 113–14 n.
22 *Op. cit.,* p. 4 [pp. 42–43].
23 *Ibid.,* p. 32 [p. 72].

of the word proof, in which this question is as amenable to it as any other of the disputed questions of philosophy. The subject is within the cognisance of the rational faculty; and neither does that faculty deal with it solely in the way of intuition. Considerations may be presented capable of determining the intellect either to give or withhold its assent to the doctrine; and this is equivalent to proof.

We shall examine presently of what nature are these considerations; in what manner they apply to the case, and what rational grounds, therefore, can be given for accepting or rejecting the utilitarian formula.[24]

The very title of chapter iv is illuminating, "Of what Sort of Proof the Principle of Utility Is Susceptible." Apparently, Mill considered that he was not so much giving a proof of the principle of utility as discussing the question of the meaning of "proof" when applied to an ethical first principle. So we find him asking, concerning the principle of utility, "What ought to be required of this doctrine—what conditions is it requisite that the doctrine should fulfil—to make good its claim to be believed?" [25]

So much, then, is obvious. Mill utterly disavows any attempt to give a strict proof of the principle of utility. Thus steps 1*A* and 1*B* cannot be interpreted as Moore and Bradley have interpreted them; for then they would be simply attempted strict deductions that, unfortunately, are failures because of the commission of fallacies that any schoolboy can detect.[26]

This result is final and quite unassailable. We now come to the more interesting and hazardous task of trying to ascertain just what is the nature of those considerations which, Mill thinks, are capable of determining the intellect to give assent to the principle of utility. And first let us call to mind the well-known, but not on that account wholly irrelevant, fact that Mill was an empiricist, an opponent of all forms of intuitionism and a priorism. That Mill himself thought

24 *Ibid.*, p. 4 [p. 43].
25 *Ibid.*, p. 32 [p. 72].
26 It would do no good were the critic of Mill to say that Mill's disavowal of strict proof applies only to his whole proof, that this latter includes step 2, which is inductive, and that therefore it is permissible to treat steps 1*A* and 1*B* as attempts at strict deduction. First, Mill would call such a combination of deduction and induction a strict proof "in the ordinary acceptation of the term." Second, his disavowal of strict proof is re-emphasized within both step 1*A* and step 1*B*.

this relevant is clear from chapter i of *Utilitarianism,* which is devoted precisely to its reiteration in application to ethics:

> According to the one opinion, the principles of morals are evident *a priori,* requiring nothing to command assent, except that the meaning of the terms be understood. According to the other doctrine, right and wrong, as well as truth and falsehood, are questions of observation and experience.[27]

Yet Mill is clear that a peculiar problem marks off ethical questions from factual. It is not possible to determine what is right or wrong in individual cases by direct perception. It is necessary, in making ethical judgments, to apply general principles that go back to an ethical first principle: ". . . the morality of an individual action is not a question of direct perception, but of the application of a law to an individual case." [28] Thus this serious question faces the ethical empiricist: How can one's ethical first principle (such as the principle of utility) be established? Self-evidence is not available, for appeal to it would be an embracing of intuitionism; nor is inductive generalization, since the rightness or wrongness of individual acts is not open to direct perception.

In this situation Mill makes use of two considerations, both of which he got from Bentham, not to *prove* the principle of utility but to *make it acceptable* to reasonable men. One of these is essentially an appeal to men's honesty. When ordinary men try to justify their moral judgments rationally, they do so by the tacit use of the principle of utility. When an ethicist attempts to show why his ethical first principle (if it differs from that of utility) should be accepted, he does so by utilitarian arguments.[29] This is not, I am convinced, the old *consensus gentium* argument, nor does it rest on a social-agreement theory of truth. If it were, a strict proof of utility would be possible. It is rather, as I have said, an appeal to intellectual honesty. It says: "My dear ethicist, whenever you are caught off guard, either in everyday situations or in arguing for some ethical principle, you find your reasons go back to a tacit assumption of utility as the first principle of ethics. What more does the

---

27 P. 2 [p. 41].
28 *Ibid.* [p. 41].
29 Cf. *ibid.,* pp. 3–4 [pp. 41–42].

utilitarian need to do than to bring this clearly to your attention?"

I do not, however, think that this was the main consideration that Mill wished to present in developing a favorable attitude toward the principle of utility. In the first place, it is not in any special sense empirical. In the second place, he adverts to it briefly in chapter i, but not at all in chapter iv, which, as we have seen, is devoted to the task of showing "of what sort of proof the principle of utility is susceptible." Chapter iv is, I wish to urge, simply an explication of a certain sort of consideration that an empiricist can use to gain acceptance for an ethical first principle, the first principle in this instance (though it is not used as a mere illustration, for Mill does wish to get his readers to accept it) being, of course, that of utility.

Let us recall that an empiricist cannot hold that we directly perceive ethical attributes of particular actions. Thus he cannot establish his ethical first principle by an inductive generalization. This, however, is true of any first principle.[30]

To be incapable of proof by reasoning is common to all first principles; to the first premises of our knowledge, as well as to those of our conduct. But the former, being matters of fact, may be the subject of a direct appeal to the faculties which judge of fact—namely, our senses, and our internal consciousness. Can an appeal be made to the same faculties on questions of practical ends? Or by what other faculty is cognisance taken of them?[31]

It is in answer to this question that Mill gives us step 1A. Now just what is the analogy that he wishes to urge upon us between visible and seen, on the one hand, and desirable and desired, on the other? I submit the following is an interpretation that at least makes sense of Mill's argument as a whole.

In the area of knowledge the empiricist cannot strictly prove his first principle. He cannot prove, by induction or by deduction from any more ultimate principle, that there are no unobserved entities, that there are no visible things never seen, audible occurrences never heard, and so on. But he can set it up as a plausible

30 The critic can rightly urge that this does not square with the traditional interpretation of Mill's justification of induction (by the use of induction). On this point the critic has, I fear, firmer ground to stand on.

31 *Op. cit.*, p. 32 [p. 72].

principle (as a "meaning criterion," as a later positivist put it) that any epistemological theory that requires visible or audible entities that are never seen or heard is talking nonsense. The only test anyone can seriously propose that a thing is visible is that it actually is seen. A theory that conflicts with this requirement will just not be accepted by reasonable people. Similarly in ethical theory. A theory that sets up, as ends desirable in themselves (i.e., good, *not* simply capable of being desired), states of affairs that nobody ever desires is just being academic and unrealistic. "If the end which the utilitarian doctrine proposes to itself were not, in theory and practice, acknowledged to be an end, nothing could ever convince any person that it was so." That is, if no one appealed to the greatest happiness to justify ethical judgments or ever in practice desired the greatest happiness, no considerations capable of getting reasonable people to accept that principle as ethically ultimate could be presented. Let us call this the requirement, directed toward any ethical first principle, of "psychological realism." Since a first principle is incapable of proof, anyone could arbitrarily set up any ethical first principle he chose, and there would be no basis for deciding between this and any other (if we eschew the intuitionist's self-evidence) unless some such requirement as that of psychological realism were set up.

Step 1*B* is to be interpreted in similar fashion, with the addition that Mill is here assuming the truth of psychological hedonism. Now, whatever one's opinion as to this latter doctrine (I believe it to be false), the design of Mill's argument is not affected. "No reason can be given why the general happiness is desirable, except that each person, so far as he believes it to be attainable, desires his own happiness." Let us remember that, for Mill, the desirability of the general happiness is a first principle that cannot be proved. The sentence just quoted, therefore, sets down no requirement as to strict proof. It rather shows what sort of consideration must be presented to lead to the acceptance of this first principle. One cannot sensibly present general happiness as desirable if it is completely unrelated to what individual people actually desire. Mill cannot and does not argue that each seeks the general happiness or that society as a whole somehow has its own motives, over and above those of its members, and that these are directed toward the general happiness. Rather, Mill simply says (anticipating the outcome of step 2 and the acceptance of the pleasure of each individual as a good) that, since the pleasure of each is a good, the sum of these must be a good: "each person's happiness is a good to that person, and the general happiness, therefore, a good to the aggregate of all persons." [32] Or, as he explains in a letter: "I merely meant in this particular sentence to argue that, since A's happiness is a good, B's a good, C's a good, &c., the sum of all these goods must be a good." [33] This may be incorrect; it may be that goods cannot be added, though surely it is not just obvious that Mill is mistaken in this matter. However that may be, Mill is clearly *not* trying to prove that *"because* everybody desired his own pleasure, *therefore* everybody desires the pleasure of everybody else." [34] He is not (if the reader will tolerate another reiteration) trying to *prove* anything. He is attempting simply to present the general-happiness principle in a way that will make it seem acceptable as an ethical first principle to people who, rejecting self-evidence in this matter, still wish to be intelligent.

The test of psychological realism condemns any ethical theory that would set up as good in themselves ends which no one actually ever seeks. The principle of utility comes through this test, in Mill's first step, unscathed. Now comes the second step as a clincher. No other ethical theory can pass this test successfully, since the only thing people ever desire is happiness. Suppose, now, for a moment, that Mill does make this out. Then, clearly, the principle of utility holds the field alone. Any acceptable ethical first principle must meet the test of psychological realism. Only the principle of utility can meet this test. When and as this is shown, utilitarianism will, as a matter of fact, be accepted. No other kind of proof is required or possible.

Mill himself admits that people do desire as ends many things besides pleasure. He tries to square this with his contention that "there is in reality nothing desired except happiness" by appeal to the sort of associationist account that goes back to John Gay. Frequent association of these other things (e.g., money or moral virtue) with pleasures to which they give rise has set up an inseparable association. Whenever we think of these things, we think of them as pleasant, and so we seek *them,* not some pleasant effect. This line

---

[32] *Ibid.*, p. 33 [p. 73].
[33] Hugh S. R. Elliot, *The Letters of John Stuart Mill* (1910), II, 116.
[34] Bradley, *op. cit.*, p. 114 n.

of thought bears different possible interpretations. It may mean simply that, though we do desire other things than pleasure, (associated) pleasure is the cause of our doing so. This is a plausible account of motivation, but it does not show that only pleasure is desired; it shows only that pleasure is the cause of our desiring whatever we do desire. Thus it is not to the point, for psychological realism does not require of an ethical theory that what it posits as good must be the cause of our desires but rather that it be something actually desired. And it is clear that Mill wants to show that only pleasure is desired for its own sake. Again Mill may mean to say that we are mistaken, we think we seek other things, but we really seek the pleasure so indissolubly associated with them that we do not, consciously, separate it. It seems, however, rather obvious that this is not what he means, as he reiterates that we do seek these other things than pleasure for their own sakes. Moreover, he says that we seek them as parts of happiness. Tentatively, then, I suggest the following: Only that which is experienced as pleasant is sought for its own sake. Many things originally not themselves experienced as pleasant come to be so through association with pleasant effects. Thus money or virtue really are desired as ends, but only so far as they are experienced as pleasant. This can then be expressed loosely by saying only pleasure is desired, yet other things are also—as concrete parts of it. It would be better to say: Only things experienced as pleasant are desired for their own sakes. Now, if this be accepted, then what does it involve if we are to suppose that the principle of utility successfully passes the test of psychological realism? It requires that that principle, when it says that happiness is the sole good, mean not that pleasantness is good but that things experienced as pleasant, and they alone, are good. Pleasure, as a property, is not good, and certainly not the sole good. Is this a tenable interpretation? I think it is. But this carries us away from the question of the proof of the principle of utility to the nature of that principle, and that will be dealt with at a later point in this paper and only very briefly.

One last word, and I am done with my criticism of the traditional way of disposing with Mill's argument. Moore finishes off his criticism of Mill's step 2 as follows:

Mill, then, has nothing better to say for himself than this. His two fundamental propositions are, in his own words, "that to think of an object as desirable (unless for the sake of its consequences), and to think of it as pleasant, are one and the same thing; and that to desire anything except in proportion as the idea of it is pleasant, is a physical and metaphysical impossibility." Both of these statements are, we have seen, merely supported by fallacies. The first seems to rest on the naturalistic fallacy; the second rests partly on this, partly on the fallacy of confusing ends and means, and partly on the fallacy of confusing a pleasant thought with the thought of a pleasure.[35]

It is clear again that Moore is thinking of Mill's argument as a strict proof. Had he read it in context, even going back one paragraph, he would have had to give up this whole interpretation. Let me set down the paragraph that immediately precedes the passage Moore quotes:

> We have now, then, an answer to the question, of what sort of proof the principle of utility is susceptible. If the opinion which I have now stated is psychologically true—if human nature is so constituted as to desire nothing which is not either a part of happiness or a means of happiness, we can have no other proof, and we require no other, that these are the only things desirable. If so, happiness is the sole end of human action, and the promotion of it the test by which to judge of all human conduct; from whence it necessarily follows that it must be the criterion of morality, since a part is included in the whole.[36]

This, so it seems to me, is just a summary of what step 2 purports to do. It says that, if there is only one sort of thing that is ever desired, then psychological realism requires one's ethical theory to square with this. This sort of plausibility is all that can be required of any ethical theory.

Turning, now, to the paragraph which is the immediate context of the passage that Moore quotes, we find that Mill simply summarizes his contention that there is only one sort of thing ever desired, that this is happiness, that utilitarianism alone, therefore, is acceptable to ethicists who are honestly realistic. However, he does fall into a loose manner of speaking, upon which a casuist is able to capitalize. He writes, "to think of an object as desirable," when the context makes clear that he meant "to desire an object." He has just written, in an earlier part of the same sentence, "de-

[35] *Op. cit.,* p. 72.
[36] Mill, *op. cit.,* p. 36 [p. 76].

siring a thing and finding it pleasant . . . are phenomena entirely inseparable," which he then reiterates in different words, "to think of a thing as desirable . . . and to think of it as pleasant, are one and the same thing." All this means is that any object desired (for its own sake) is inseparably associated with pleasure. I find no evidence that this commits the naturalistic fallacy in any of its three senses. Mill does use the infelicitous term "desirable" here. But he could have used "good" in the same loose and colloquial sense; i.e., he could have said, in accordance with frequent popular usage, "to think of an object as good" when he meant "to desire an object."

In summary, the argument of chapter iv of Mill's *Utilitarianism* is extremely simple and (in the main) sensible. To an empiricist who eschews all intuitive self-evidence, no ethical first principle can be strictly proved. All that one can do is to present considerations that will lead honest and reasonable people to accept such a principle. These considerations, for an empiricist, must turn on what people actually desire. Each person desires his own happiness. Therefore, a first principle that makes happiness good will prove acceptable to honest men when they consider it. And if the happiness of each is good, then the sum of happiness of all is good. Thus the principle of utility is something that men, constituted as they are, can honestly accept. But no other ethical first principle can meet this simple test of psychological realism; for (and here the reasoning is not too clear) the only thing people seek (for its own sake) is happiness. At least a plausible interpretation of this last consideration is that happiness is not a sum of pleasures in the sense of an amount of sheer pleasantness but is a sum of things experienced (whether by one's original nature or through long association) as pleasant.

It must be admitted that this whole interpretation presupposes a fundamental distinction, a distinction which intuitionists [37] like Moore and Sidgwick, thinking they can rest their case on the self-evidence of their first principles, apparently ignore. I refer to the distinction between a statement in a theory and a statement about a theory, which here takes the form of the distinction be-

---

[37] Sometimes by "intuitionistic ethics" is meant not an ethics whose first principles are taken to be self-evident but simply an ethics that claims that there is some value term (such as "good") whose reference is uniquely nondescriptive. In this sense, I claim, both Bentham and Mill are intuitionists.

tween a proof within an ethical system and a proof of an ethical system. A first principle in an ethical system (or in an epistemological or ontological system) obviously cannot be proved in that system. It is possible to deal with an ethical system whose first principles are, within that system, self-evident, as a whole, and to ask, "Of what proof is it susceptible?" But this would put it on all fours with other systems and would lose for it the advantage of the supposed certainty which its self-evident first principles give it. In fact, to say that a principle is self-evident may mean just that it is a first principle; in *that* system in which it is self-evident it is not to be questioned; the possibility of its falsehood would just be the possibility of a contradiction in the system. In any other sense the self-evidence of a first principle takes us outside the system. But that brings up the serious question of how a whole ethical system can be established, a question that such an intuitionist as Moore never clearly faced just because he never saw this ambiguity in the concept of self-evidence.

It may, indeed, be contended that Moore meant by "self-evident" simply being a first principle in a system. In fact, Moore explicitly says: "When I call [propositions asserting that something is good in itself] 'intuitions' I mean *merely* to assert that they are incapable of proof; I imply nothing whatever as to the manner or origin of our cognition of them." [38] And again, he says:

> The expression "self-evident" means properly that the proposition so called is evident or true, *by itself* alone; that it is not an inference from some proposition other than *itself*. The expression does *not* mean that the proposition is true, because it is evident to you or me or all mankind, because in other words it appears to be true. That a proposition appears to be true can never be a valid argument that true it really is.[39]

I am not sure that in his later writings Moore so clearly distinguished self-evidence from psychological conviction. His frequent contention that he could be certain about the truth of such propositions as "This is a hand" and that philosophical analysis must start with such indubitable propositions seems to indicate that he

[38] *Op. cit.*, p. x [p. 105].
[39] *Ibid.*, p. 143.

did come to confuse first principles and propositions that are psychologically indubitable. But for the present purpose I need only point out that he was not aware in *Principia Ethica* that to be a first principle is always relative to a system. He assumes that self-evident propositions just are true. He does not see that the fact that they are not, in a given system, deduced from other propositions but serve as ultimate premises indicates nothing whatever as to their truth save as that is an intra-systemic matter. Whether the system in which their truth is fundamental to all else is as a whole true or is more acceptable than rival systems is a question he completely fails to see. That is, he fails to distinguish between the question of how a whole ethical system, with its first principles, can in any way be established, and the question of proof within such a system. Mill, in his loose, common-sensical way, is trying to state this distinction and to answer the question, "What kind of proof of an ethical system is possible?" He is saying that an ethical system as a whole cannot be established in any other way than by making it acceptable to reasonable men; and this is done just by showing that it and it alone (in its first principles, though not as theoretically elaborated) is actually accepted by men when outside the philosopher's closet. Mill simply asks ethicists to square their professionally elaborated ethics with the common-sense ethics of every man, including themselves. His statement of his problem and his answer are not clear-cut; but what, in essentials, he was trying to do should be obvious to any sympathetic reader. All the more so because, in the main, he is just following Bentham, and Bentham did the same thing very clearly.

Having made a case that Mill is arguing *about* his system, not *in* it, and that his argument amounts to an appeal to the honesty of his readers in admitting that only utilitarianism squares with their actual motives, I need not take the space necessary to argue for a similar interpretation of Bentham. I need only point out some passages which show that, particularly in chapter i of *An Introduction to the Principles of Morals and Legislation*, Bentham was doing quite clearly what Mill did somewhat more blunderingly.

"Is the principle of utility susceptible of any direct proof?" asks Bentham. "It should seem not: for that which is used to prove everything else, cannot itself be proved: a chain of proofs must have their commencement somewhere. To give such proof is as impossible as it is needless." [40] However, there are those who do not accept utility as their ethical first principle. To such a one Bentham says: "If he thinks the settling of his opinions on such a subject worth the trouble, let him take the following steps, and at length, perhaps, he may reconcile himself to it." [41] If his alternative is the absence of all first principles whatever, then, in all consistency, he must admit that his ethical judgments are without foundation. If his first principle be merely an expression of some sentiment or approbation of his own, will not his whole system be founded on caprice? Can he claim objectivity for it? Does he give the like right to everyone else to found his ethics on an individual feeling? If so, let him ask himself

whether it is not anarchial, and whether at this rate there are not as many different standards of right and wrong as there are men? and whether even to the same man, the same thing, which is right today, may not (without the least change in its nature) be wrong tomorrow? and whether the same thing is not right and wrong in the same place at the same time? and in either case, whether all argument is not at an end? and whether, when two men have said, "I like this" and "I don't like it," they can (upon such a principle) have any thing more to say?" [42]

All this may sound highly rhetorical, but at least Bentham is not fooling himself or others—he is offering no proof of his first principle, he is persuading people to accept it by showing them that they would not consider the alternatives to it to be sensible if they understood them. And this can hardly be said of G. E. Moore's famous elaboration (in his *Ethics* and in "The Nature of Moral Philosophy") of this last passage from Bentham. Moore thinks that the consequence of subjectivism pointed out by Bentham, viz., that disagreement on moral matters becomes impossible, *disproves* subjectivism, in some strict sense.

But to resume. Bentham saves for the last his most telling appeal—the need for psychological realism:

[40] *Introduction to the Principles of Morals and Legislation,* chap. i, § xi [p. 18].

[41] *Ibid.,* § xiv [p. 19].

[42] *Ibid.,* § xiv [pp. 19–20].

Admitting any other principle than the principle of utility to be a right principle, a principle that it is right for a man to pursue; admitting (what is not true) that the word *right* can have a meaning without reference to utility, let him say whether there there is any such thing as a *motive* that a man can have to pursue the dictates of it: if there is, let him say what that motive is, and how it is to be distinguished from those which enforce the dictates of utility: if not, then lastly let him say what it is this other principle can be good for? [43]

This rhetorical question is clearly meant to have a negative answer—no other first principle sets up as good anything that anyone has any motive to seek. Bentham is, of course, assuming the truth of psychological hedonism. Besides this list (which I have here shortened) of rhetorical questions, a serious consideration of which, Bentham believes, will lead any doubter to be reconciled to the principle of utility, Bentham has one other device for making that principle appear plausible. He points out that, "when a man attempts to combat the principle of utility, it is with reasons drawn, without his being aware of it, from that very principle itself." [44] Also, most men, without thinking of it, order their lives or at least found their judgments of people's actions by assuming this principle. Since this is the case, it is only being intellectually honest to accept that principle explicitly when our universal dependence upon it is pointed out to us.

But G. E. Moore, though not quite so vitriolic as he is against Mill, is inclined to believe that Bentham's case rests on a commission of naturalistic fallacy. Here again he follows Sidgwick:

"Bentham," says Sidgwick, "explains that his fundamental principle 'states the greatest happiness of all those whose interest is in question as being the right and proper end of human action' ": and yet "his language in other passages of the same chapter would seem to imply" that he *means* by the word "right" "conducive to the general happiness." Prof. Sidgwick sees that, if you take these two statements together, you get the absurd result that "greatest happiness is the end of human action, which is conducive to the general happiness." [45]

[43] *Ibid.,* § xiv, 10 [p. 20].
[44] *Ibid.,* § xiii [p. 18].
[45] Moore, *op. cit.,* p. 17 [p. 116].

This absurdity is due to "the naturalistic fallacy, which is implied in Bentham's statements." [46] Now, apparently Moore does not wish to condemn Bentham's definition (on Sidgwick's authority) of "right" as "conducive to general happiness." This alone would be no commission of the naturalistic fallacy. (It must be remembered that Moore himself at the time accepted a very similar definition of "right.") What he wishes to condemn is Bentham's use (still on Sidgwick's authority) of this definition to prove that the greatest happiness is the only right end of human action.

[Bentham] applies the word "right," therefore, to the end, as such, not only to the means which are conducive to it; and, that being so, right can no longer be defined as "conducive to the general happiness," without involving the fallacy in question. For now it is obvious that the definition of right as conducive to general happiness can be used by him in support of the fundamental principle that general happiness is the right end; instead of being itself derived from that principle. . . . What I am maintaining is that the *reasons* which he actually gives for his ethical proposition are fallacious ones so far as they consist in a definition of right. What I suggest is that he did not perceive them to be fallacious; that, if he had done so, he would have been led to seek for other reasons in support of his Utilitarianism; and that, had he sought for other reasons, he *might* have found none which he thought to be sufficient. In that case he would have changed his whole system—a most important consequence.[47]

It is clear here that Moore is interpreting Bentham as trying to give a strict proof of the principle of utility, by means of a definition of "right" which commits the naturalistic fallacy (since, even though right is complex, it includes a nonnatural or value component and hence cannot be identified with the referent of "conducive to the general happiness," which embraces no nonnatural property). This, however, flies directly in the face of the whole organization of chapter i, in which, as we have seen, Bentham not only disavows a strict proof of that principle, but shows clearly what sort of proof is here possible.

But let us look more closely at the passages that, pulled out of their context, have led to this misinterpretation. It is quite correct

---

[46] *Ibid.*, p. 18 [p. 116].
[47] *Ibid.*, pp. 18–19 [pp. 117–18].

that Bentham does specify the principle of utility as ". . . that principle which states the greatest happiness of all those whose interest
is in question, as being the right and proper, and only right and
proper and universally desirable, end of human action." [48] But
where in this same chapter does he use language indicating that he
means to *define* "right" as conducive to the greatest happiness? I
find only two passages that could be construed in this way. The
first is:

> Of an action that is conformable to the principle of utility, one may
> always say either that it is one that ought to be done, or at least that it is
> not one that ought not to be done. One may say also, that it is right it
> should be done; at least that it is not wrong it should be done: that it is a
> right action; at least that it is not a wrong action. When thus interpreted,
> the words *ought,* and *right* and *wrong,* and others of that stamp, have a
> meaning: when otherwise, they have none. [49]

The other, which I have already quoted, runs: ". . . admitting
(what is not true) that the word *right* can have a meaning without
reference to utility, let him say whether there is any such thing as a
motive that a man can have to pursue the dictates of it. . . ."

If these passages are taken to mean that Bentham arbitrarily
defines "right" as "conformity to general happiness," then the principle of utility follows immediately and tautologically. And Bentham is quite wrong in saying that it is an ethical first principle that
cannot be proved and that all one can do is to get people to consider
it honestly. But, if these passages are not to be taken thus, how are
they to be interpreted? Bentham, note, does not say, "right" *means*
"conformable to the greatest happiness." He says we may say of an
action conformable to utility that it is right; that, when so used,
"right" has a meaning, otherwise not; and again that "right" can
have no meaning without reference to utility. Now this is perfectly
consonant with the view that, though "right" does not refer to utility, what it does refer to is regularly related to utility, is present only
when utility is. Moreover, it squares with the use of psychological
realism as a test: that is, only when "right" is so used that it points
out acts that do have utility does it fit with people's actual motives;

[48] Bentham, *op. cit.,* chap. i, § i n [p. 15].
[49] *Ibid.,* § x [p. 18].

thus any other first principle than utility would make "right" and other ethical terms meaningless, in the sense that these terms would no longer agree with people's actual motives and judgments. This is a perfectly plausible interpretation that has the merit of fitting these passages into Bentham's thought rather than speculating on them in isolation. But it has the consequence that the principle of utility is no tautology and does not involve the naturalistic fallacy in any of its forms. Can this be made out? I think it can, and without any forcing.

In the first place, though Bentham embraces psychological hedonism, he does not confuse this with ethical hedonism. The first three sentences of his *Principles* make this unmistakable: "Nature has placed mankind under the governance of two sovereign masters, *pain* and *pleasure*. It is for them alone to point out what we ought to do, as well as to determine what we shall do. On the one hand the standard of right and wrong, on the other the chain of causes and effects, are fastened to their throne." [50] It is true, he goes on to say, that "the *principle of utility* recognises the subjection, and assumes it for the foundation of that system, the object of which is to rear the fabric of felicity by the hands of reason and of law." [51] But here he is clearly speaking of his attempts to write a handbook for the judge and legislator that will square with actual human motives and thus deter from crime and encourage obedience to law. The twofold character of pleasure, as a test of what is desirable and as an object of desire, is made, as it were, the cornerstone of his whole attempt at legal codification and reform: "Pleasures then, and the avoidance of pains, are the *ends* which the legislator has in view [i.e., are the ends he should aim at]. . . . Pleasures and pains are the *instruments* he has to work with. . . ." [52] This distinction, between pleasure as marking the good and pleasure as controlling human action, is present throughout Bentham's whole discussion of principles of legislation: of cases unmeet for punishment, of rules governing the proper proportion between punishments and offenses, etc. His basic principle, that one is never justified in inflicting more pain (through punishment) than is necessary to deter from crime, would be meaningless without it.

[50] *Ibid.*, § i [p. 15].
[51] *Ibid.* [pp. 15–16].
[52] *Ibid.*, chap. iv, § i [p. 35].

Thus the principle of utility is definitely an ethical principle (a "standard of right and wrong," as he calls it). Though realistically geared to or paralleling a hedonistic law of human motivation, it is not that law, nor is it proved by that law. It is no identity statement, or definition, in nonethical terms, of basic ethical words, such as "right" or "desirable end." It is clearly a synthetic statement to the effect that the only situation desirable as an end in itself, and in terms of which human actions can be judged good or bad as they tend to promote or hinder its achievement, is that which exemplifies the greatest happiness of all concerned. This cannot be proved within the utilitarian system because that system is simply a development of it (plus an indefinite number of empirical laws connected directly or indirectly with the occurrence of happiness). But the utilitarian system is capable of the sort of "proof" open to any ethical system. It can be made to appear plausible, it can be presented so that people who try honestly to be reasonable will be led to accept it. And this is done, so Bentham thinks, by showing that it, and it alone of all ethical theories, squares with our unsophisticated moral judgments and reasonings and sets up as morally good something which, by the basic law of human motivation, actually is sought by people.

Now I can imagine an objector arguing in the following vein: Granted that you have shown that the proof of the principle of utility as formulated in Bentham and Mill does not rest on the set of fallacies traditionally ascribed to it, haven't you, on the other hand, made of it little more than a farce? You point out that it is no proof at all, it is merely an appeal to people's belief. It is just an attempt to get people to accept utilitarianism. It is reduced to so much propaganda.

This is no place for an extended statement of method in ethics. But since, as indicated at the outset, this paper was written largely from a methodological rather than a historical interest, a few concluding words on this head may not be inappropriate.

First, it seems to me that Bentham and Mill are right in saying that any ethical theory must contain at least one first principle that cannot be proved; for to prove it would involve deriving it from some more basic principle, which latter would, then, be part of the theory. And, as Mill indicates, this is true of theories in other branches of philosophy. Examples would be the correspondence theory of truth in epistemology, the tautological theory of entailment in the philosophy of logic, the nominalistic theory of existence in ontology. Though I think it proper to demand that theories in different philosophic disciplines be harmoniously fitted together to make a categorically unified metaphysics, they are not derivable from anything more basic. This is their peculiarity as philosophical. They are self-contained.

Second, proofs, both inductive and deductive, are possible within a philosophical theory or system. In fact, however, a great deal of the development of such a theory is strictly neither deductive nor inductive but involves a sort of consistency that may perhaps be designated as "fittingness" or "appropriateness." Philosophic competence in developing a theory is a curious amalgam of technical logical and linguistic skill and philosophic insight and imagination.

Third, however competently developed, there still remains the question of the acceptability of a philosophic theory as a whole. This is in part just a matter of actual success or failure in getting people who turn their attention to such matters to accept the theory. But this is not quite all; for it must be admitted that there are good and bad ways of going about this. Appeal to authority—whether of a church, a great tradition in philosophy, the writings of a certain individual philosopher, or the tenets of a particular school of thought—is a bad way. Another bad way is through confusion as to what one is doing. An important instance is the confusion between talking within a system and about a system, which, no doubt, springs from the desire for certainty and seems to be the source of that curious delusion that there are self-evident first principles. A good way of going about gaining acceptance of a philosophic system is to show that, though clearer and more consistent, it yet squares in some over-all large fashion with common sense, with those ways of organizing experience that we all adopt when not in the closet of philosophic speculation. Why is this a good way? In the first place, it is the way most likely to succeed in the long run. We humans are basically intellectually honest, I optimistically believe, and will not for long accept a philosophic theory that we cannot in any way integrate with our everyday fashion of looking at things. In the second place, common sense, so far as relevant in this matter, is itself metaphysics—only half-thought-out, full of confusions and even contradictions, yet the residue of attempts through the centuries of untold numbers of men to categorize experience. It is, then, with all its need of clarification, a more reliable basis than any one man's speculations for determining what categorical systems can and what ones cannot be permanently successful in ordering experience.

Fourth, implicit in all of the third point is a metaphysics. There are people who do accept and reject philosophic systems. There is experience that can be categorized in different ways. And so on. All this, of course, I accept in my own metaphysics. And it is consonant with my method of "proving" that metaphysics by appeal to common sense. But what of another metaphysics that might reject all this, and thus the whole method it embraces? What can I do with it? Nothing, except to say it will not be accepted for long by many, which, of course, is to bring it within my metaphysics. Yet this is the peculiar situation a metaphysical system is in. And so here we must stop.

This may seem a long way from Bentham and Mill, but I am convinced that a sympathetic reading of the "proof" of utilitarianism by these men shows that they were trying to face, in ethics, the sort of peculiar difficulty that any philosophic theory is in when questions about establishing it, as contrasted with proving things within it and by means of it, are honestly faced. And, though I do not wish to condone laxity of formulation, I do wish to condemn that sort of casuistry which fastens to another man's words and neglects his sentences or, in reading a sentence, ignores the paragraphs and chapters.

The Interpretation of
the Moral Philosophy
of J. S. Mill

J. O. Urmson

It is a matter which should be of great interest to those who study the psychology of philosophers that the theories of some great philosophers of the past are studied with the most patient and accurate scholarship, while those of others are so burlesqued and travestied by critics and commentators that it is hard to believe that their works are ever seriously read with a sympathetic interest, or even that they are read at all. Amongst those who suffer most in this way John Stuart Mill is an outstanding example. With the exception of a short book by Reginald Jackson,[1] there is no remotely accurate account of his views on deductive logic, so that, for example, the absurd view that the syllogism involves *petitio principii* is almost invariably fathered on him; and, as Von Wright says, 'A good systematic and critical monograph on Mill's Logic of Induction still remains to be written'.[2] But even more perplexing is the almost universal misconstruction placed upon Mill's ethical doctrines; for his *Utilitarianism* is a work which every undergraduate is set to read and which one would therefore expect Mill's critics to have read at least once. But this, apparently, is not so; and instead of Mill's own doctrines a travesty is discussed, so that the most common criticisms of him are simply irrelevant. It will not be the thesis of this paper that Mill's views are immune to criticism, or that they

Reprinted with the permission of the author and editor, from *Philosophical Quarterly*, Vol. 3 (1953), pp. 33–39.

1 *An Examination of the Deductive Logic of J. S. Mill* (1941).
2 *A Treatise on Induction and Probability* (1951), p. 164.

are of impeccable clarity and verbal consistency; it will be maintained that, if interpreted with, say, half the sympathy automatically accorded to Plato, Leibniz, and Kant, an essentially consistent thesis can be discovered which is very superior to that usually attributed to Mill and immune to the common run of criticisms.

One further note must be made on the scope of this paper. Mill, in his *Utilitarianism* attempts to do two things; first, he attempts to state the place of the conception of a *summum bonum* in ethics, secondly, he attempts to give an account of the nature of this ultimate end. We shall be concerned only with the first of these two parts of Mill's ethical theory; we shall not ask what Mill thought the ultimate end was, and how he thought that his view on this point could be substantiated, but only what part Mill considered that the notion of an ultimate end, whatever it be, must play in a sound ethical theory. This part of Mill's doctrine is logically independent of his account of happiness.

Two Mistaken Interpretations of Mill

Some of Mill's expositors and critics have thought that Mill was attempting to analyse or define the notion of right in terms of the *summum bonum*. Thus Mill is commonly adduced as an example of an ethical naturalist by those who interpret his account of happiness naturalistically, as being one who defined rightness in terms of the natural consequences of actions. Moore, for example, while criticising Mill's account of the ultimate end says: 'In thus insisting that what is right must mean what produces the best possible results Utilitarianism is fully justified'.[3] Others have been less favourable in their estimation of this alleged view of Mill's. But right or wrong, it seems clear to me that Mill did not hold it. Mill's only reference to this analytic problem is on page 27 (of the Everyman edition, to which all references will be made [p. 67]), where he refers to a person 'who sees in moral obligation a transcendent fact, an objective reality belonging to the province of "Things in themselves" ', and goes on to speak of this view as an irrelevant opinion 'on this point of Ontology', as though the

---

[3] *Principia Ethica,* reprinted 1948, p. 106.

analysis of ethical terms was not part of ethical philosophy at all as he conceived it, but part of ontology. It seems clear that when Mill speaks of his quest being for the 'criterion of right and wrong' (p. 1 [p. 39]), 'concerning the foundation of morality' (p. 1 [p. 39]) for a 'test of right and wrong' (p. 2 [p. 40]), he is looking for a 'means of ascertaining what is right or wrong' (p. 2 [p. 40]), not for a definition of these terms. We shall not, therefore, deal further with this interpretation of Mill; if a further refutation of it is required it should be sought in the agreement of the text with the alternative exposition shortly to be given.

The other mistaken view avoids the error of this first view, and indeed is incompatible with it. It is, probably, the received view. On this interpretation Mill is looking for a test of right or wrong as the ultimate test by which one can justify the <u>ascription</u> of rightness or wrongness to courses of action, rightness and wrongness being taken to be words which we understand. This test is taken to be whether the course of action does or does not tend to promote the ultimate end (which Mill no doubt says is the general happiness). So far there is no cause to quarrel with the received view, for it is surely correct. But in detail the view is wrong. For it is further suggested that for Mill this ultimate test is also the immediate test; the rightness or wrongness of any particular action is to be decided by considering whether it promotes the ultimate end. We may, it might be admitted, on Mill's view sometimes act, by rule of thumb or in a hurry, without actually raising this question; but the actual justification, if there is one, must be directly in terms of consequences, including the consequences of the example that we have set. On this view, then, Mill holds that an action, a particular action, is right if it promotes the ultimate end better than any alternative, and otherwise it is wrong. However we in fact make up our minds in moral situations, so far as justification goes no other factor enters into the matter. It is clear that on this interpretation Mill is immediately open to two shattering objections; first, it is obviously and correctly urged, if one has, for example, promised to do something it is one's duty to do it at least partly because one has promised to do it and not merely because of consequences, even if these consequences are taken to include one's example in promise-breaking. Secondly, it is correctly pointed out that on this view a man who, *ceteris paribus,* chooses the in-

[margin handwritten note: def. preachers words ascribing praise to god at end of sermon]

ferior of two musical comedies for an evening's entertainment has
done a moral wrong, and this is preposterous.[4] If this were in fact
the view of Mill, he would indeed be fit for little more than the
halting eristic of philosophical infants.

A Revised Interpretation of Mill

I shall now set out in a set of propositions what I take to be
in fact Mill's view and substantiate them afterwards from the text.
This will obscure the subtleties but will make clearer the main lines
of interpretation.

A.   A particular action is justified as being right by showing that
it is in accord with some moral rule. It is shown to be wrong
by showing that it transgresses some moral rule.

B.   A moral rule is shown to be correct by showing that the recognition of that rule promotes the ultimate end.

C.   Moral rules can be justified only in regard to matters in which
the general welfare is more than negligibly affected.

D.   Where no moral rule is applicable the question of the rightness or wrongness of particular acts does not arise, though the
worth of the actions can be estimated in other ways.

As a terminological point it should be mentioned that where the
phrase 'moral rule' occurs above Mill uses the phrase 'secondary
principle' more generally, though he sometimes says 'moral law'. By
these terms, whichever is preferred, Mill is referring to such precepts as 'Keep promises', 'Do no murder', or 'Tell no lies'. A list of
which Mill approves is to be found in *On Liberty* (p. 135).

There is, no doubt, need of further explanation of these propositions; but that, and some caveats, can best be given in the process
of establishing that these are in fact Mill's views. First, then, to establish from the text that in Mill's view particular actions are
shown to be right or wrong by showing that they are or are not in
accord with some moral rule. (i) He says with evident approbation
on p. 2 [pp. 40–41]: 'The intuitive, no less than what may be termed
the inductive, school of ethics, insists on the necessity of general
laws. They both agree that the morality of an individual action is

---

[4] For one example of this interpretation of Mill and the first and more important objection, see Carritt, *The Theory of Morals*, Ch. IV.

not a question of direct perception, but of the application of a law to an individual case. They recognise also, to a great extent, the same moral laws'. Mill reproaches these schools only with being unable to give a unifying rationale of these laws (as he will do in proposition *B*). (ii) He says on page 22 [p. 62]: 'But to consider the rules of morality as improvable is one thing; to pass over the intermediate generalisations entirely, and endeavour to test each individual action directly by the first principle, is another. It is a strange notion that the acknowledgement of a first principle is inconsistent with the admission of secondary ones'. He adds, with feeling: 'Men really ought to leave off talking a kind of nonsense on this subject which they would neither talk nor listen to on other matters of practical concernment'. (iii) Having admitted on p. 23 [p. 63] that 'rules of conduct cannot be so framed as to require no exceptions', he adds (p. 24 [p. 64]) 'We must remember that only in these cases of conflict between secondary principles is it requisite that first principles should be appealed to. There is no case of moral obligation in which some secondary principle is not involved; and if only one, there can seldom be any real doubt which one it is, in the mind of any person by whom the principle itself is recognised'. This quotation supports both propositions *A* and *D*. It shows that for Mill moral rules are not merely rules of thumb which aid the unreflective man in making up his mind, but an essential part of moral reasoning. The relevance of a moral rule is the criterion of whether we are dealing with a case of right or wrong or some other moral or prudential situation. (iv) The last passage which we shall select to establish this interpretation of Mill (it would be easy to find more) is also a joint confirmation of propositions *A* and *D*, showing that our last was not an *obiter dictum* on which we have placed too much weight. In the chapter entitled 'On the connection between justice and utility', Mill has maintained that it is a distinguishing mark of a just act that it is one required by a specific rule or law, positive or moral, carrying also liability to penal sanctions. He then writes this important paragraph (p. 45 [pp. 85–86]), which in view of its importance and the neglect that it has suffered must be quoted at length: 'The above is, I think, a true account, as far as it goes, of the origin and progressive growth of the idea of justice. But we must observe, that it contains, as yet, nothing to distinguish that obligation from moral obligation in general. For the truth is, that

the idea of penal sanction, which is the essence of law, enters not
only into the conception of injustice, but into that of any kind of
wrong. We do not call anything wrong, unless we mean to imply
that a person ought to be punished in some way or other for doing
it; if not by law, by the opinion of his fellow-creatures; if not by
opinion, by the reproaches of his own conscience. This seems to be
the real turning point of the distinction between morality and
simple expediency. It is a part of the notion of Duty in every one
of its forms, that a person may rightfully be compelled to fulfil it.
Duty is a thing which may be exacted from a person, as one exacts
a debt. Unless we think that it may be exacted from him, we do
not call it his duty. . . . There are other things, on the contrary,
which we wish that people should do, which we like or admire
them for doing, perhaps dislike or despise them for not doing, but
yet admit that they are not bound to do; it is not a case of moral
obligation; we do not blame them, that is, we do not think that
they are proper objects of punishment. . . . I think there is no
doubt that this distinction lies at the bottom of the notions of right
and wrong; that we call any conduct wrong, or employ, instead,
some other term of dislike or disparagement, according as we think
that the person ought, or ought not, to be punished for it; and we
say, it would be right to do so and so, or merely that it would be
desirable or laudable, according as we would wish to see the person
whom it concerns, compelled, or only persuaded and exhorted, to
act in that manner'. How supporters of the received view have
squared it with this passage I do not know; they do not mention
it. If they have noticed it at all it is, presumably, regarded as an
example of Mill's inconsistent eclecticism. Mill here makes it quite
clear that in his view right and wrong are derived from moral rules;
in other cases where the ultimate end is no doubt affected appraisal
of conduct must be made in other ways. For example, if one's own
participation in the ultimate end is impaired without breach of
moral law, it is (*Liberty,* p. 135) imprudence or lack of self-respect,
it is not wrong-doing. So much for the establishment of this interpretation of Mill, in a positive way, as regards points *A* and *D*.
We must now ask whether there is anything in Mill which is inconsistent with it and in favour of the received view.

    It is impossible to show positively that there is nothing in
Mill which favours the received view against the interpretation here
given, for it would require a complete review of everything that

Mill says. We shall have to be content with examining two points which might be thought to tell in favour of the received view.

(*a*)   On p. 6 [pp. 44–45] Mill says: 'The creed which accepts as the foundation of morals, Utility, or the Greatest Happiness Principle, holds that actions are right in proportion as they tend to promote happiness, wrong as they tend to promote the reverse of Happiness'. This seems to be the well-known sentence which is at the bottom of the received interpretation. Of course, it could be taken as a loose and inaccurate statement of the received view, if the general argument required it. But note that strictly one can say that a certain action tends to produce a certain result only if one is speaking of type- rather than token-actions. Drinking alcohol may tend to promote exhilaration, but my drinking this particular glass either does or does not produce it. It seems, then, that Mill can well be interpreted here as regarding moral rules as forbidding or enjoining types of action, in fact as making the point that the right moral rules are the ones which promote the ultimate end (my proposition *B*), not as saying something contrary to proposition *A*. And this, or something like it, is the interpretation which consistency requires. Mill's reference to 'tendencies of actions' at the top of p. 22 [p. 6] supports the stress here laid on the word 'tend', and that context should be examined by those who require further conviction.

(*b*)   Mill sometimes refers to moral rules as 'intermediate generalisations' (e.g., p. 22 [p. 62]) from the supreme principle, or as 'corollaries' of it (also p. 22 [p. 62]). These are probably the sort of phrases which lead people to think that they play a purely heuristic role in ethical thinking for Mill. As for the expression 'intermediate generalisation', Mill undoubtedly thinks that we should, and to some extent do, arrive at and improve our moral rules by such methods as observing that a certain type of action has had bad results of a social kind in such an overwhelming majority of cases that it ought to be banned. (But this is an over-simplification; see the note on p. 58 [pp. 99–100] on how we ought to arrive at moral rules, and the pessimistic account of how we in fact arrive at them in *Liberty*, p. 69–70). But this account of the genesis of moral rules does not require us to interpret them as being anything but rules when once made. It really seems unnecessary to say much of the expression 'corollary'; Mill obviously cannot wish it to be taken literally; in fact it is hard to state the relation of moral rules to a justifying principle with exactitude and Mill, in a popular article in *Fraser,* did not try very hard to do so.

Moral Rules and the Ultimate End

We have already been led in our examination of possible objections to proposition A to say something in defence of the view that Mill thought that a moral rule is shown to be correct by showing that the recognition of that rule promotes the ultimate end (proposition *B*). A little more may be added on this point, though it seems fairly obvious that if we are right in saying that the supreme principle is not to be evoked, in Mill's view, in the direct justification of particular right acts, it must thus come in in an indirect way in view of the importance that Mill attached to it. And it is hard to think what the indirect way is if not this. (i) On p. 3 [p. 41] Mill reproaches other moral philosophers with not giving a satisfactory account of moral rules in terms of a fundamental principle, though they have correctly placed moral rules as governing particular actions. It would be indeed the mark of an inconsistent philosopher if he did not try to repair the one serious omission which he ascribes to others. (ii) Mill ascribes to Kant (p. 4 [p. 42]) the use of utilitarian arguments because, Mill alleges, he in fact supports the rules of morality by showing the evil consequences of not adopting them or adopting alternatives. Thus Mill is here regarding as distinctively utilitarian the justification or rejection of moral rules on the ground of consequences. He could hardly have wished to suggest that Kant would directly justify, even inadvertently, particular actions on such grounds. But it is perhaps not to the point to argue this matter more elaborately. If anyone has been convinced by what has gone before, he will not need much argument on this point; with others it is superfluous to make the attempt.

In What Fields Are Moral Rules of Right and Wrong Applicable?

The applicability of moral rules is, says Mill, 'the characteristic difference which marks off, not justice, but morality in general, from the remaining provinces of Expediency and Worthiness' (p. 46 [p. 86]). Mill says little or nothing in *Utilitarianism* about the boundary between morality and worthiness (surely it would be better to have said the boundary between right and wrong on the one hand and other forms of both moral and non-moral appraisal on the other?). It seems reasonable to suppose that he would have recognised that the use of moral rules must be confined to matters in which the kind of consequence is sufficiently invariable for there not to be too many exceptions. But this is a pragmatic limitation; Mill does have something to say about a limitation in principle in *Liberty* which I have crudely summarised in my proposition C— moral rules can be justifiably maintained in regard only to matters in which the general welfare is more than negligibly affected.

It is important to note that Mill in *Liberty* is concerned with freedom from moral sanctions as well as the sanctions of positive law. The distinction between self-regarding and other actions is regarded by him as relevant to moral as well as to political philosophy. The most noteworthy passage which bears on the scope of moral rules is on page 135. Here he mentions such things as encroachment on the rights of others as being 'fit objects of moral reprobation, and, in grave cases, of moral retribution and punishment'. But self-regarding faults (low tastes and the like) are 'not properly immoralities and to whatever pitch they are carried, do not constitute wickedness . . . . The term duty to oneself, when it means anything more than prudence, means self-respect or self-development'. Self-regarding faults render the culprit 'necessarily and properly a subject of distaste, or, in extreme cases, even of contempt', but this is in the sphere of worthiness not of right and wrong.

So much then for Mill's account of the logic of moral reasoning. It must be emphasised that no more has been attempted than a skeleton plan of Mill's answer, and that Mill puts the matter more richly and more subtly in his book. Even on the question of general interpretation more store must be laid on the effect of a continuous reading in the light of the skeleton plan than on the effect of the few leading quotations introduced in this paper. It is emphatically not the contention of this paper that Mill has given a finally correct account of these matters which is immune to all criticism; an attempt has been made only to give a sympathetic account without any criticism favourable or unfavourable. But I certainly do maintain that the current interpretations of Mill's *Utilitarianism* are so unsympathetic and so incorrect that the majority of criticisms which have in fact been based on them are irrelevant and worthless.

Interpretations of Mill's *Utilitarianism*

J. D. Mabbott

Professor Urmson's article 'The Interpretation of the Moral Philosophy of J. S. Mill' in *The Philosophical Quarterly* for January 1953 (Vol. 3, No. 10 [pp. 151–60]) is a most interesting and stimulating piece of work. The main point Urmson makes is that previous critics have interpreted Mill to hold, as G. E. Moore certainly did hold, that 'it is always the duty of every agent to do that one, among all the actions which he *can* do on any given occasion, whose *total consequence* will have the greatest intrinsic value' (Moore, *Ethics*, p. 232). But, on Urmson's view, Mill's real position was as follows. 'A. A particular action is justified as being right by showing that it is in accord with some moral rule. It is shown to be wrong by showing that it transgresses some moral rule. B. A moral rule is shown to be correct by showing that the recognition of that rule promotes the ultimate end (sc. the greatest happiness of the greatest number)' (p. 35 [p. 154]). I think in the second clause there are two slight amendments to be made. 'Recognition' is not enough; practice according to the rule is required. And 'promotes' suggests that all defensible moral rules are in fact recognised or obeyed; I should prefer 'would promote' (at least as an elucidation of Mill).

Now from these two principles there follow two crucial differences between the orthodox interpretation of utilitarianism and that of Urmson. (1) On the orthodox interpretation it is never right to do an action when some alternative action would produce more good (cf. the Moore quotation above). But on Urmson's view it may

Reprinted with the permission of the author and editor from *Philosophical Quarterly*, Vol. VI (1956), pp. 115–120.

be right to do an action which is in accord with a moral rule, even if that particular action does less good than some alternative action—on the ground that the general practice of the rule does more good than the omission of such practice or the practice of an alternative rule. (2) On the orthodox interpretation (again compare G. E. Moore) the rightness of an action is determined by its *actual* consequences; on Urmson's interpretation by *hypothetical* consequences, by what *would happen if* the rule which the action follows were generally practised.

Now there is one passage in *Utilitarianism* (Everyman Edition —to which all other references will be given—pp. 17–18 [p. 57]) in which Mill explicitly accepts both these important corollaries; though Urmson does not quote it, it is one of the most striking pieces of evidence in favour of his interpretation. 'In the case of abstinences indeed—of things which people forbear to do from moral considerations, *though the consequences in the particular case might be beneficial*—it would be unworthy of an intelligent agent not to be consciously aware that the action is of a kind which, *if practised generally, would be generally injurious,* and that this is the ground of the obligation to abstain from it'.

Re-reading Mill in the light of Urmson's comments reveals many passages such as this in his support, passages whose significance certainly seems to have escaped previous critics. But it seems to me doubtful whether Mill is as clearly and consistently committed to the Urmson view as he suggests. Many passages fit the old orthodox interpretation and I doubt whether Mill himself realized the fundamental differences between the two views. The remainder of this paper is intended not only to show the difficulties which some passages in Mill present to Urmson's thesis but also to use these difficulties to bring out more sharply the differences between the two views.

The main point of the new interpretation is that the first principle is not relevant to determine the rightness of any particular act. Mill says there is only one exception to this, namely the case in which two rules conflict. 'We must remember that only in these cases of conflict between secondary principles is it requisite that first principles should be appealed to. There is no case of moral obligation in which some secondary principle is not involved; and, if only one, there can seldom be any doubt which one it is' (p. 24

[p. 64]). But when two rules conflict what question do I ask? How do I apply the first principle to escape my dilemma? Do I ask whether keeping the one rule *in general* do more good than keeping the other? This would seem, on Urmson's interpretation, to be the right question, but it would be very difficult to answer. Or do I ask whether keeping the one rule *on this particular occasion* will do more good than keeping the other? But then I might as well have left out all reference to the rules and just asked whether act A which happens to accord with rule X will do more good than act B which happens to accord with rule Y. Mill gives no guidance to the question which he would approve.

The passage quoted above maintains that the *only* exception to the ban on deciding particular actions by reference to the first principle is that of conflict of secondary principles. But there is another exception which Mill elsewhere allows. The 'chief exception' to the rule against lying is said to be where withholding the truth 'would save an individual from great and unmerited evil' (p. 21 [p. 61]). The word "unmerited' may seem to import a conflicting secondary principle—'to each his due'; but I do not think this is the main point. Mill is admitting what all would admit, that when the consequences of keeping a secondary rule are very bad indeed (or of breaking it very good) an exception may be made. Now this other exception (and it is called the 'chief exception') also produces a further difficulty in Urmson's interpretation. Mill also says, in the passage quoted above from p. 24 [p. 64], that there is no case of moral obligation in which a secondary principle is not involved. What of the case where no secondary principle is involved and yet some act open to me can produce very good results or avert very bad ones? Would not such an act be moral, right, my duty? Yet the only principle here is the first principle. It may be recalled that alongside his *prima facie* duties of keeping faith, etc., which correspond to Mill's secondary principles, Sir David Ross lists *prima facie* duties of beneficence and non-maleficence. One way of putting the two present difficulties is that on Urmson's interpretation of Mill the production of the greatest happiness would have to be (*a*) a *prima facie* obligation (i.e. relevant to determine the rightness of particular acts), (*b*) the basis of every other *prima facie* obligation (or secondary principle), (*c*) the arbiter between conflicting *prima facie* obligations.

The third difficulty, and one admitted by Urmson, is that Mill calls the secondary principles 'corollaries' of the first principle (p. 22 [p. 62]). But they can hardly be corollaries if in a particular case they contradict the first principle when I abstain from a particular act in order to obey a rule 'though the consequence in the particular case might be beneficial' (p. 18, cited above [p. 57]). The term 'corollary' suggests, as Urmson agrees, that the value of secondary principles is purely heuristic; and this is borne out by Mill's metaphors. 'It is a strange notion that the acknowledgement of a first principle is inconsistent with the admission of secondary ones. . . . To inform the traveller of a destination is not to forbid the use of land-marks and direction-posts on the way' (pp. 22–3 [p. 62]). But a land-mark or signpost may on a particular occasion fail to point the best way to a destination. I may be on foot and there is an obvious short-cut across the fields; or the signposted road may be visibly blocked by floods or drifts. We should then say 'neglect the signpost'. But what happens when we cash the metaphor? The destination is the greatest happiness of the greatest number; the signpost the secondary rule. What happens when a signpost visibly fails to point the best route? Shall we neglect it? On Urmson's interpretation Mill must say 'No, there are occasions when, though you see another route leads to the general happiness, you must follow the signpost—the secondary rule'. Similarly with the comparison (p. 23 [p. 62]) with an almanack (which saves the navigator from having to calculate on each occasion what course to set). No problem arises if the almanack is held to be infallible. But the almanack of secondary principles does not in every case provide sailing directions leading to the maximum happiness. Yet even when it does not, Mill must maintain (on Urmson's interpretation) that we should follow it.

It might be suggested to meet that difficulty, as it is by Burke and by G. E. Moore (*Principia Ethica*, p. 162), that the reason why we should follow a rule even when breaking it will visibly produce better consequences is that the rule enshrines the stored wisdom of generations of men with their experience and traditions and that the individual is therefore likely to be mistaken in his judgment that better consequences will result from breaking it, especially as bias or prejudice may influence his judgment. But it is easy to find cases where bias and prejudice are excluded, and such a view as Moore's would prescribe a rigid adherence to rules, which no one would defend.

A further difficulty closely related to the preceding one arises when Mill tries to explain away the case where we have a duty to follow a rule when more good would be done by some alternative action. 'It may be held that it is expedient for some immediate object, some temporary purpose, to violate a rule whose observation is expedient in a much higher degree'. Thus 'it would often be expedient to obtain some object useful to ourselves or others to tell a lie' (p. 21 [p. 60]). But Mill then goes on to argue that in fact telling the lie in such a case would not have better results than telling the truth. He has already foreshadowed his argument by calling the good results of telling the lie 'temporary' and 'immediate'. He says telling the truth will do more good in the long run for two reasons 'inasmuch as the cultivation in ourselves of a sensitive feeling on the subject of veracity is one of the most useful, and the enfeeblement of that feeling one of the most hurtful, things to which our conduct can be instrumental; and inasmuch as any, even unintentional, deviation from truth does that much towards weakening the trustworthiness of human assertion' (p. 21 [p. 60]). Now the crucial point to notice is that Mill is here relying on the consequences of telling this particular truth now and not on the consequences of truth-telling in general.

It is perhaps worth noticing that the two arguments themselves are inconclusive, since they are the arguments usually used by utilitarians of the orthodox or non-Urmson type to explain why a rule should be kept on some occasions when more good would be done to those directly concerned by breaking it. Keeping the rule will do indirect or long-term good in two ways: (1) by strengthening in the agent the habit of keeping the rule; (2) by fostering the reliance others will place in the keeping of it. I shall discuss these arguments in the reverse order for reasons which will appear in the discussion.

Ross raised the vital difficulty for the 'fostering-reliance' argument. If my breaking of the rule is not known to anyone else, general reliance on the rule will be unaffected. In *The Right and the Good* Ross illustrated this point by what Mr. Nowell-Smith has called an instance of 'desert-island morality' (*Ethics*, p. 240). This is unfair, for Ross in his later book, *Foundations of Ethics*, gives a simple real life example. It is important to see that real life examples are frequent and easy to find. I quoted two from my own experience in my article on 'Punishment' in *Mind* (April 1939), which turns throughout on this very distinction between orthodox and Urmson-type utilitarianism with which we are here concerned, and a third in 'Moral Rules' (*Proceedings of the British Academy*, 1953). As the point is vital, I offer yet another. An ex-pupil of mine was secretary to a very rich man. His employer had ordered him to put all begging letters in the wastepaper basket unanswered. He was liberal to his chosen causes and life was too short to verify the *bona fides* of every begging letter. His employer also had a habit of leaving bundles of notes in the pockets of his suits. These the secretary regularly extracted before sending suits to be cleaned, and returned them to his employer who at once put them into another pocket uncounted. One slack morning the secretary read the begging letters out of curiosity and found among them one which made a good case. A few minutes earlier he had found a bundle of notes in a blazer pocket. He told me that he had wondered whether to pick off five of the notes and send them to the writer of the letter. 'My boss would never have known'. I asked him whether he did, and he replied 'No, it wasn't my money'. This is not a utilitarian reason; and, in particular the fact that his boss would never have known removes the 'fostering-reliance' argument. But, it may be said, there is one person who would know and that is the secretary himself, and here the utilitarian will fall back on the other argument. The secretary, if he sent the money, would enfeeble his tendency not to take other people's property and on other occasions this enfeeblement would have bad results. But this argument also is no good. For a utilitarian secondary rules are not to be applied without exception and therefore rigid habits should not be acquired. The following dialogue at a bridge table will illustrate the fallacy. I am third player on the first trick; the second player has played the ace; I hold the King. I remember I have been told that third player should play high. I whisper to my mentor standing behind me 'What do I play?' He says 'The King'. 'But it will do no good; the ace has been played'. 'Never mind that. You must play your King; otherwise you will enfeeble your tendency to play high as third player'. 'But is this rule an absolute rule?' 'No, there are exceptions'. 'What are they?' 'When it will do no good to play high.' 'But this is such a case'. 'Never mind. You must not weaken your good habits'.

There is an interesting parallel to this last point in Mill's treatment of rights. In his essay *On Liberty* he argues that a man should not be prevented from publishing his scientific opinions. He argues this on the grounds that his opinion may be true or part of the truth, in which case it will be useful for it to become known. Even if it is false it will serve the useful purpose of keeping the holders of the true opinion alert and preventing the true opinion from becoming a dead dogma. The point of special interest here is that he recognizes that some might say that a man has a right to publish his scientific opinions even if publishing them will have none of these beneficial results. His comment is 'It is proper to state that I forego any advantage which could be derived to my argument from the idea of abstract right as a thing independent of utility'. It might be supposed that he is admitting there is such an advantage. But he goes on 'I regard utility as the ultimate appeal in all ethical questions, but it must be utility in the largest sense grounded in the permanent interests of man as an intelligent being' (Everyman Edition, p. 74). He is appealing here, as in the case of truth-telling, to the long-term results of publication in the particular case. Now I have come across a little periodical devoted to maintaining that the earth is flat. It can hardly be held that this is the whole truth. That part of the truth which it might be said to enshrine (that a small part of the earth's surface is very nearly flat) has already been included in the orthodox view. And it is difficult to believe that the publication of this little periodical keeps the Astronomer Royal on his toes. Yet most of us would reject the suppression of the periodical. But we need not call this an abstract right (or a self-evident or natural right). We can say that it is *generally* useful to have this rule and to apply it in all cases, even though in some cases no good will accrue from its application. This would be the Urmson interpretation, but it does not seem to be Mill's argument.

This paper is not concerned with the rival merits of the two types of utilitarianism. I argued that issue in my papers on 'Punishment' (1939) and 'Moral Rules' (1953) cited above. I have taken Mill's text as a means of sharpening the distinctions between them.

It is interesting that in an article entitled 'Two Concepts of Rules' (*Philosophical Review*, Vol. LXIV, Jan. 1955 [pp. 201–29]) Mr. J. B. Rawls discusses the same issue and illustrates his points by reference to another great utilitarian, John Austin. He shows convincingly that Austin in his 'Lectures on Jurisprudence' (Vol. I, p. 116) states very clearly the Urmson interpretation of utilitarianism. But when he goes on to discuss and defend it he slides away from it into the orthodox interpretation, just as I have tried to show Mill does in his essay.

Some Merits of
One Form of
Rule-Utilitarianism

Richard Brandt

1. Utilitarianism is the thesis that the moral predicates of an act—at least its objective rightness or wrongness, and sometimes also its moral praiseworthiness or blameworthiness—are functions in some way, direct or indirect, of consequences for the welfare of sentient creatures, and of nothing else. Utilitarians differ about what precise function they are; and they differ about what constitutes welfare and how it is to be measured. But they agree that all one needs to know, in order to make moral appraisals correctly, is the consequences of certain things for welfare.

Utilitarianism is thus a normative ethical thesis and not, at least not necessarily, a meta-ethical position—that is, a position about the meaning and justification of ethical statements. It is true that some utilitarians have declared that the truth of the normative thesis follows, given the ordinary, or proper, meaning of moral terms such as "right." I shall ignore this further, meta-ethical claim. More recently some writers have suggested something very similar, to the effect that our concept of "morality" is such that we could not call a system of rules a "moral system" unless it were utilitarian in some sense.

This latter suggestion is of special interest to us, since the general topic of the present conference is "the concept of morality,"

A revised version of a paper presented to a conference on moral philosophy held at the University of Colorado in October, 1965. Reprinted with the permission of the author and editors from the *University of Colorado Series in Philosophy,* Number 3 (1967), pp. 39–65.

and I wish to comment on it very briefly. It is true that there is a connection between utilitarianism and the concept of morality; at least I believe—and shall spell out the contention later—that utilitarianism cannot be explained, at least in its most plausible form, without making use of the concept of "morality" and, furthermore, without making use of an analysis of this concept. But the reverse relationship does not hold: it is not true that the concept "morality" is such that we cannot properly call a system of rules a morality unless it is a thoroughly utilitarian system, although possibly we would not call a system of rules a "morality" if it did not regulate at all the forms of conduct which may be expected to do good or harm to sentient persons. One reason why it is implausible to hold that any morality is necessarily utilitarian is that any plausible form of utilitarianism will be a rather complex thesis, and it seems that the concept of morality is hardly subtle enough to entail anything so complex—although, of course, such reasoning does not exclude the possibility of the concept of morality entailing some simple and unconvincing form of utilitarianism. A more decisive reason, however, is that we so use the term "morality" that we can say consistently that the morality of a society contains some prohibitions which considerations of utility do not support, or are not even thought to support: for example, some restrictions on sexual behavior. (Other examples are mentioned later.) Thus there is no reason to think that only a utilitarian code could properly be called a "moral code" or a "morality," as these terms are ordinarily used.

In any case, even if "non-utilitarian morality" (or "right, but harmful") were a contradiction in terms, utilitarianism as a normative thesis would not yet be established; for it would be open to a non-utilitarian to advocate changing the meaning of "morality" (or "right") in order to allow for his normative views. There is, of course, the other face of the coin: even if, as we actually use the term "morality" (or "right"), the above expressions are not contradictions in terms, it might be a good and justifiable thing for people to be taught to use words so that these expressions would become self-contradictory. But if there are good reasons for doing the last, presumably there are good and convincing reasons for adopting utilitarianism as a normative thesis, without undertaking such a roundabout route to the goal. I shall, therefore, discuss utilitarianism as a normative thesis, without supposing that it can be supported by arguing that a non-utilitarian morality is a contradiction in terms.

2. If an analysis of concepts like "morally wrong" and "morality" and "moral code" does not enable us to establish the truth of the utilitarian thesis, the question arises what standard a normative theory like utilitarianism has to meet in order for a reasonable presumption to be established in its favor. It is well known that the identity and justification of any such standard can be debated at length. In order to set bounds to the present discussion, I shall state briefly the standard I shall take for granted for purposes of the present discussion. Approximately this standard would be acceptable to a good many writers on normative ethics. However this may be, it would be agreed that it is worth knowing whether some form of utilitarianism meets this standard better than any other form of utilitarian theory, and it is this question which I shall discuss.

The standard which I suggest an acceptable normative moral theory has to meet is this: The theory must contain no unintelligible concepts or internal inconsistencies; it must not be inconsistent with known facts; it must be capable of precise formulation so that its implications for action can be determined; and—most important— its implications must be acceptable to thoughtful persons who have had reasonably wide experience, when taken in the light of supporting remarks that can be made, and when compared with the implications of other clearly statable normative theories. It is not required that the implications of a satisfactory theory be consonant with the uncriticized moral intuitions of intelligent and experienced people, but only with those intuitions which stand in the light of supporting remarks, etc. Furthermore, it is not required of an acceptable theory that the best consequences would be produced by people adopting that theory, in contrast to other theories by which they might be convinced. (The theory might be so complex that it would be a good thing if most people did not try their hand at applying it to concrete situations!) It may be a moving *ad hominem* argument, if one can persuade an act-utilitarian that it would have bad consequences for people to try to determine the right act according to that theory, and to live by their conclusions; but such a showing would not be a reasonable ground for rejecting that normative theory.

3. Before turning to the details of various types of utilitarian theory, it may be helpful to offer some "supporting remarks" which will explain some reasons why some philosophers are favorably disposed toward a utilitarian type of normative theory.

(a)   The utilitarian principle provides a clear and definite procedure for determining which acts are right or wrong (praiseworthy or blameworthy), by observation and the methods of science alone and without the use of any supplementary intuitions (assuming that empirical procedures can determine when something maximizes utility), for all cases, including the complex ones about which intuitions are apt to be mute, such as whether kleptomanic behavior is blameworthy or whether it is right to break a confidence in certain circumstances. The utilitarian presumably frames his thesis so as to conform with enlightened intuitions which are clear, but his thesis, being general, has implications for all cases, including those about which his intuitions are not clear. The utilitarian principle is like a general scientific theory, which checks with observations at many points, but can also be used as a guide to beliefs on matters inaccessible to observation (like the behavior of matter at absolute zero temperature).

         Utilitarianism is not the only normative theory with this desirable property; egoism is another, and, with some qualifications, so is Kant's theory.

(b)   Any reasonably plausible normative theory will give a large place to consequences for welfare in the moral assessment of actions, for this consideration enters continuously and substantially into ordinary moral thinking. Theories which ostensibly make no appeal of this sort either admit utilitarian considerations by the back door, or have counterintuitive consequences. Therefore the ideal of simplicity leads us to hope for the possibility of a pure utilitarian theory. Moreover, utilitarianism avoids the necessity of weighing disparate things such as justice and utility.

(c)   If a proposed course of action does not raise moral questions, it is generally regarded as rational, and its agent well-advised to perform it, if and only if it will maximize expectable utility for the agent. In a similar vein, it can be argued that society's "choice" of an institution of morality is rational and well-

advised, if and only if having it will maximize expectable social utility—raise the expectable level of the average "utility
curve" of the population. If morality is a system of traditional
and arbitrary constraints on behavior, it cannot be viewed as
a rational institution. But it can be, if the system of morality is
utilitarian. In that case the institution of morality can be recommended to a person of broad human sympathies, as an institution which maximizes the expectation of general welfare;
and to a selfish person, as an institution which, in the absence
of particular evidence about his own case, may be expected to
maximize his own expectation of welfare (his own welfare
being viewed as a random sample from the population). To
put it in other words, a utilitarian morality can be "vindi-
cated" by appeal either to the humanity or to the selfishness
of human beings.

To say this is not to deny that non-utilitarian moral principles may be capable of vindication in a rather similar way.
For instance, to depict morality as an institution which fosters
human equality is to recommend it by appeal to something
which is perhaps as deep in man as his sympathy or humanity.[1]

4. The type of utilitarianism on which I wish to focus is a
form of rule-utilitarianism, as contrasted with act-utilitarianism.
According to the latter type of theory (espoused by Sidgwick and
Moore), an act is objectively right if no other act the agent could
perform would produce better consequences. (On this view, an act
is blameworthy if and only if it is right to perform the act of blam-
ing or condemning it; the principles of blameworthiness are a special case of the principle of objectively right actions.) Act-utilitarianism is hence a rather atomistic theory: the rightness of a single act
is fixed by its effects on the world. Rule-utilitarianism, in contrast,
is the view that the rightness of an act is fixed, not by its relative
utility, but by the utility of having a relevant moral rule, or of most
or all members of a certain class of acts being performed.

The implications of act-utilitarianism are seriously counter-

---

1 It would not be impossible to combine a restricted principle of utility
with a morality of justice or equality. For instance, it might be said that an act
is right only if it meets a certain condition of justice, and also if it is one which,
among all the just actions open to the agent, meets a requirement of utility as
well as any other.

intuitive, and I shall ignore it except to consider whether some ostensibly different theories really are different.

5. Rule-utilitarianisms may be divided into two main groups, according as the rightness of a particular act is made a function of ideal rules in some sense, or of the actual and recognized rules of a society. The variety of theory I shall explain more fully is of the former type.

According to the latter type of theory, a person's moral duties or obligations in a particular situation are determined, with some exceptions, solely by the moral rules, or institutions, or practices prevalent in the society, and not by what rules (etc.) it would ideally be best to have in the society. (It is sometimes held that actual moral rules, practices, etc., are only a necessary condition of an act's being morally obligatory or wrong.) Views roughly of this sort have been held in recent years by A. MacBeath, Stephen Toulmin, John Rawls, P. F. Strawson, J. O. Urmson, and B. J. Diggs. Indeed, Strawson says in effect that for there to be a moral obligation on one is just for there to be a socially sanctioned demand on him, in a situation where he has an interest in the system of demands which his society is wont to impose on its members, and where such demands are generally acknowledged and respected by members of his society.[2] And Toulmin asserts that when a person asks, "Is this the right thing to do?" what he is normally asking is whether a proposed action "conforms to the moral code" of his group, "whether the action in question belongs to a class of actions generally approved of in the agent's community." In deliberating about the question what is right to do, he says, "there is no more general 'reason' to be given beyond one which related the action . . . to an accepted social practice."[3]

So far the proposal does not appear to be a form of utilitarianism at all. The theory is utilitarian, however, in the following way: it is thought that what is relevant for a decision whether to try to change moral codes, institutions, etc., or for a justification of them, is the relative utility of the code, practice, etc. The recognized code

---

[2] P. F. Strawson, "Social Morality and Individual Ideal," *Philosophy* 36 (1961): 1–17.

[3] Stephen Toulmin, *An Examination of the Place of Reason in Ethics*, Cambridge University Press, 1950, pp. 144–45. See various acute criticisms, with which I mostly agree, in Rawls' review, *Philos. Rev.* 60 (1951): 572–580.

or practice determines the individual's moral obligations in a particular case; utility of the code or practice determines whether it is justified or ought to be changed. Furthermore, it is sometimes held that utilitarian considerations have some relevance to the rightness of a particular action. For instance, Toulmin thinks that in case the requirements of the recognized code or practice conflict in a particular case, the individual ought (although strictly, he is not morally obligated) to do what will maximize utility in the situation, and that in case an individual can relieve the distress of another, he ought (strictly, is not morally obligated) to do so, even if the recognized code does not require him to.[4]

This theory, at least in some of its forms or parts, has such conspicuously counterintuitive implications that it fails to meet the standard for a satisfactory normative theory. In general, we do not believe that an act's being prohibited by the moral code of one's society is sufficient to make it morally wrong. Moral codes have prohibited such things as work on the Sabbath, marriage to a divorced person, medically necessary abortion, and suicide; but we do not believe it was really wrong for persons living in a society with such prohibitions, to do these things.[5]

Neither do we think it a necessary condition of an act's being wrong that it be prohibited by the code of the agent's society, or of an act's being obligatory that it be required by the code of his society. A society may permit a man to have his wife put to death for

4 Toulmin and Rawls sometimes go further, and suggest that a person is morally free to do something which the actual code or practice of his society prohibits, if he is convinced that the society would be better off if the code or practice were rewritten so as to permit that sort of thing, and he is prepared to live according to the ideally revised code. If their theory were developed in this direction, it need not be different from some "ideal" forms of rule-utilitarianism, although, as stated, the theory makes the recognized code the standard for moral obligations, with exceptions granted to individuals who hold certain moral opinions. See Toulmin, *op. cit.*, pp. 151–152, and Rawls, "Two Concepts of Rules," *Philos. Rev.* 64 (1955), pp. 28–29 [pp. 225–26], especially ftnt. 25. It should be noticed that Rawls' proposal is different from Toulmin's in an important way. He is concerned with only a segment of the moral code, the part which can be viewed as the rules of practices. As he observes, this may be only a small part of the moral code.

5 Does a stranger living in a society have a moral obligation to conform to its moral code? I suggest we think that he does not, unless it is the right moral code or perhaps at least he thinks it is, although we think that offense he might give to the feelings of others should be taken into account, as well as the result his nonconformity might have in weakening regard for moral rules in general.

infidelity, or to have a child put to death for almost any reason; but
we still think such actions wrong. Moreover, a society may permit
a man absolute freedom in divorcing his wife, and recognize no obligations on his part toward her; but we think, I believe, that a man
has some obligations for the welfare of a wife of thirty years' standing (with some qualifications), whatever his society may think.[6]

Some parts of the theory in some of its forms, however, appear
to be correct. In particular, the theory in some forms implies that,
if a person has a certain recognized obligation in an institution or
practice (e.g., a child to support his aged parent, a citizen to pay
his taxes), then he morally does have this obligation, with some exceptions, irrespective of whether in an ideal institution he would or
would not have. This we do roughly believe, although we need not
at the same time accept the reasoning which has been offered to
explain how the fact of a practice or institution leads to the moral
obligation. The fact that the theory seems right in this would be
a strong point in its favor if charges were correct that "ideal" forms
of rule-utilitarianism necessarily differ at this point. B. J. Diggs, for
instance, has charged that the "ideal" theories imply that:

> one may freely disregard a rule if ever he discovers that action on the
> rule is not maximally felicific, and in this respect makes moral rules like
> 'practical maxims.' . . . It deprives social and moral rules of their authority
> and naturally is in sharp conflict with practice. On this alternative rule
> utilitarianism collapses into act utilitarianism. Surely it is a mistake to
> maintain that a set of rules, thought to be ideally utilitarian or felicific,
> is the criterion of right action . . . If we are presented with a list [of
> rules], but these are not rules in practice, the most one could reasonably
> do is to try to get them adopted.[7]

I believe, however, and shall explain in detail later that this charge
is without foundation.

6. Let us turn now to "ideal" forms of rule-utilitarianism,
which affirm that whether it is morally obligatory or morally right
to do a certain thing in a particular situation is fixed, not by the

[6] It is a different question whether we should hold offenders in such
societies seriously morally blameworthy. People cannot be expected to rise much
above the level of recognized morality, and we condemn them little when they
do not.

[7] "Rules and Utilitarianism," *Amer. Philos. Quarterly,* I (1964), 32–44.

actual code or practice of the society (these may be indirectly relevant, as forming part of the situation), but by some "ideal" rule—that is, by the utility of having a certain general moral rule, or by the utility of all or most actions being performed which are members of a relevant class of actions.

If the rightness of an act is fixed by the utility of a relevant rule (class), are we to say that the rule (class) which qualifies must be the optimific rule (class), the one which maximizes utility, or must the rule (class) meet only some less stringent requirement (e.g., be better than the absence of any rule regulating the type of conduct in question)? And, if it is to be of the optimific type, are all utilities to be counted, or perhaps only "negative" utilities, as is done when it is suggested that the rule (class) must be the one which minimizes suffering? [8]

The simplest proposal—that the rule (class) which qualifies is the one that maximizes utility, with all utilities, whether "positive" or "negative," being counted—also seems to me to be the best, and it is the one I shall shortly explain more fully. Among the several possible theories different from this one I shall discuss briefly only one, which seems the most plausible of its kind, and is at least closely similar to the view defended by Professor Marcus Singer.

According to this theory, an action (or inaction) at time t in circumstances C is wrong if and only if, were everyone in circumstances C to perform a relevantly similar action, harm would be done—meaning by "doing harm" that affected persons would be made worse off by the action (or inaction) than they already were at time t. (I think it is not meant that the persons must be put in a state of "negative welfare" in some sense, but simply made worse off than they otherwise would have been.) Let us suppose a person is deciding whether to do A in circumstances C at t. The theory, then, implies the following: (1) If everyone doing A in circumstances C would make people worse off than they already were at t (A can be inaction, such as failing to pull a drowning man from the water)

[8] In a footnote to Chapter 9 of *The Open Society*, Professor Popper suggested that utilitarianism would be more acceptable if its test were minimizing suffering rather than maximizing welfare, to which J. J. C. Smart replied (*Mind*, 1958, pp. 542–543) that the proposal implies that we ought to destroy all living beings, as the surest way to eliminate suffering. It appears, however, that Professor Popper does not seriously advocate what seemed to be the position of the earlier footnote (Addendum to fourth edition, p. 386).

whereas some other act would not make them so, then it is wrong for anyone to do *A*. (2) If everyone doing *A* would not make people worse off, then even if everyone doing something else would make them better off, it is not wrong to do *A*. (3) If everyone doing *A* would make people worse off, but if there is no alternative act, the performance of which by everyone would avoid making people worse off, then it is right to do *A*, even though doing *A* would make people relatively much worse off than they would have been made by the performance of some other action instead. The "optimific rule" theory, roughly, would accept (1), but reject (2) and (3).

Implication (3) of the theory strikes me as clearly objectionable; I am unable to imagine circumstances in which we should think it not morally incumbent on one to avoid very bad avoidable consequences for others, even though a situation somewhat worse than the status quo could not be avoided. Implication (2) is less obviously dubious. But I should think we do have obligations to do things for others, when we are not merely avoiding being in the position of making them worse off. For instance, if one sees another person at a cocktail party, standing by himself and looking unhappy, I should suppose one has some obligation to make an effort to put him at his ease, even though doing nothing would hardly make him worse off than he already is.

Why do proponents of this view, like Professor Singer, prefer his view to the simpler, "maximize utility" form of rule-utilitarianism? This is not clear. One objection sometimes raised is that an optimific theory implies that every act is morally weighty and none morally indifferent. And one may concede that this is a consequence of some forms of utilitarianism, even rule-utilitarianism of the optimific variety; but we shall see that it is by no means a consequence of the type of proposal described below. For the theory below will urge that an action is not morally indifferent only if it falls under some prescription of an optimific moral code, and, since there are disadvantages in a moral code regulating actions, optimific moral codes will prohibit or require actions of a certain type only when there are significant utilitarian reasons for it. As a consequence, a great many types of action are morally indifferent, according to the theory. Professor Singer also suggests that optimific-type theories have objectionable consequences for state-of-nature situations; [9] we

[9] M. G. Singer, *Generalization in Ethics* (New York, A. A. Knopf, Inc., 1961), p. 192.

may postpone judgment on this until we have examined these consequences of the theory here proposed, at a later stage. Other objections to the optimizing type of rule-utilitarianism with which I am familiar either confuse rule-utilitarianism with act-utilitarianism, or do not distinguish among the several possible forms of optimizing rule-utilitarianisms.

7. I propose, then, that we tentatively opt for an "ideal" rule-utilitarianism, of the "maximizing utility" variety. This decision, however, leaves various choices still to be made, between theories better or worse fitted to meet various problems. Rather than attempt to list alternatives, and explain why one choice rather than another between them would work out better, I propose to describe in some detail the type of theory which seems most plausible. I shall later show how this theory meets the one problem to which the "actual rule" type theories seemed to have a nice solution; and I shall discuss its merits, as compared with another quite similar type of theory which has been suggested by Jonathan Harrison and others.

The theory I wish to describe is rather similar to one proposed by J. D. Mabbott in his 1953 British Academy lecture, "Moral Rules." It is also very similar to the view defended by J. S. Mill in *Utilitarianism,* although Mill's formulation is ambiguous at some points, and he apparently did not draw some distinctions he should have drawn (I shall revert to this historical point).

For convenience I shall refer to the theory as the "ideal moral code" theory. The essence of it is as follows. Let us first say that a moral code is "ideal" if its currency in a particular society would produce at least as much good per person (the total divided by the number of persons) as the currency of any other moral code. (Two different codes might meet this condition, but, in order to avoid complicated formulations, the following discussion will ignore this possibility.) Given this stipulation for the meaning of "ideal," the Ideal Moral Code theory consists in the assertion of the following thesis: *An act is right if and only if it would not be prohibited by the moral code ideal for the society; and an agent is morally blameworthy (praiseworthy) for an act if, and to the degree that, the moral code ideal in that society would condemn (praise) him for it.* It is a virtue of this theory that it is a theory both about objective rightness and about moral blameworthiness (praiseworthiness) of actions, but the assertion about blameworthiness will be virtually ignored in what follows.

8. In order to have a clear proposal before us, however, the foregoing summary statement must be filled out in three ways: (1) by explaining what it is for a moral code to have currency; (2) by making clear what is the difference between the rules of a society's moral code and the rules of its institutions; and (3) by describing how the relative utility of a moral code is to be estimated.

First, then, the notion of a moral code having currency in a society.

For a moral code to have currency in a society, two things must be true. First, a high proportion of the adults in the society must subscribe to the moral principles, or have the moral opinions, constitutive of the code. Exactly how high the proportion should be, we can hardly decide on the basis of the ordinary meaning of "the moral code"; but probably it would not be wrong to require at least ninety percent agreement. Thus, if at least 90 percent of the adults subscribe to principle *A,* and 90 percent to principle *B,* etc., we may say that a code consisting of *A* and *B* (etc.) has currency in the society, provided the second condition is met. Second, we want to say that certain principles *A, B,* etc. belong to the moral code of a society only if they are recognized as such. That is, it must be that a large proportion of the adults of the society would respond correctly if asked, with respect to *A* and *B,* whether most members of the society subscribed to them. (It need not be required that adults base their judgments on such good evidence as recollection of moral discussions; it is enough if for some reason the correct opinion about what is accepted is widespread.) It is of course possible for certain principles to constitute a moral code with currency in a society even if some persons in the society have no moral opinions at all, or if there is disagreement, e.g., if everyone in the society disagrees with every other person with respect to at least one principle.

The more difficult question is what it is for an individual to subscribe to a moral principle or to have a moral opinion. What is it, then, for someone to think sincerely that any action of the kind *F* is wrong? (1) He is to some extent motivated to avoid actions which he thinks are *F,* and often, if asked why he does not perform such an action when it appears to be to his advantage, offers, as one of his reasons, that it is *F.* In addition, the person's motivation to avoid *F*-actions does not derive entirely from his belief that *F*-actions on his part are likely to be harmful to him or to persons to whom he is somehow attached. (2) If he thinks he has just performed an F-action, he feels guilty or remorseful or uncomfortable about it, unless he thinks he has some excuse—unless, for instance, he knows that at the time of action he did not think his action would be an F-action. "Guilt" (etc.) is not to be understood as implying some special origin such as interiorization of parental prohibitions, or as being a vestige of anxiety about punishment. It is left open that it might be an unlearned emotional response to the thought of being the cause of the suffering of another person. Any feeling which must be viewed simply as anxiety about anticipated consequences, for one's self or person to whom one is attached, is not, however, to count as a "guilt" feeling. (3) If he believes that someone has performed an F-action, he will tend to admire him less as a person, unless he thinks that the individual has a good excuse. He thinks that action of this sort, without excuse, reflects on character—this being spelled out, in part, by reference to traits like honesty, respect for the rights of others, and so on. (4) He thinks that these attitudes of his are correct or well justified, in some sense, but with one restriction: it is not enough if he thinks that what justifies them is simply the fact that they are shared by all or most members of his society. This restriction corresponds with our distinction between a moral conviction and something else. For instance, we are inclined to think no moral attitude is involved if an Englishman disapproves of something but says that his disapproval is justified by the fact that it is shared by "well-bred Englishmen." In such cases we are inclined to say that the individual subscribes only to a custom, or to a rule of etiquette or manners. On the other hand, if the individual thinks that what justifies his attitude unfavorable to F-actions is that F-actions are contrary to the will of God (and the individual's attitude is not merely a prudential one), or inconsistent with the welfare of mankind, or contrary to human nature, we are disposed to say the attitude is a moral attitude and the opinions expressed a moral one. And the same if he thinks his attitude justified, but can give no reason. There are perhaps other restrictions we should make on acceptable justifications (perhaps to distinguish a moral code from a code of honor), and other types of justification we should wish to list as clearly acceptable (perhaps an appeal to human equality).

9. It is important to distinguish between the moral code of a

society and its institutions, or the rules of its institutions. It is especially important for the Ideal Moral Code theory, for this theory involves the conception of a moral code ideal for a society in the context of its institutions, so that it is necessary to distinguish the moral code which a society does or might have from its institutions and their rules. The distinction is also one we actually do make in our thinking, although it is blurred in some cases. (For instance, is "Honor thy father and thy mother" a moral rule, or a rule of the family institution, in our society?) [10]

An institution is a set of positions or statuses, with which certain privileges and jobs are associated. (We can speak of these as "rights" and "duties" if we are careful to explain that we do not mean moral rights and duties.) That is, there are certain, usually nameable, positions which consist in the fact that anyone who is assigned to the position is expected to do certain things, and at the same time is expected to have certain things done for him. The individuals occupying these positions are a group of cooperating agents in a system which as a whole is thought to have the aim of serving certain ends. (E.g., a university is thought to serve the ends of education, research, etc.) The rules of the system concern jobs that must be done in order that the goals of the institutions be achieved; they allocate the necessary jobs to different positions. Take, for instance, a university. There are various positions in it: the presidency, the professorial ranks, the registrars, librarians, etc. It is understood that one who occupies a certain post has certain duties, say teaching a specified number of classes or spending time working on research in the case of the instructing staff. Obviously the university cannot achieve its ends unless certain persons do the teaching, some tend to the administration, some do certain jobs in the library, and so on. Another such system is the family. We need not speculate on the "purpose" of the family, whether it is primarily a device for producing a new generation, etc. But it is clear that

[10] The confusion is compounded by the fact that terms like "obligation" and "duty" are used sometimes to speak about moral obligations and duties, and sometimes not. The fact that persons have a certain legal duty in certain situations is a rule of the legal institutions of the society; a person may not have a moral duty to do what is his legal duty. The fact that a person has an obligation to invite a certain individual to dinner is a matter of manners or etiquette, and at least may not be a matter of moral obligation. See R. B. Brandt, "The Concepts of Duty and Obligation," *Mind*, LXXII (1964), especially pp. 380–384.

when a man enters marriage, he takes a position to which certain jobs are attached, such as providing support for the family to the best of his ability, and to which also certain rights are attached, such as exclusive sexual rights with his wife, and the right to be cared for should he become incapacitated.

If an "institution" is defined in this way, it is clear that the moral code of a society cannot itself be construed as an institution, nor its rules as rules of an institution. The moral code is society-wide, so if we were to identify its rules as institutional rules, we should presumably have to say that everyone belongs to this institution. But what is the "purpose" of society as a whole? Are there any distinctions of status, with rights and duties attached, which we could identify as the "positions" in the moral system? Can we say that moral rules consist in the assignment of jobs in such a way that the aims of the institution may be achieved? It is true that there is a certain analogy: society as a whole might be said to be aiming at the good life for all, and the moral rules of the society might be viewed as the rules with which all must conform in order to achieve this end. But the analogy is feeble. Society as a whole is obviously not an organization like a university, an educational system, the church, General Motors, etc.; there is no specific goal in the achievement of which each position has a designated role to play. Our answer to the above questions must be in the negative: morality is not an institution in the explained sense; nor are moral rules institutional expectations or rules.

The moral code of a society may, of course, have implications that bear on institutional rules. For one thing, the moral code may imply that an institutional system is morally wrong and ought to be changed. Moreover, the moral code may imply that a person has also a moral duty to do something which is his institutional job. For instance, it may be a moral rule that a person ought to do whatever he has undertaken to do, or that he ought not to accept the benefits of a position without performing its duties. Take for instance the rules, "A professor should meet his classes" or "Wives ought to make the beds." Since the professor has undertaken to do what pertains to his office, and the same for a wife, and since these tasks are known to pertain to the respective offices, the moral rule that a person is morally bound (with certain qualifications) to do what he has undertaken to do implies, in context, that the professor is morally bound to meet his classes and the wife to make the beds, other things being equal (viz., there being.no contrary moral obligations in the situation). But these implications are not themselves part of the moral code. No one would say that a parent had neglected to teach his child the moral code of the society if he had neglected to teach him that professors must meet classes, and that wives must make the beds. A person becomes obligated to do these things only by participating in an institution, by taking on the status of professor or wife. Parents do not teach children to have guilt feelings about missing classes, or making beds. The moral code consists only of more general rules, defining what is to be done in certain types of situations in which practically everyone will find himself. ("Do what you have promised!")

Admittedly some rules can be both moral and institutional: "Take care of your father in his old age" might be both an institutional rule of the family organization and also a part of the moral code of a society. (In this situation, one can still raise the question whether this moral rule is optimific in a society with that institutional rule; the answer could be negative.)

It is an interesting question whether "Keep your promises" is a moral rule, an institutional rule (a rule of an "institution" of promises), or both. Obviously it is a part of the moral code of western societies. But is it also a rule of an institution? There are difficulties in the way of affirming that it is. There is no structure of cooperating individuals with special functions, which serves to promote certain aims. Nor, when one steps into the "role" of a promiser, does one commit one's self to any specific duties; one fixes one's own duties by what one promises. Nor, in order to understand what one is committing one's self to by promising, need one have any knowledge of any system of expectations prevalent in the society. A three-year-old, who has never heard of any duties incumbent on promisers, can tell his friends, who wish to play baseball that afternoon, that he will bring the ball and bat, and that they need give no thought to the availability of these items. His invitation to rely on him for something needed for their common enjoyment, and his assurance that he will do something and his encouraging them thereby to set their minds at rest, *is* to make a promise. No one need suppose that the promiser is stepping into a socially recognized position, with all the rights and duties attendant on the same, although it is true he has placed himself in a position where he will properly be held responsible for the disappointment if he fails, and where inferences about his reliability as a person will properly be drawn if he forgets, or worse, if it turns out he was never in a position to perform. The bindingness of a promise is no more dependent on a set of expectations connected with an institution, than is the wrongness of striking another person without justifying reason.

Nevertheless, if one thinks it helpful to speak of a promise as an institution or a practice, in view of certain analogies (promiser and promisee may be said to have rights and duties like the occupants of roles in an institution, and there is the ritual-word "promise" the utterance of which commits the speaker to certain performances), there is no harm in this. The similarities and dissimilarities are what they are, and as long as these are understood it seems to make little difference what we say. Nevertheless, even if making a promise is participating in a practice or institution, there is still the *moral* question whether one is morally bound to perform, and in what conditions, and for what reasons. This question is left open, given the institution is whatever it is—as in the case with all rules of institutions.

10. It has been proposed above that an action is right if and only if it would not be prohibited by the moral code ideal for the society in which it occurs, where a moral code is taken to be "ideal" if and only if its currency would produce at least as much good per person as the currency of any other moral code.[11] We must now give more attention to the conception of an ideal moral code, and how it may be decided when a given moral code will produce as much good per person as any other. We may, however, reasonably bypass the familiar problems of judgments of comparative utilities, especially when different persons are involved, since these problems are faced by all moral theories that have any plausibility. We shall simply assume that rough judgments of this sort are made and can be justified.

(*a*) We should first notice that, as "currency" has been explained above, a moral code could not be current in a society if it

---

11 Some utilitarians have suggested that the right act is determined by the total net intrinsic good produced. This view can have embarrassing consequences for problems of population control. The view here advocated is that the right act is determined by the per person, average, net intrinsic good produced.

186 Richard Brandt

were too complex to be learned or applied. We may therefore confine our consideration to codes simple enough to be absorbed by human beings, roughly in the way in which people learn actual moral codes.

(b) We have already distinguished the concept of an institution and its rules from the concept of a moral rule, or a rule of the moral code. (We have, however, pointed out that in some cases a moral rule may prescribe the same thing that is also an institutional expectation. But this is not a necessary situation, and a moral code could condemn an institutional expectation.) Therefore, in deciding how much good the currency of a specific moral system would do, we consider the institutional setting as it is, as part of the situation. We are asking which moral code would produce the most good in the long run in this setting. One good to be reckoned, of course, might be that the currency of a given moral code would tend to change the institutional system.

(c) In deciding which moral code will produce the most per person good, we must take into account the probability that certain types of situation will arise in the society. For instance, we must take for granted that people will make promises and subsequently want to break them, that people will sometimes assault other persons in order to achieve their own ends, that people will be in distress and need the assistance of others, and so on. We may not suppose that, because an ideal moral code might have certain features, it need not have other features because they will not be required; for instance, we may not suppose, on the ground that an ideal moral system would forbid everyone to purchase a gun, that such a moral system needs no provisions about the possession and use of guns— just as our present moral and legal codes have provisions about self-defense, which would be unnecesary if everyone obeyed the provision never to assault anyone.

It is true that the currency of a moral code with certain provisions might bring about a reduction in certain types of situation, e.g., the number of assaults or cases of dishonesty. And the reduction might be substantial, if the moral code were current which prohibited these offenses very strongly.

(We must remember that an ideal moral code might differ from the actual one not only in what it prohibits or enjoins, but also in how strongly it prohibits or enjoins.) But it is consistent to suppose that a moral code prohibits a certain form of behavior very severely, and yet that the behavior will occur, since the "currency" of a moral code requires only 90 percent subscription to it, and a "strong" subscription, on the average, permits a great range from person to person. In any case there must be doubt whether the best moral code will prohibit many things very severely, since there are serious human costs in severe prohibitions: the burden of guilt feelings, the traumas caused by the severe criticism by others which is a part of having a strong injunction in a code, the risks of any training process which would succeed in interiorizing a severe prohibition, and so on.

(d) It would be a great oversimplification if, in assessing the comparative utility of various codes, we confined ourselves merely to counting the benefits of people doing (refraining from doing) certain things, as a result of subscribing to a certain code. To consider only this would be as absurd as estimating the utility of some feature of a legal system by attending only to the utility of people behaving in the way the law aims to make them behave—and overlooking the fact that the law only reduces and does not eliminate misbehavior, as well as the disutility of punishment to the convicted, and the cost of the administration of criminal law. In the case of morals, we must weigh the benefit of the improvement in behavior as a result of the restriction built into conscience, against the cost of the restriction—the burden of guilt feelings, the effects of the training process, etc. There is a further necessary refinement. In both law and morals we must adjust our estimates of utility by taking into account the envisaged system of excuses. That *mens rea* is required as a condition of guilt in the case of most legal offenses is most important; and it is highly important for the utility of a moral system whether accident, intent, and motives are taken into account in deciding a person's liability to moral criticism. A description of a moral code is incomplete until we have specified the severity of condemnation (by conscience or the criticism of others) to be attached to various actions, along with the excuses to be allowed as exculpating or mitigating.

11. Philosophers have taken considerable interest in the question what implications forms of rule-utilitarianism have for the moral relevance of the behavior of persons other than the agent. Such implications, it is thought, bring into focus the effective difference between any form of rule-utilitarianism, and act-utilitarianism. In particular, it has been thought that the implications of rule-utilitarianisms for two types of situation are especially significant: (a) for situations in which persons are generally violating the recognized moral code, or some feature of it; and (b) for situations in which, because the moral code is generally respected, maximum utility would be produced by violation of the code by the agent. An example of the former situation (sometimes called a "state of nature" situation) would be widespread perjury in making out income-tax declarations. An example of the latter situation would be widespread conformity to the rule forbidding walking on the grass in a park.

What are the implications of the suggested form of rule-utilitarianism for these types of situation? Will it prescribe conduct which is not utility-maximizing in these situatons? If it does, it will clearly have implications discrepant with those of act-utilitarianism —but perhaps unpalatable to some people.

It is easy to see how to go about determining what is right or wrong in such situations, on the above-described form of rule-utilitarianism—it is a question of what an "ideal" moral code would prescribe. But it is by no means easy to see where a reasonable person would come out, after going through such an investigation. Our form of rule-utilitarianism does not rule out, as morally irrelevant, reference to the behavior of other persons; it implies that the behavior of others is morally relevant precisely to the extent to which an optimific moral code (the one the currency of which is optimific) would take it into account. How far, then, we might ask, would an optimific moral code take into account the behavior of other persons, and what would its specific prescriptions be for the two types of situations outlined?

It might be thought, and it has been suggested, that an ideal moral code could take no cognizance of the behavior of other persons, and in particular of the possibility that many persons are ignoring some prohibitions of the code, sometimes for the reason, apparently, that it is supposed that a code of behavior would be self-defeating if it prescribed for situations of its own breach, on a wide scale. It is a sufficient answer to this suggestion, to point out that our actual moral code appears to contain some such prescriptions. For instance, our present code seems to permit, for the case in which almost everyone is understating his income, that others do the same, on the ground that otherwise they will be paying more than their fair share. It is, of course, true that a code simple enough to be learned and applied cannot include prescriptions for all possible types of situation involving the behavior of other persons; but it can contain some prescriptions pertinent to some general features of the behavior of others.

Granted, then, that an ideal moral code may contain some special prescriptions which pay attention to the behavior of other persons, how in particular will it legislate for special situations such as the examples cited above? The proper answer to this question is that there would apparently be no blanket provision for all cases of these general types, and that a moral agent faced with such a concrete situation would have to think out what an ideal moral code would imply for his type of concrete situation. Some things do seem clear. An ideal moral code would not provide that a person is permitted to be cruel in a society where most other persons are cruel; there could only be loss of utility in any special provision permitting that. On the other hand, if there is some form of cooperative activity which enhances utility only if most persons cooperate, and nonparticipation in which does not reduce utility when most persons are not cooperating, utility would seem to be maximized if the moral code somehow permitted all to abstain—perhaps by an abstract formula stating this very condition. (This is on the assumption that the participation by some would not, by example, eventually bring about the participation of most or all.) Will there be any types of situation for which an ideal moral code would prescribe infringement of a generally respected moral code, by a few, when a few infringements (provided there are not many) would maximize utility? The possibility of this is not ruled out. Obviously there will be some regulations for emergencies; one may cut across park grass in order to rush a heart-attack victim to a hospital. And there will be rules making special exceptions when considerable utility is involved; the boy with no other place to play may use the grass in the park. But, when an agent has no special claim which others could not make, it is certainly not clear that ideal moral rules will make him an exception on the ground that some benefit will come to him, and that restraint by him is unnecessary in view of the cooperation of others.

The implications of the above form of rule-utilitarianism, for these situations, are evidently different from those of act-utilitarianism.[12]

12. The Ideal Moral Code theory is very similar to the view put forward by J. S. Mill in *Utilitarianism.*

Mill wrote that his creed held that "actions are right in proportion as they tend to promote happiness; wrong as they tend to produce the reverse of happiness." Mill apparently did not intend by this any form of act-utilitarianism. He was—doubtless with much less than full awareness—writing of act-*types,* and what he meant was that an act of a certain type is morally obligatory (wrong) if and only if acts of that type tend to promote happiness (the reverse). Mill supposed that it is known that certain kinds of acts, e.g., murder and theft, promote unhappiness, and that therefore we can say, with exceptions only for very special circumstances, that murder and theft are wrong. Mill recognized that there can be a discrepancy between the tendency of an act-type, and the probable effects, in context, of an individual act. He wrote: "In the case of abstinences, indeed—of things which people forbear to do from moral considerations, though the consequences in the particular case might be beneficial—, it would be unworthy of an intelligent agent not to be consciously aware that the action is of a class which, if practiced generally, would be generally injurious, and that this is the ground of the obligation to abstain from it." [13] Moreover, he

---

[12] The above proposal is different in various respects from that set forth in the writer's "Toward a Credible Form of Utilitarianism," in Castaneda and Nakhnikian, *Morality and the Language of Conduct,* 1963. The former paper did not make a distinction between institutional rules and moral rules. (The present paper, of course, allows that both may contain a common prescription.) A result of these differences is that the present theory is very much simpler, and avoids some counter-intuitive consequences which some writers have pointed out in criticism of the earlier proposal.

[13] *Utilitarianism,* Library of Liberal Arts, New York, 1957, p. 25 [p. 57].

specifically denied that one is morally obligated to perform (avoid) an act just on the ground that it can be expected to produce good consequences; he says that "there is no case of moral obligation in which some secondary principle is not involved." (*op. cit.*, p. 33 [p. 64]).

It appears, however, that Mill did not quite think that it is morally obligatory to perform (avoid) an act according as its general performance would promote (reduce) happiness in the world. For he said (p. 60 [pp. 85–86]) that "We do not call anything wrong unless we mean to imply that a person ought to be punished in some way or other for doing it—if not by law, by the opinion of his fellow creatures; if not by opinion, by the reproaches of his own conscience. This seems the real turning point of the distinction between morality and simple expediency." The suggestion here is that it is morally obligatory to perform (avoid) an act according as it is beneficial to have a system of sanctions (with what this promises in way of performance), whether formal, informal (criticism by others), or internal (one's own conscience), for enforcing the performance (avoidance) of the type of act in question. This is very substantially the Ideal Moral Code theory.

Not that there are no differences. Mill is not explicit about details, and the theory outlined above fills out what he actually said. Moreover, Mill noticed that an act can fall under more than one secondary principle and that the relevant principles may give conflicting rulings about what is morally obligatory. In such a case, Mill thought, what one ought to do (but it is doubtful whether he believed there is a strict moral obligation in this situation) is what will maximize utility in the concrete situation. This proposal for conflicts of "ideal moral rules" is not a necessary part of the Ideal Moral Code theory as outlined above.

13. It is sometimes thought that a rule-utilitarianism rather like Mill's cannot differ in its implication about what is right or wrong from the act-utilitarian theory. This is a mistake.

The contention would be correct if two dubious assumptions happened to be true. The first is that one of the rules of an optimific moral code will be that a person ought always to do whatever will maximize utility. The second is that, when there is a conflict between the rules of an optimific code, what a person ought to do is to maximize utility. For then, either the utilitarian rule is the only one that applies (and it always will be relevant), in which case the person ought to do what the act-utilitarian directs; or if there is a conflict among the relevant rules, the conflict-resolving principle takes over, and this, of course, prescribes exactly what act-utilitarianism prescribes. Either way, we come out where the act-utilitarianian comes out.

But there is no reason at all to suppose that there will be a utilitarian rule in an optimific moral code. In fact, obviously there will not be. It is true that there should be a directive to relieve the distress of others, when this can be done, say, at relatively low personal cost; and there should be a directive not to injure other persons, except in special situations. And so on. But none of this amounts to a straight directive to do the most good possible. Life would be chaotic if people tried to observe any such moral requirement.

The second assumption was apparently acceptable to Mill. But a utilitarian principle is by no means the only possible conflict-resolving principle. For if we say, with the Ideal Moral Code theory, that what is right is fixed by the content of the moral system with maximum utility, the possibility is open that the utility-maximizing moral system will contain some rather different device for resolving conflicts between lowest-level moral rules. The ideal system might contain several higher-level conflict-resolving principles, all different from Mill's. Or, if there is a single one, it could be a directive to maximize utility; it could be a directive to do what an intelligent person who had fully interiorized the rest of the ideal moral system would feel best satisfied with doing; and so on. But the final court of appeal need not be an appeal to direct utilities. Hence the argument that Mill-like rule-utilitarianism must collapse into direct utilitarianism is doubly at fault.[14]

In fact, far from "collapsing" into act-utilitarianism, the Ideal Moral Code theory appears to avoid the serious objections which have been leveled at direct utilitarianism. One objection to the latter view is that it implies that various immoral actions (mur-

[14] Could some moral problems be so unique that they would not be provided for by the set of rules it is best for the society to have? If so, how should they be appraised morally? Must there be some appeal to rules covering cases most closely analogous, as seems to be the procedure in law? If so, should we say that an act is right if it is not prohibited, either explicitly or by close analogy, by an ideal moral code? I shall not attempt to answer these questions.

dering one's elderly father, breaking solemn promises) are right or even obligatory if only they can be kept secret. The Ideal Moral Code theory has no such implication. For it obviously would not maximize utility to have a moral code which condoned secret murders or breaches of promise. W. D. Ross criticized act-utilitarianism on the ground that it ignored the personal relations important in ordinary morality, and he listed a half-dozen types of moral rule which he thought captured the main themes of thoughtful morality: obligations of fidelity, obligations of gratitude, obligations to make restitution for injuries, obligations to help other persons, to avoid injuring them, to improve one's self, and to bring about a just distribution of good things in life. An ideal moral code, however, would presumably contain substantially such rules in any society, doubtless not precisely as Ross stated them. So the rule-utilitarian need not fail to recognize the personal character of morality.

14. In contrast to the type of theory put forward by Toulmin and others, the Ideal Moral Code theory has the advantage of implying that the moral rules recognized in a given society are not necessarily morally binding. They are binding only in so far as they maximize welfare, as contrasted with other possible moral rules. Thus if, in a given society, it is thought wrong to work on the Sabbath, to perform socially desirable abortions, or to commit suicide, it does not follow, on the Ideal Moral Code theory, that these things are necessarily wrong. The question is whether a code containing such prohibitions would maximize welfare. Similarly, according to this theory, a person may act wrongly in doing certain things which are condoned by his society.

A serious appeal of theories like Toulmin's is, however, their implications for institutional obligations. For instance, if in society *A* it is a recognized obligation to care for one's aged father, Toulmin's theory implies that it really is a moral obligation for a child in that society to care for his aged parent (with some qualifications); whereas if in society *B* it is one's recognized obligation not to care for one's aged father, but instead for one's aged maternal uncle, his theory implies that it really is the moral obligation of a person in that society to care for his aged maternal uncle—even if a better institutional system would put the responsibilities in different places. This seems approximately what we do believe.

The Ideal Moral Code theory, however, has much the same

implications. According to it, an institutional system forms the setting within which the best (utility-maximizing) moral code is to be
applied, and one's obligation is to follow the best moral rules in
that institutional setting—not to do what the best moral rules
would require for some other, more ideal, setting.

Let us examine the implications of the Ideal Moral Code
theory by considering a typical example. Among the Hopi Indians,
a child is not expected to care for his father (he is always in a different clan), whereas he is expected to care for his mother, maternal
aunt, and maternal uncle, and so on up the female line (all in the
same clan). It would be agreed by observers that this system does
not work very well. The trouble with it is that the lines of institutional obligation and the lines of natural affection do not coincide, and, as a result, an elderly male is apt not to be cared for by
anyone.

Can we show that an "ideal moral code" would call on a young
person to take care of his maternal uncle, in a system of this sort?
(It might also imply he should try to change the system, but that
is another point.) One important feature of the situation of the
young man considering whether he should care for his maternal
uncle is that, the situation including the expectations of others
being what it is, if he does nothing to relieve the distress of his
maternal uncle, it is probable that it will not be relieved. His situation is very like that of the sole observer of an automobile accident; he is a mere innocent bystander, but the fact is that if he
does nothing, the injured persons will die. So the question for us
is whether an ideal moral code will contain a rule that, if someone is in a position where he can relieve serious distress, and where
it is known that in all probability it will not be relieved if he does
not do so, he should relieve the distress. The answer seems to be
that it will contain such a rule: we might call it an "obligation
of humanity." But there is a second, and more important point.
Failure of the young person to provide for his maternal uncle
would be a case of unfairness or free-riding. For the family system
operates like a system of insurance; it provides one with various
sorts of privileges or protections, in return for which one is expected to make certain payments, or accept the risk of making certain payments. Our young man has already benefited by the system,
and stands to benefit further; he has received care and education

as a child, and later on his own problems of illness and old-age will be provided for. On the other hand, the old man, who has (we assume) paid such premiums as the system calls on him to pay in life, is now properly expecting, in accordance with the system, certain services from a particular person whom the system designates as the one to take care of him. Will the ideal moral code require such a person to pay the premium in such a system? I suggest that it will, and we can call the rule in question an "obligation of fairness." [15] So, we may infer that our young man will have a moral obligation to care for his maternal uncle, on grounds both of humanity and fairness.

We need not go so far as to say that such considerations mean that an ideal moral code will underwrite morally every institutional

[15] See John Rawls, in "Justice as Fairness," *Philosophical Review*, LXVII (1958), 164–194, especially pp. 179–184.

It seems to be held by some philosophers that an ideal moral code would contain no rule of fairness. The line of argument seems to be as follows: Assume we have an institution involving cooperative behavior for an end which will necessarily be of benefit to all in the institution. Assume further that the cooperative behavior required is burdensome. Assume finally that the good results will be produced even if fewer than all cooperate—perhaps 90 percent is sufficient. It will then be to an individual's advantage to shirk making his contribution, since he will continue to enjoy the benefits. Shirking on the part of some actually maximizes utility, since the work is burdensome, and the burdensome effort of those who shirk (provided there are not too many) is useless.

I imagine that it would be agreed that, in this sort of system, there should be an agreed and known rule for exempting individuals from useless work. (E.g., someone who is ill would be excused.) In the absence of this, a person should feel free to excuse himself for good and special reason. Otherwise, I think we suppose everyone should do his share, and that it is not a sufficient reason for shirking, to know that enough are cooperating to produce the desired benefits. Let us call this requirement, of working except for special reason (etc.) a "rule of fairness."

Would an ideal moral code contain a rule of fairness? At least, there could hardly be a public rule permitting people to shirk while a sufficient number of others work. For what would the rule be? It would be all too easy for most people to believe that a sufficient number of others were working (like the well-known difficulty in farm-planning, that if one plants what sold at a good price the preceding year, one is apt to find that prices for that product will drop, since most other farmers have the same idea). Would it even be a good idea to have a rule to the effect that if one absolutely knows that enough others are working, one may shirk? This seems highly doubtful.

Critics of rule-utilitarianism seem to have passed from the fact that the best system would combine the largest product with the least effort, to the conclusion that the best moral code would contain a rule advising not to work when there are enough workers already. This is a *non sequitur*.

obligation. An institution may be grossly inequitable; or some part of it may serve no purpose at all but rather be injurious (as some legal prohibitions may be). But I believe we can be fairly sure that Professor Diggs went too far in saying that a system of this sort "deprives social and moral rules of their authority and naturally is in sharp conflict with practice" and that it "collapses into act-utilitarianism."

15. It may be helpful to contrast the Ideal Moral Code theory with a rather similar type of rule-utilitarianism, which in some ways is simpler than the Ideal Moral Code theory, and which seems to be the only form of rule-utilitarianism recognized by some philosophers. This other type of theory is suggested in the writings of R. F. Harrod, Jonathan Harrison, perhaps John Hospers and Marcus Singer, although, as I shall describe it, it differs from the exact theory proposed by any of these individuals, in more or less important ways.

The theory is a combination of act-utilitarianism with a Kantian universalizability requirement for moral action. It denies that an act is necessarily right if it will produce consequences no worse than would any other action the agent might perform; rather, it affirms that an act is right if and only if universal action on the "maxim" of the act would not produce worse consequences than universal action on some other maxim on which the agent could act. Or, instead of talking of universal action on the "maxim" of the act in question, we can speak of all members of the class of relevantly similar actions being performed; then the proposal is that an action is right if and only if universal performance of the class of relevantly similar acts would not have worse consequences than universal performance of the class of acts relevantly similar to some alternative action the agent might perform. Evidently it is important how we identify the "maxim" of an act or the class of "relevantly similar" acts.

One proceeds as follows. One may begin with the class specified by the properties one thinks are the morally significant ones of the act in question. (One could as well start with the class defined by all properties of the act, if one practically could do this!) One then enlarges the class by omitting from its definition those properties which would not affect the average utility which would result from all the acts in the class being performed. (The total utility might be affected simply by enlarging the size of the class; merely enlarging the class does not affect the average utility.) Conversely, one must also narrow any proposed class of "relevantly similar" acts if it is found that properties have been omitted from the specification of it, the presence of which would affect the average utility which would result if all the acts in the class were performed. The relevant class must not be too large, because of omission of features which define subclasses with different utilities; or too small, because of the presence of features which make no difference to the utilities.

An obvious example of an irrelevant property is that of the agent having a certain name (in most situations), or being a certain person. On the other hand, the fact that the agent wants (does not want) to perform a certain act normally is relevant to the utility of the performance of that act.

So much by way of exposition of the theory.

For many cases this theory and the Ideal Moral Code theory have identical implications. For, when it is better for actions of type *A* to be performed in a certain situation than for actions of any other type to be perfomed, it will often be a good thing to have type *A* actions prescribed by the moral code, directly or indirectly.

The theory also appears more simple than the Ideal Moral Code theory. In order to decide whether a given act is right or wrong we are not asked to do anything as grand as decide what some part of an ideal moral code would be like, but merely whether it would be better, or worse, for all in a relevant class of acts to be performed, as compared with some other relevant class. Thus it offers simple answers to questions such as whether one should vote ("What if nobody did?"), pick wildflowers along the road ("What if everyone did?"), join the army in wartime, or walk on the grass in a park.[16] Furthermore, the theory has a simple way of dealing

---

16 One should not, however, overemphasize the simplicity. Whether one should vote in these circumstances is not decided by determining that it would have bad consequences if no one voted at all. It is a question whether it would be the best thing for all those people to vote (or not vote) in the class of situations relevantly similar to this one. It should be added, however, that if I am correct in my (below) assessment of the identity of this theory with act-utilitarianism, in the end it is simple, on the theory, to answer these questions.

It hardly seems that an ideal moral code would contain prescriptions as

with conflicts of rules: one determines whether it would be better, or worse, for all members of the more complex class (about which the rules conflict) of actions to be performed (e.g., promises broken in the situation where the breach would save a life).

In one crucial respect, however, the two theories are totally different. For, in contrast with the Ideal Moral Code theory, this theory implies that exactly those acts are objectively right which are objectively right on the act-utilitarian theory. Hence the implications of this theory for action include the very counterintuitive ones which led its proponents to seek an improvement over act-utilitarianism.

It must be conceded that this assessment of the implications of the theory is not yet a matter of general agreement,[17] and depends on a rather complex argument. In an earlier paper (*loc. cit.*) I argued that the theory does have these consequences, although my statement of the theory was rather misleading. More recently Professor David Lyons has come to the same conclusion, after an extensive discussion in which he urges that the illusion of a difference between the consequences of this theory and those of act-utilitarianism arises because of failure to notice certain important features of the context of actions, primarily the relative frequency of similar actions at about the same time, and "threshold effects" which an action may have on account of these features.[18]

It may be worthwhile to draw attention to the features of the Ideal Moral Code theory which avoid this particular result. In the first place, the Ideal Moral Code theory sets a limit to the number and complexity of the properties which define a class of morally similar actions. For, on this theory, properties of an act make a difference to its rightness, only if a moral principle referring to

---

specific as rules about these matters. But the implications for such matters would be fairly direct if, as suggested above, an ideal moral code would contain a principle enjoining fairness, i.e., commanding persons to do their share in common enterprises (or restraints), when everyone benefits if most persons do their share, when persons find doing their share a burden, and when it is not essential that everyone do his share although it is essential that most do so, for the common benefit to be realized.

[17] See, for instance, the interesting paper by Michael A. G. Stocker, *Consistency in Ethics, Analysis* supplement, vol. 25, January 1965, pp. 116–122.

[18] David Lyons, *Forms and Limits of Utilitarianism*, Clarendon Press, Oxford, 1965.

them (directly or indirectly) can be learned as part of the optimific moral code. Actual persons, with their emotional and intellectual limitations, are unable to learn a moral code which incorporates all the distinctions the other theory can recognize as morally relevant; and even if they could learn it, it would not be utility-maximizing for them to try to apply it. In the second place, we noted that to be part of a moral code a proscription must be public, believed to be part of what is morally disapproved of by most adults. Thus whereas some actions (e.g., some performed in secret) would be utility-maximizing, the Ideal Moral Code theory may imply that they are wrong, because it would be a bad thing for it to be generally recognized that a person is free to do that sort of thing.

16. I do not know of any reason to think that the Ideal Moral Code theory is a less plausible normative moral theory than any other form of utilitarianism. Other types of rule-utilitarianism are sufficiently like it, however, that it might be that relatively minor changes in formulation would make their implications for conduct indistinguishable from those of the Ideal Moral Code theory.

Two questions have not here been discussed. One is whether the Ideal Moral Code theory is open to the charge that it implies that some actions are right which are unjust in such an important way that they cannot be right. The second question is one a person would naturally wish to explore if he concluded that the right answer to the first question is affirmative: it is whether a rule-utilitarian view could be combined with some other principles like a principle of justice in a plausible way, without loss of all the features which make utilitarianism attractive. The foregoing discussion has not been intended to provide an answer to these questions.

Two Concepts of Rules

John Rawls

In this paper I want to show the importance of the distinction between justifying a practice [1] and justifying a particular action falling under it, and I want to explain the logical basis of this distinction and how it is possible to miss its significance. While the distinction has frequently been made,[2] and is now becoming commonplace, there remains the task of explaining the tendency either to overlook it altogether, or to fail to appreciate its importance.

To show the importance of the distinction I am going to de-

This is a revision of a paper given at the Harvard Philosophy Club on April 30, 1954. Reprinted with the permission of the author and editors from *The Philosophical Review,* Vol. LXIV (1955), pp. 3–32.

1 I use the word "practice' throughout as a sort of technical term meaning any form of activity specified by a system of rules which defines offices, roles, moves, penalties, defenses, and so on, and which gives the activity its structure. As examples one may think of games and rituals, trials and parliaments.

2 The distinction is central to Hume's discussion of justice in *A Treatise of Human Nature,* bk. III, pt. 11, esp. secs. 2–4. It is clearly stated by John Austin in the second lecture of *Lectures on Jurisprudence* (4th ed.; London, 1873), I, 116ff. (1st ed., 1832). Also it may be argued that J. S. Mill took it for granted in *Utilitarianism;* on this point cf. J. O. Urmson, "The Interpretation of the Moral Philosophy of J. S. Mill," *Philosophical Quarterly,* Vol. III (1953 [pp. 151–60]). In addition to the arguments given by Urmson there are several clear statements of the distinction in *A System of Logic* (8th ed.; London, 1872), bk. VI, ch. xii, pars. 2, 3, 7. The distinction is fundamental to J. D. Mabbott's important paper, "Punishment," *Mind,* n.s., vol. XLVIII (April, 1939). More recently the distinction has been stated with particular emphasis by S. E. Toulmin in *The Place of Reason in Ethics* (Cambridge, 1950), see esp. ch. xi, where it plays a major part in his account of moral reasoning. Toulmin doesn't explain the basis of the distinction, nor how one might overlook its importance, as I try to in this paper, and in my review of his book (*Philosophical Review,* Vol. LX [October, 1951]), as some of my criticisms show, I failed to understand the force of it. See also H. D. Aiken, "The Levels of Moral Discourse," *Ethics,* vol. LXII (1952), A. M. Quinton, "Punishment," *Analysis,* vol. XIV (June, 1954), and P. H. Nowell-Smith, *Ethics* (London, 1954), pp. 236–239, 271–273.

fend utilitarianism against those objections which have traditionally been made against it in connection with punishment and the obligation to keep promises. I hope to show that if one uses the distinction in question then one can state utilitarianism in a way which makes it a much better explication of our considered moral judgments than these traditional objections would seem to admit.[3] Thus the importance of the distinction is shown by the way it strengthens the utilitarian view regardless of whether that view is completely defensible or not.

To explain how the significance of the distinction may be overlooked, I am going to discuss two conceptions of rules. One of these conceptions conceals the importance of distinguishing between the justification of a rule or practice and the justification of a particular action falling under it. The other conception makes it clear why this distinction must be made and what is its logical basis.

I

The subject of punishment, in the sense of attaching legal penalties to the violation of legal rules, has always been a troubling moral question.[4] The trouble about it has not been that people disagree as to whether or not punishment is justifiable. Most people have held that, freed from certain abuses, it is an acceptable institution. Only a few have rejected punishment entirely, which is rather surprising when one considers all that can be said against it. The difficulty is with the justification of punishment: various arguments for it have been given by moral philosophers, but so far none of them has won any sort of general acceptance; no justification is without those who detest it. I hope to show that the use of the aforementioned distinction enables one to state the utilitarian view in a way which allows for the sound points of its critics.

For our purposes we may say that there are two justifications

[3] On the concept of explication see the author's paper *Philosophical Review*, Vol. LX (April, 1951).

[4] While this paper was being revised, Quinton's appeared; footnote 2 supra. There are several respects in which my remarks are similar to his. Yet as I consider some further questions and rely on somewhat different arguments, I have retained the discussion of punishment and promises together as two test cases for utilitarianism.

of punishment. What we may call the retributive view is that punishment is justified on the grounds that wrongdoing merits punishment. It is morally fitting that a person who does wrong should suffer in proportion to his wrongdoing. That a criminal should be punished follows from his guilt, and the severity of the appropriate punishment depends on the depravity of his act. The state of affairs where a wrongdoer suffers punishment is morally better than the state of affairs where he does not; and it is better irrespective of any of the consequences of punishing him.

What we may call the utilitarian view holds that on the principle that bygones are bygones and that only future consequences are material to present decisions, punishment is justifiable only by reference to the probable consequences of maintaining it as one of the devices of the social order. Wrongs committed in the past are, as such, not relevant considerations for deciding what to do. If punishment can be shown to promote effectively the interest of society it is justifiable, otherwise it is not.

I have stated these two competing views very roughly to make one feel the conflict between them: one feels the force of *both* arguments and one wonders how they can be reconciled. From my introductory remarks it is obvious that the resolution which I am going to propose is that in this case one must distinguish between justifying a practice as a system of rules to be applied and enforced, and justifying a particular action which falls under these rules; utilitarian arguments are appropriate with regard to questions about practices, while retributive arguments fit the application of particular rules to particular cases.

We might try to get clear about this distinction by imagining how a father might answer the question of his son. Suppose the son asks, "Why was *J* put in jail yesterday?" The father answers, "Because he robbed the bank at *B*. He was duly tried and found guilty. That's why he was put in jail yesterday." But suppose the son had asked a different question, namely, "Why do people put other people in jail?" Then the father might answer, "To protect good people from bad people" or "To stop people from doing things that would make it uneasy for all of us; for otherwise we wouldn't be able to go to bed at night and sleep in peace." There are two very different questions here. One question emphasizes the proper name: it asks why *J* was punished rather than someone else, or it asks what he was punished for. The other question asks why we have the institution of punishment: why do people punish one another rather than, say, always forgiving one another?

Thus the father says in effect that a particular man is punished, rather than some other man, because he is guilty, and he is guilty because he broke the law (past tense). In his case the law looks back, the judge looks back, the jury looks back, and a penalty is visited upon him for something he did. That a man is to be punished, and what his punishment is to be, is settled by its being shown that he broke the law and that the law assigns that penalty for the violation of it.

On the other hand we have the institution of punishment itself, and recommend and accept various changes in it, because it is thought by the (ideal) legislator and by those to whom the law applies that, as a part of a system of law impartially applied from case to case arising under it, it will have the consequence, in the long run, of furthering the interests of society.

One can say, then, that the judge and the legislator stand in different positions and look in different directions: one to the past, the other to the future. The justification of what the judge does, *qua* judge, sounds like the retributive view; the justification of what the (ideal) legislator does, *qua* legislator, sounds like the utilitarian view. Thus both views have a point (this is as it should be since intelligent and sensitive persons have been on both sides of the argument); and one's initial confusion disappears once one sees that these views apply to persons holding different offices with different duties, and situated differently with respect to the system of rules that make up the criminal law.[5]

One might say, however, that the utilitarian view is more fundamental since it applies to a more fundamental office, for the judge carries out the legislator's will so far as he can determine it. Once the legislator decides to have laws and to assign penalties for their violation (as things are there must be both the law and the penalty) an institution is set up which involves a retributive conception of particular cases. It is part of the concept of the criminal law as a system of rules that the application and enforcement of these rules in particular cases should be justifiable by arguments of a retributive character. The decision whether or not to use law

---

[5] Note the fact that different sorts of arguments are suited to different offices. One way of taking the differences between ethical theories is to regard them as accounts of the reasons expected in different offices.

rather than some other mechanism of social control, and the decision as to what laws to have and what penalties to assign, may be settled by utilitarian arguments; but if one decides to have laws then one has decided on something whose working in particular cases is retributive in form.[6]

The answer, then, to the confusion engendered by the two views of punishment is quite simple: one distinguishes two offices, that of the judge and that of the legislator, and one distinguishes their different stations with respect to the system of rules which make up the law; and then one notes that the different sorts of considerations which would usually be offered as reasons for what is done under the cover of these offices can be paired off with the competing justifications of punishment. One reconciles the two views by the time-honored device of making them apply to different situations.

But can it really be this simple? Well, this answer allows for the apparent intent of each side. Does a person who advocates the retributive view necessarily advocate, as an *institution*, legal machinery whose essential purpose is to set up and preserve a correspondence between moral turpitude and suffering? Surely not.[7] What retributionists have rightly insisted upon is that no man can be punished unless he is guilty, that is, unless he has broken the law. Their fundamental criticism of the utilitarian account is that, as they interpret it, it sanctions an innocent person's being punished (if one may call it that) for the benefit of society.

On the other hand, utilitarians agree that punishment is to be inflicted only for the violation of law. They regard this much as understood from the concept of punishment itself.[8] The point

---

6 In this connection see Mabbott, *op. cit.*, pp. 163–164.

7 On this point see Sir David Ross, *The Right and the Good* (Oxford, 1930), pp. 57–60.

8 See Hobbes's definition of punishment in *Leviathan*, ch. xxviii; and Bentham's definition in *The Principle of Morals and Legislation*, ch. xii, par. 36, ch. xv, par. 28, and in *The Rationale of Punishment*, (London, 1830), bk. I, ch. i. They could agree with Bradley that: "Punishment is punishment only when it is deserved. We pay the penalty, because we owe it, and for no other reason; and if punishment is inflicted for any other reason whatever than because it is merited by wrong, it is a gross immorality, a crying injustice, an abominable crime, and not what it pretends to be." *Ethical Studies* (2nd ed.; Oxford, 1927), pp. 26–27. Certainly by definition it isn't what it pretends to be. The innocent can only be punished by mistake; deliberate "punishment" of the innocent necessarily involves fraud.

of the utilitarian account concerns the institution as a system of rules: utilitarianism seeks to limit its use by declaring it justifiable only if it can be shown to foster effectively the good of society. Historically it is a protest against the indiscriminate and ineffective use of the criminal law.[9] It seeks to dissuade us from assigning to penal institutions the improper, if not sacrilegious, task of matching suffering with moral turpitude. Like others, utilitarians want penal institutions designed so that, as far as humanly possible, only those who break the law run afoul of it. They hold that no official should have discretionary power to inflict penalties whenever he thinks it for the benefit of society; for on utilitarian grounds an institution granting such power could not be justified.[10]

The suggested way of reconciling the retributive and the utilitarian justifications of punishment seems to account for what both sides have wanted to say. There are, however, two further questions which arise, and I shall devote the remainder of this section to them.

First, will not a difference of opinion as to the proper criterion of just law make the proposed reconciliation unacceptable to retributionists? Will they not question whether, if the utilitarian principle is used as the criterion, it follows that those who have broken the law are guilty in a way which satisfies their demand that those punished deserve to be punished? To answer this difficulty, suppose that the rules of the criminal law are justified on utilitarian grounds (it is only for laws that meet his criterion that the utilitarian can be held responsible). Then it follows that the actions which the criminal law specifies as offenses are such that, if they were tolerated, terror and alarm would spread in society. Conse-

[9] Cf. Leon Radzinowicz, *A History of English Criminal Law: The Movement for Reform 1750–1833* (London, 1948), esp. ch. xi on Bentham.

[10] Bentham discusses how corresponding to a punitory provision of a criminal law there is another provision which stands to it as an antagonist and which needs a name as much as the punitory. He calls it, as one might expect, the *anaetiosostic,* and of it he says: "The punishment of guilt is the object of the former one: the preservation of innocence that of the latter." In the same connection he asserts that it is never thought fit to give the judge the option of deciding whether a thief (that is, a person whom he believes to be a thief, for the judge's belief is what the question must always turn upon) should hang or not, and so the law writes the provision: "The judge shall not cause a thief to be hanged unless he have been duly convicted and sentenced in course of law" (*The Limits of Jurisprudence Defined,* ed. C. W. Everett [New York, 1945], pp. 238–239).

quently, retributionists can only deny that those who are punished deserve to be punished if they deny that such actions are wrong. This they will not want to do.

The second question is whether utilitarianism doesn't justify too much. One pictures it as an engine of justification which, if consistently adopted, could be used to justify cruel and arbitrary institutions. Retributionists may be supposed to concede that utilitarians *intend* to reform the law and to make it more humane; that utilitarians do not *wish* to justify any such thing as punishment of the innocent; and that utilitarians may appeal to the fact that punishment presupposes guilt in the sense that by punishment one understands an institution attaching penalties to the infraction of legal rules, and therefore that it is logically absurd to suppose that utilitarians in justifying *punishment* might also have justified punishment (if we may call it that) of the innocent. The real question, however, is whether the utilitarian, in justifying punishment, hasn't used arguments which commit him to accepting the infliction of suffering on innocent persons if it is for the good of society (whether or not one calls this punishment). More generally, isn't the utilitarian committed in principle to accepting many practices which he, as a morally sensitive person, wouldn't want to accept? Retributionists are inclined to hold that there is no way to stop the utilitarian principle from justifying too much except by adding to it a principle which distributes certain rights to individuals. Then the amended criterion is not the greatest benefit of society *simpliciter,* but the greatest benefit of society subject to the constraint that no one's rights may be violated. Now while I think that the classical utilitarians proposed a criterion of this more complicated sort, I do not want to argue that point here.[11] What I want to show is that there is *another* way of preventing the utilitarian principle from justifying too much, or at least of making it much less likely to do so: namely, by stating utilitarianism in a way which accounts for the distinction between the justification of an institution and the justification of a particular action falling under it.

I begin by defining the institution of punishment as follows: a person is said to suffer punishment whenever he is legally deprived of some of the normal rights of a citizen on the ground that he has

11 By the classical utilitarians I understand Hobbes, Hume, Bentham, J. S. Mill, and Sidgwick.

violated a rule of law, the violation having been established by trial
according to the due process of law, provided that the deprivation
is carried out by the recognized legal authorities of the state, that
the rule of law clearly specifies both the offense and the attached
penalty, that the courts construe statutes strictly, and that the stat-
ute was on the books prior to the time of the offense.[12] This definition specifies what I shall understand by punishment. The question
is whether utilitarian arguments may be found to justify institutions
widely different from this and such as one would find cruel and arbitrary.

This question is best answered, I think, by taking up a particular accusation. Consider the following from Carritt:

> . . . the utilitarian must hold that we are justified in inflicting pain al-
> ways and only to prevent worse pain or bring about greater happiness.
> This, then, is all we need to consider in so-called punishment, which must
> be purely preventive. But if some kind of very cruel crime becomes com-
> mon, and none of the criminals can be caught, it might be highly ex-
> pedient, as an example, to hang an innocent man, if a charge against him
> could be so framed that he were universally thought guilty; indeed this
> would only fail to be an ideal instance of utilitarian 'punishment' because
> the victim himself would not have been so likely as a real felon to com-
> mit such a crime in the future; in all other respects it would be perfectly
> deterrent and therefore felicific.[13]

Carritt is trying to show that there are occasions when a utilitarian
argument would justify taking an action which would be generally
condemned; and thus that utilitarianism justifies too much. But the
failure of Carritt's argument lies in the fact that he makes no distinction between the justification of the general system of rules
which constitutes penal institutions and the justification of particular applications of these rules to particular cases by the various
officials whose job it is to administer them. This becomes perfectly
clear when one asks who the "we" are of whom Carritt speaks. Who
is this who has a sort of absolute authority on particular occasions
to decide that an innocent man shall be "punished" if everyone can
be convinced that he is guilty? Is this person the legislator, or the

---

[12] All these features of punishment are mentioned by Hobbes; cf. *Leviathan,* ch. xxviii.

[13] *Ethical and Political Thinking* (Oxford, 1947), p. 65.

judge, or the body of private citizens, or what? It is utterly crucial to know who is to decide such matters, and by what authority, for all of this must be written into the rules of the institution. Until one knows these things one doesn't know what the institution is whose justification is being challenged; and as the utilitarian principle applies to the institution one doesn't know whether it is justifiable on utilitarian grounds or not.

Once this is understood it is clear what the countermove to Carritt's argument is. One must describe more carefully what the *institution* is which his example suggests, and then ask oneself whether or not it is likely that having this institution would be for the benefit of society in the long run. One must not content oneself with the vague thought that, when it's a question of *this* case, it would be a good thing if *somebody* did something even if an innocent person were to suffer.

Try to imagine, then, an institution (which we may call "telishment") which is such that the officials set up by it have authority to arrange a trial for the condemnation of an innocent man whenever they are of the opinion that doing so would be in the best interests of society. The discretion of officials is limited, however, by the rule that they may not condemn an innocent man to undergo such an ordeal unless there is, at the time, a wave of offenses similar to that with which they charge him and telish him for. We may imagine that the officials having the discretionary authority are the judges of the higher courts in consultation with the chief of police, the minister of justice, and a committee of the legislature.

Once one realizes that one is involved in setting up an *institution,* one sees that the hazards are very great. For example, what check is there on the officials? How is one to tell whether or not their actions are authorized? How is one to limit the risks involved in allowing such systematic deception? How is one to avoid giving anything short of complete discretion to the authorities to telish anyone they like? In addition to these considerations, it is obvious that people will come to have a very different attitude towards their penal system when telishment is adjoined to it. They will be uncertain as to whether a convicted man has been punished or telished. They will wonder whether or not they should feel sorry for him. They will wonder whether the same fate won't at any time fall on them. If one pictures how such an institution would actually work, and the enormous risks involved in it, it seems clear that it would serve no useful purpose. A utilitarian justification for this institution is most unlikely.

It happens in general that as one drops off the defining features of punishment one ends up with an institution whose utilitarian justification is highly doubtful. One reason for this is that punishment works like a kind of price system: by altering the prices one has to pay for the performance of actions it supplies a motive for avoiding some actions and doing others. The defining features are essential if punishment is to work in this way; so that an institution which lacks these features, e.g., an institution which is set up to "punish" the innocent, is likely to have about as much point as a price system (if one may call it that) where the prices of things change at random from day to day and one learns the price of something after one has agreed to buy it.[14]

If one is careful to apply the utilitarian principle to the institution which is to authorize particular actions, then there is *less* danger of its justifying too much. Carritt's example gains plausibility by its indefiniteness and by its concentration on the particular case. His argument will only hold if it can be shown that there are utilitarian arguments which justify an institution whose publicly ascertainable offices and powers are such as to permit officials to exercise that kind of discretion in particular cases. But the requirement of having to build the arbitrary features of the par-

---

[14] The analogy with the price system suggests an answer to the question how utilitarian considerations insure that punishment is proportional to the offense. It is interesting to note that Sir David Ross, after making the distinction between justifying a penal law and justifying a particular application of it, and after stating that utilitarian considerations have a large place in determining the former, still holds back from accepting the utilitarian justification of punishment on the grounds that justice requires that punishment be proportional to the offense, and that utilitarianism is unable to account for this. Cf. *The Right and the Good*, pp. 61–62. I do not claim that utilitarianism can account for this requirement as Sir David might wish, but it happens, nevertheless, that if utilitarian considerations are followed penalties will be proportional to offenses in this sense: the order of offenses according to seriousness can be paired off with the order of penalties according to severity. Also the absolute level of penalties will be as low as possible. This follows from the assumption that people are rational (i.e., that they are able to take into account the "prices" the state puts on actions), the utilitarian rule that a penal system should provide a motive for preferring the less serious offense, and the principle that punishment as such is an evil. All this was carefully worked out by Bentham in *The Principles of Morals and Legislation*, chs. xiii–xv.

ticular decision into the institutional practice makes the justification much less likely to go through.

II

I shall now consider the question of promises. The objection to utilitarianism in connection with promises seems to be this: it is believed that on the utilitarian view when a person makes a promise the only ground upon which he should keep it, if he should keep it, is that by keeping it he will realize the most good on the whole. So that if one asks the question "Why should I keep *my* promise?" the utilitarian answer is understood to be that doing so in *this* case will have the best consequences. And this answer is said, quite rightly, to conflict with the way in which the obligation to keep promises is regarded.

Now of course critics of utilitarianism are not unaware that one defense sometimes attributed to utilitarians is the consideration involving the practice of promise-keeping.[15] In this connection they are supposed to argue something like this: it must be admitted that we feel strictly about keeping promises, more strictly than it might seem our view can account for. But when we consider the matter carefully it is always necessary to take into account the effect which our action will have on the practice of making promises. The promisor must weigh, not only the effects of breaking his promise on the particular case, but also the effect which his breaking his promise will have on the practice itself. Since the practice is of great utilitarian value, and since breaking one's promise always seriously damages it, one will seldom be justified in breaking one's promise. If we view our individual promises in the wider context of the practice of promising itself we can account for the strictness of the obligation to keep promises. There is always one very strong utilitarian consideration in favor of keeping them,

---

[15] Ross, *The Right and the Good*, pp. 37–39, and *Foundations of Ethics* (Oxford, 1939), pp. 92–94. I know of no utilitarian who has used this argument except W. A. Pickard-Cambridge in "Two Problems about Duty," *Mind*, n.s., XLI (April, 1932), 153–157, although the argument goes with G. E. Moore's version of utilitarianism in *Principia Ethica* (Cambridge, 1903). To my knowledge it does not appear in the classical utilitarians; and if one interprets their view correctly this is no accident.

and this will insure that when the question arises as to whether
or not to keep a promise it will usually turn out that one should,
even where the facts of the particular case taken by itself would
seem to justify one's breaking it. In this way the strictness with
which we view the obligation to keep promises is accounted for.

Ross has criticized this defense as follows: [16] however great the
value of the practice of promising, on utilitarian grounds, there
must be some value which is greater, and one can imagine it to be
obtainable by breaking a promise. Therefore there might be a case
where the promisor could argue that breaking his promise was justified as leading to a better state of affairs on the whole. And the
promisor could argue in this way no matter how slight the advantage won by breaking the promise. If one were to challenge the
promisor his defense would be that what he did was best on the
whole in view of all the utilitarian considerations, which in this
case *include* the importance of the practice. Ross feels that such a
defense would be unacceptable. I think he is right insofar as he is
protesting against the appeal to consequences in general and without
further explanation. Yet it is extremely difficult to weigh the force
of Ross's argument. The kind of case imagined seems unrealistic and
one feels that it needs to be described. One is inclined to think that
it would either turn out that such a case came under an exception
defined by the practice itself, in which case there would not be an
appeal to consequences in general on the particular case, or it would
happen that the circumstances were so peculiar that the conditions
which the practice presupposes no longer obtained. But certainly
Ross is right in thinking that it strikes us as wrong for a person to
defend breaking a promise by a general appeal to consequences. For
a general utilitarian defense is not open to the promisor: it is not
one of the defenses allowed by the practice of making promises.

Ross gives two further counterarguments: [17] First, he holds
that it overestimates the damage done to the practice of promising
by a failure to keep a promise. One who breaks a promise harms his
own name certainly, but it isn't clear that a broken promise always

[16] Ross, *The Right and the Good*, pp. 38–39.
[17] Ross, *ibid.*, p. 39. The case of the nonpublic promise is discussed again in
Foundations of Ethics, pp. 95–96, 104–105. It occurs also in Mabbott, "Punishment," *op. cit.*, pp. 155–157, and in A. I. Melden, "Two Comments on Utilitarianism," *Philosophical Review*, Vol. LX (October, 1951), 519–523, which discusses
Carritt's example in *Ethical and Political Thinking*, p. 64.

damages the practice itself sufficiently to account for the strictness of the obligation. Second, and more important, I think, he raises the question of what one is to say of a promise which isn't known to have been made except to the promisor and the promisee, as in the case of a promise a son makes to his dying father concerning the handling of the estate.[18] In this sort of case the consideration relating to the practice doesn't weigh on the promisor at all, and yet one feels that this sort of promise is as binding as other promises. The question of the effect which breaking it has on the practice seems irrelevant. The only consequence seems to be that one can break the promise without running any risk of being censured; but the obligation itself seems not the least weakened. Hence it is doubtful whether the effect on the practice ever weighs in the particular case; certainly it cannot account for the strictness of the obligation where it fails to obtain. It seems to follow that a utilitarian account of the obligation to keep promises cannot be successfully carried out.

From what I have said in connection with punishment, one can foresee what I am going to say about these arguments and counter-arguments. They fail to make the distinction between the justification of a practice and the justification of a particular action falling under it, and therefore they fall into the mistake of taking it for granted that the promisor, like Carritt's official, is entitled without restriction to bring utilitarian considerations to bear in deciding whether to keep *his* promise. But if one considers what the practice of promising is one will see, I think, that it is such as not to allow this sort of general discretion to the promisor. Indeed, the point of the practice is to abdicate one's title to act in accordance with utilitarian and prudential considerations in order that the future may be tied down and plans coordinated in advance. There are obvious utilitarian advantages in having a practice which denies to the promisor, as a defense, any general appeal to the utilitarian principle in accordance with which the practice itself may be justified. There is nothing contradictory, or surprising, in this: utilitarian (or aesthetic) reasons might properly be given in arguing that the game

---

18 Ross's example is described simply as that of two men dying alone where one makes a promise to the other. Carritt's example (cf. n. 17 supra) is that of two men at the North Pole. The example in the text is more realistic and is similar to Mabbott's. Another example is that of being told something in confidence by one who subsequently dies. Such cases need not be "desert-island arguments" as Nowell-Smith seems to believe (cf. his *Ethics*, pp. 239–244).

of chess, or baseball, is satisfactory just as it is, or in arguing that it should be changed in various respects, but a player in a game cannot properly appeal to such considerations as reasons for his making one move rather than another. It is a mistake to think that if the practice is justified on utilitarian grounds then the promisor must have complete liberty to use utilitarian arguments to decide whether or not to keep his promise. The practice forbids this general defense; and it is a purpose of the practice to do this. Therefore what the above arguments presuppose—the idea that if the utilitarian view is accepted then the promisor is bound if, and only if, the application of the utilitarian principle to his own case shows that keeping it is best on the whole—is false. The promisor is bound because he promised: weighing the case on its merits is not open to him.[19]

Is this to say that in particular cases one cannot deliberate whether or not to keep one's promise? Of course not. But to do so is to deliberate whether the various excuses, exceptions and defenses, which are understood by, and which constitute an important part of, the practice, apply to one's own case.[20] Various defenses for not keeping one's promise are allowed, but among them there isn't the one that, on general utilitarian grounds, the promisor (truly) thought his action best on the whole, even though there may be the defense that the consequences of keeping one's promise would have been *extremely* severe. While there are too many complexities here to consider all the necessary details, one can see that the general defense isn't allowed if one asks the following question: what would one say of someone who, when asked why he broke his promise, replied simply that breaking it was best on the whole? Assuming that his reply is sincere, and that his belief was reasonable (i.e., one need not consider the possibility that he was mistaken), I think that one would question whether or not he knows what it means to say "I promise" (in the appropriate circumstances). It would be said of someone who used this excuse without further explanation that he didn't understand what defenses the practice, which defines a promise, allows to him. If a child were to use this excuse one would cor-

---

[19] What I have said in this paragraph seems to me to coincide with Hume's important discussion in the *Treatise of Human Nature*, bk. III, pt. II, sec. 5; and also sec. 6, par. 8.

[20] For a discussion of these, see H. Sidgwick, *The Methods of Ethics* (6th ed.; London, 1901), bk. III, ch. vi.

rect him; for it is part of the way one is taught the concept of a promise to be corrected if one uses this excuse. The point of having the practice would be lost if the practice did allow this excuse.

It is no doubt part of the utilitarian view that every practice should admit the defense that the consequences of abiding by it would have been extremely severe; and utilitarians would be inclined to hold that some reliance on people's good sense and some concession to hard cases is necessary. They would hold that a practice is justified by serving the interests of those who take part in it; and as with any set of rules there is understood a background of circumstances under which it is expected to be applied and which need not—indeed which cannot—be fully stated. Should these circumstances change, then even if there is no rule which provides for the case, it may still be in accordance with the practice that one be released from one's obligation. But this sort of defense allowed by a practice must not be confused with the general option to weigh each particular case on utilitarian grounds which critics of utilitarianism have thought it necessarily to involve.

The concern which utilitarianism raises by its justification of punishment is that it may justify too much. The question in connection with promises is different: it is how utilitarianism can account for the obligation to keep promises at all. One feels that the recognized obligation to keep one's promise and utilitarianism are incompatible. And to be sure, they are incompatible if one interprets the utilitarian view as necessarily holding that each person has complete liberty to weigh every particular action on general utilitarian grounds. But must one interpret utilitarianism in this way? I hope to show that, in the sorts of cases I have discussed, one cannot interpret it in this way.

III

So far I have tried to show the importance of the distinction between the justification of a practice and the justification of a particular action falling under it by indicating how this distinction might be used to defend utilitarianism against two long-standing objections. One might be tempted to close the discussion at this point by saying that utilitarian considerations should be understood as applying to practices in the first instance and not to particular actions falling under them except insofar as the practices admit of it. One might say that in this modified form it is a better account of our considered moral opinions and let it go at that. But to stop here would be to neglect the interesting question as to how one can fail to appreciate the significance of this rather obvious distinction and can take it for granted that utilitarianism has the consequence that particular cases may always be decided on general utilitarian grounds.[21] I want to argue that this mistake may be connected with misconceiving the logical status of the rules of practices; and to show this I am going to examine two conceptions of rules, two ways of placing them within the utilitarian theory.

The conception which conceals from us the significance of the distinction I am going to call the summary view. It regards rules in the following way: one supposes that each person decides what he shall do in particular cases by applying the utilitarian principle; one supposes further that different people will decide the same particular case in the same way and that there will be recurrences of cases similar to those previously decided. Thus it will happen that in cases of certain kinds the same decision will be made either by the same person at different times or by different persons at the same time. If a case occurs frequently enough one supposes that a rule is formulated to cover that sort of case. I have called this conception the summary view because rules are pictured as summaries of past decisions arrived at by the *direct* application of the utilitarian principle to particular cases. Rules are regarded as reports that cases of

----

[21] So far as I can see it is not until Moore that the doctrine is expressly stated in this way. See, for example, *Principia Ethica,* p. 147, where it is said that the statement "I am morally bound to perform this action" is identical with the statement "*This* action will produce the procedure of the greatest possible amount of good in the Universe" (my italics). It is important to remember that those whom I have called the classical utilitarians were largely interested in social institutions. They were among the leading economists and political theorists of their day, and they were not infrequently reformers interested in practical affairs. Utilitarianism historically goes together with a coherent view of society, and is not simply an ethical theory, much less an attempt at philosophical analysis in the modern sense. The utilitarian principle was quite naturally thought of, and used, as a criterion for judging social institutions (practices) and as a basis for urging reforms. It is not clear, therefore, how far it is necessary to amend utilitarianism in its classical form. For a discussion of utilitarianism as an integral part of a theory of society, see L. Robbins, *The Theory of Economic Policy in English Classical Political Economy* (London, 1952).

a certain sort have been found on *other* grounds to be properly decided in a certain way (although, of course, they do not *say* this).

There are several things to notice about this way of placing rules within the utilitarian theory.[22]

22 This footnote should be read after sec. 3 and presupposes what I have said there. It provides a few references to statements by leading utilitarians of the summary conception. In general it appears that when they discussed the logical features of rules the summary conception prevailed and that it was typical of the way they talked about moral rules. I cite a rather lengthy group of passages from Austin as a full illustration.

John Austin in his *Lectures on Jurisprudence* meets the objection that deciding in accordance with the utilitarian principle case by case is impractical by saying that this is a misinterpretation of utilitaranism. Accordng to the utilitarian view ". . . our conduct would conform to *rules* inferred from the tendencies of actions, but would not be determined by a direct resort to the principle of general utility. Utility would be the test of our conduct, ultimately, but not immediately: the immediate test of the rules to which our conduct would conform, but not the immediate test of specific or individual actions. Our rules would be fashioned on utility; our conduct, on our rules" (vol. I, p. 116). As to how one decides on the tendency of an action he says: "If we would try the tendency of a specific or individual act, we must not contemplate the act as if it were single and insulated, but must look at the class of acts to which it belongs. We must suppose that acts of the class were generally done or omitted, and consider the probable effect upon the general happiness or good. We must guess the consequences which would follow, if the class of acts were general; and also the consequences which would follow, if they were generally omitted. We must then compare the consequences on the positive and negative sides, and determine on which of the two the *balance* of advantage lies. . . . If we truly try the tendency of a specific or individual act, we try the tendency of the class to which that act belongs. The *particular* conclusion which we draw, with regard to the single act, implies a *general* conclusion embracing all similar acts. . . . To the rules thus inferred, and lodged in the memory, our conduct would conform *immediately* if it were truly adjusted to utility" (*ibid.*, p. 117). One might think that Austin meets the objection by stating the practice conception of rules; and perhaps he did intend to. But it is not clear that he has stated this conception. Is the generality he refers to of the statistical sort? This is suggested by the notion of tendency. Or does he refer to the utility of setting up a practice? I don't know; but what suggests the summary view is his subsequent remarks. He says: "To consider the specific consequences of single or individual acts, would *seldom* [my italics] consist with that ultimate principle" (*ibid.*, p. 117). But would one ever do this? He continues: ". . . this being admitted, the necessity of pausing and calculating, which the objection in question supposes, is an imagined necessity. To preface each act or forbearance by a conjecture and comparison of consequences, were clearly *superfluous* [my italics] and mischievous. It were clearly superfluous, inasmuch as the *results of that process* [my italics] would be embodied in a known *rule*. It were clearly mischievous, inasmuch as the *true* result would be expressed by that rule, whilst the process would probably be faulty, if it were done on the spur of the occasion" (*ibid.*, pp. 117–118). He goes on: "If our experience and observation of particulars were not *generalized,* our

a.   The point of having rules derives from the fact that similar
cases tend to recur and that one can decide cases more quickly
if one records past decisions in the form of rules. If similar
cases didn't recur, one would be required to apply the utilitarian principle directly, case by case, and rules reporting past
decisions would be of no use.

---

experience and observation of particulars would seldom avail us in *practice*. . . .
The inferences suggested to our minds by repeated experience and observation
are, therefore, drawn in *principles,* or compressed into *maxims*. These we carry
about us ready for use, and apply to individual cases promptly . . . without re-
verting to the process by which they were obtained; or without recalling, and
arraying before our minds, the numerous and intricate considerations of which
they are *handy abridgments* [my italics]. . . . True theory is a *compendium* of
particular truths. . . . Speaking then, generally, human conduct is inevitably
guided [my italics] by *rules,* or by *principles* or *maxims*" (*ibid.,* pp. 117–118). I
need not trouble to show how all these remarks incline to the summary view.
Further, when Austin comes to deal with cases "of comparatively rare occurrence"
he holds that specific considerations may outweigh the general. "Looking at the
reasons from which we had inferred the rule, it were absurd to think it inflex-
ible. We should therefore dismiss the *rule;* resort directly to the *principle* upon
which our rules were fashioned; and calculate *specific* consequences to the best
of our knowledge and ability" (*ibid.,* pp. 120–121). Austin's view is interesting
because it shows how one may come close to the practice conception and then
slide away from it.
     In *A System of Logic,* bk. VI, ch. xii, par. 2, Mill distinguishes clearly
between the position of judge and legislator and in doing so suggests the distinction between the two concepts of rules. However, he distinguishes the two positions to illustrate the difference between cases where one is to apply a rule already established and cases where one must formulate a rule to govern subsequent conduct. It's the latter case that interests him and he takes the "maxim
of policy" of a legislator as typical of rules. In par. 3 the summary conception is
very clearly stated. For example, he says of rules of conduct that they should be
taken provisionally, as they are made for the most numerous cases. He says that
they "point out" the manner in which it is least perilous to act; they serve as an
"admonition" that a certain mode of conduct has been found suited to the most
common occurrences. In *Utilitarianism,* ch. ii, par. 24 [p. 62], the summary conception appears in Mill's answer to the same objection Austin considered. Here
he speaks of rules as "corollaries" from the principle of utility; these "secondary"
rules are compared to "landmarks" and "direction-posts." They are based on
long experience and so make it unnecessary to apply the utilitarian principle to
each case. In par. 25 [p. 63], Mill refers to the task of the utilitarian principle in
adjudicating between competing moral rules. He talks here as if one then applies
the utilitarian principle directly to the particular case. On the practice view one
would rather use the principle to decide which of the ways that make the
practice consistent is the best. It should be noted that while in par. 10 [pp. 49–50],
Mill's definition of utilitarianism makes the utilitarian principle apply to
morality, i.e., to the rules and precepts of human conduct, the definition in
par. 2 [pp. 44–45], uses the phrase "actions are right in *proportion* as they *tend* to
promote happiness" [my italics] and this inclines towards the summary view. In

b. The decisions made on particular cases are logically prior to rules. Since rules gain their point from the need to apply the utilitarian principle to many similar cases, it follows that a particular case (or several cases similar to it) may exist whether or not there is a rule covering that case. We are pictured as recognizing particular cases prior to there being a rule which covers them, for it is only if we meet with a number of cases of a certain sort that we formulate a rule. Thus we are able to describe a particular case as a particular case of the requisite sort whether there is a rule regarding *that* sort of case or not. Put another way: what the *A*'s and the *B*'s refer to in rules of the form 'Whenever *A* do *B*' may be described as *A*'s and *B*'s whether or not there is the rule 'Whenever *A* do *B*', or whether or not there is any body of rules which make up a practice of which that rule is a part.

To illustrate this consider a rule, or maxim, which could arise in this way: suppose that a person is trying to decide whether to tell someone who is fatally ill what his illness is when he has been asked to do so. Suppose the person to reflect and then decide, on utilitarian grounds, that he should not answer truthfully; and suppose that on the basis of this and other like occasions he formulates a rule to the effect that when asked by someone fatally ill what his illness is,

---

the last paragraph of the essay "On the Definition of Political Economy," *Westminster Review* (October, 1836), Mill says that it is only in art, as distinguished from science, that one can properly speak of exceptions. In a question of practice, if something is fit to be done "in the majority of cases" then it is made the rule. "We may . . . in talking of art *unobjectionably* speak of the *rule* and the *exception,* meaning by the rule the cases in which there exists a preponderance . . . of inducements for acting in a particular way; and by the exception, the cases in which the preponderance is on the contrary side." These remarks, too, suggest the summary view.

In Moore's *Principia Ethica,* ch. v, there is a complicated and difficult discussion of moral rules. I will not examine it here except to express my suspicion that the summary conception prevails. To be sure, Moore speaks frequently of the utility of rules as generally followed, and of actions as generally practiced, but it is possible that these passages fit the statistical notion of generality which the summary conception allows. This conception is suggested by Moore's taking the utilitarian principle as applying directly to particular actions (pp. 147–148) and by his notion of a rule as something indicating which of the few alternatives likely to occur to anyone will generally produce a greater total good in the immediate future (p. 154). He talks of an "ethical law" as a prediction, and as a generalization (pp. 146, 155). The summary conception is also suggested by his discussion of exceptions (pp. 162–163) and of the force of examples of breaching a rule (pp. 163–164).

one should not tell him. The point to notice is that someone's being fatally ill and asking what his illness is, and someone's telling him, are things that can be described as such whether or not there is this rule. The performance of the action to which the rule refers doesn't require the stage-setting of a practice of which this rule is a part. This is what is meant by saying that on the summary view particular cases are logically prior to rules.

c.   Each person is in principle always entitled to reconsider the correctness of a rule and to question whether or not it is proper to follow it in a particular case. As rules are guides and aids, one may ask whether in past decisions there might not have been a mistake in applying the utilitarian principle to get the rule in question, and wonder whether or not it is best in this case. The reason for rules is that people are not able to apply the utilitarian principle effortlessly and flawlessly; there is need to save time and to post a guide. On this view a society of rational utilitarians would be a society without rules in which each person applied the utilitarian principle directly and smoothly, and without error, case by case. On the other hand, ours is a society in which rules are formulated to serve as aids in reaching these ideally rational decisions on particular cases, guides which have been built up and tested by the experience of generations. If one applies this view to rules, one is interpreting them as maxims, as "rules of thumb"; and it is doubtful that anything to which the summary conception did apply would be called a *rule*. Arguing as if one regarded rules in this way is a mistake one makes while doing philosophy.

d.   The concept of a *general* rule takes the following form. One is pictured as estimating on what percentage of the cases likely to arise a given rule may be relied upon to express the correct decision, that is, the decision that would be arrived at if one were to correctly apply the utilitarian principle case by case. If one estimates that by and large the rule will give the correct decision, or if one estimates that the likelihood of making a mistake by applying the utilitarian principle directly on one's own is greater than the likelihood of making a mistake by following the rule, and if these considerations held of persons generally, then one would be justified in urging its adoption as a general rule. In this way *general* rules might be accounted for on the summary view. It will still make sense, however, to speak of applying the utilitarian principle case by case, for it was by trying to foresee the results of doing this that one got the initial estimates upon which acceptance of the rule depends. That one is taking a rule in accordance with the summary conception will show itself in the naturalness with which one speaks of the rule as a guide, or as a maxim, or as a generalization from experience, and as something to be laid aside in extraordinary cases where there is no assurance that the generalization will hold and the case must therefore be treated on its merits. Thus there goes with this conception the notion of a particular exception which renders a rule suspect on a particular occasion.

The other conception of rules I will call the practice conception. On this view rules are pictured as defining a practice. Practices are set up for various reasons, but one of them is that in many areas of conduct each person's deciding what to do on utilitarian grounds case by case leads to confusion, and that the attempt to coordinate behavior by trying to foresee how others will act is bound to fail. As an alternative one realizes that what is required is the establishment of a practice, the specification of a new form of activity; and from this one sees that a practice necessarily involves the abdication of full liberty to act on utilitarian and prudential grounds. It is the mark of a practice that being taught how to engage in it involves being instructed in the rules which define it, and that appeal is made to those rules to correct the behavior of those engaged in it. Those engaged in a practice recognize the rules as defining it. The rules cannot be taken as simply describing how those engaged in the practice in fact behave: it is not simply that they act as if they were obeying the rules. Thus it is essential to the notion of a practice that the rules are publicly known and understood as definitive; and it is essential also that the rules of a practice can be taught and can be acted upon to yield a coherent practice. On this conception, then, rules are not generalizations from the decisions of individuals applying the utilitarian principle directly and independently to recurrent particular cases. On the contrary, rules define a practice and are themselves the subject of the utilitarian principle.

To show the important differences between this way of fitting rules into the utilitarian theory and the previous way, I shall consider the differences between the two conceptions on the points previously discussed.

a. In contrast with the summary view, the rules of practices are logically prior to particular cases. This is so because there cannot be a particular case of an action falling under a rule of a practice unless there is the practice. This can be made clearer as follows: in a practice there are rules setting up offices, specifying certain forms of action appropriate to various offices, establishing penalties for the breach of rules, and so on. We may think of the rules of a practice as defining offices, moves, and offenses. Now what is meant by saying that the practice is logically prior to particular cases is this: given any rule which specifies a form of action (a move), a particular action which would be taken as falling under this rule given that there is the practice would not be *described as* that sort of action unless there was the practice. In the case of actions specified by practices it is logically impossible to perform them outside the stage-setting provided by those practices, for unless there is the practice, and unless the requisite proprieties are fulfilled, whatever one does, whatever movements one makes, will fail to count as a form of action which the practice specifies. What one does will be described in some *other* way.

One may illustrate this point from the game of baseball. Many of the actions one performs in a game of baseball one can do by oneself or with others whether there is the game or not. For example, one can throw a ball, run, or swing a peculiarly shaped piece of wood. But one cannot steal base, or strike out, or draw a walk, or make an error, or balk; although one can do certain things which appear to resemble these actions such as sliding into a bag, missing a grounder and so on. Striking out, stealing a base, balking, etc., are all actions which can only happen in a game. No matter what a person did, what he did would not be described as stealing a base or striking out or drawing a walk unless he could also be described as playing baseball, and for him to be doing this presupposes the rule-like practice which constitutes the game. The practice is logically prior to particular cases: unless there is the practice the terms referring to actions specified by it lack a sense.[23]

b. The practice view leads to an entirely different conception of the authority which each person has to decide on the propriety of following a rule in particular cases. To engage in a practice, to perform those actions specified by a practice, means to follow the appropriate rules. If one wants to do an action which a certain practice specifies then there is no way to do it except to follow the rules which define it. Therefore, it doesn't make sense for a person to raise the question whether or not a rule of a practice correctly applies to *his* case where the action he contemplates is a form of action defined by a practice. If someone were to raise such a question, he would simply show that he didn't understand the situation in which he was acting. If one wants to perform an action specified by a practice, the only legitimate question concerns the nature of the practice itself ("How do I go about making a will?").

This point is illustrated by the behavior expected of a player in games. If one wants to play a game, one doesn't treat the rules of the game as guides as to what is best in particular cases. In a game of baseball if a batter were to ask "Can I have four strikes?" it would be assumed that he was asking what the rule was; and if, when told what the rule was, he were to say that he meant that on this occasion he thought it would be best on the whole for him to have four strikes rather than three, this would be most kindly taken as a joke. One might contend that baseball would be a better game if four strikes were allowed instead of three; but one cannot picture the rules as guides to what is best on the whole in particular cases, and question their applicability to particular cases as particular cases.

---

[23] One might feel that it is a mistake to say that a practice is logically prior to the forms of action it specifies on the grounds that if there were never any instances of actions falling under a practice then we should be strongly inclined to say that there wasn't the practice either. Blue-prints for a practice do not make a practice. That there is a practice entails that there are instances of people having been engaged and now being engaged in it (with suitable qualifications). This is correct, but it doesn't hurt the claim that any given particular instance of a form of action specified by a practice presupposes the practice. This isn't so on the summary picture, as each instance must be "there" prior to the rules, so to speak, as something from which one gets the rule by applying the utilitarian principle to it directly.

c.   and *d.* To complete the four points of comparison with the
summary conception, it is clear from what has been said that
rules of practices are not guides to help one decide particular
cases correctly as judged by some higher ethical principle. And
neither the quasi-statistical notion of generality, nor the notion
of a particular exception, can apply to the rules of practices.
A more or less general rule of a practice must be a rule which
according to the structure of the practice applies to more or
fewer of the kinds of cases arising under it; or it must be a
rule which is more or less basic to the understanding of the
practice. Again, a particular case cannot be an exception to
a rule of a practice. An exception is rather a qualification or
a further specification of the rule.

It follows from what we have said about the practice conception of rules that if a person is engaged in a practice, and if he is
asked why *he* does what *he* does, or if he is asked to defend what he
does, then his explanation, or defense, lies in referring the ques-
tioner to the practice. He cannot say of *his* action, if it is an action
specified by a practice, that he does it rather than some other because he thinks it is best on the whole.[24] When a man engaged in a
practice is queried about his action he must assume that the ques-
tioner either doesn't know that he is engaged in it ("Why are you
in a hurry to pay him?" "I promised to pay him today") or doesn't
know what the practice is. One doesn't so much justify one's particular action as explain, or show, that it is in accordance with the
practice. The reason for this is that it is only against the stage-setting
of the practice that one's particular action is described as it is. Only
by reference to the practice can one *say* what one is doing. To explain or to defend one's own action, as a particular action, one fits it
into the practice which defines it. If this is not accepted it's a sign
that a different question is being raised as to whether one is justified
in accepting the practice, or in tolerating it. When the challenge is
to the practice, citing the rules (saying what the practice is) is naturally to no avail. But when the challenge is to the particular action
defined by the practice, there is nothing one can do but refer to the
rules. Concerning particular actions there is only a question for one

----

[24] A philosophical joke (in the mouth of Jeremy Bentham): "When I run
to the other wicket after my partner has struck a good ball I do so because it is
best on the whole."

who isn't clear as to what the practice is, or who doesn't know that it is being engaged in. This is to be contrasted with the case of a maxim which may be taken as pointing to the correct decision on the case as decided on *other* grounds, and so giving a challenge on the case a sense by having it question whether these other grounds really support the decision on this case.

If one compares the two conceptions of rules I have discussed, one can see how the summary conception misses the significance of the distinction between justifying a practice and justifying actions falling under it. On this view rules are regarded as guides whose purpose it is to indicate the ideally rational decision on the given particular case which the flawless application of the utilitarian principle would yield. One has, in principle, full option to use the guides or to discard them as the situation warrants without one's moral office being altered in any way: whether one discards the rules or not, one always holds the office of a rational person seeking case by case to realize the best on the whole. But on the practice conception, if one holds an office defined by a practice then questions regarding one's actions in this office are settled by reference to the rules which define the practice. If one seeks to question these rules, then one's office undergoes a fundamental change: one then assumes the office of one empowered to change and criticize the rules, or the office of a reformer, and so on. The summary conception does away with the distinction of offices and the various forms of argument appropriate to each. On that conception there is one office and so no offices at all. It therefore obscures the fact that the utilitarian principle must, in the case of actions and offices defined by a practice, apply to the practice, so that general utilitarian arguments are not available to those who act in offices so defined.[25]

---

25 How do these remarks apply to the case of the promise known only to father and son? Well, at first sight the son certainly holds the office of promisor, and so he isn't allowed by the practice to weigh the particular case on general utilitarian grounds. Suppose instead that he wishes to consider himself in the office of one empowered to criticize and change the practice, leaving aside the question as to his right to move from his previously assumed office to another. Then he may consider utilitarian arguments as applied to the practice; but once he does this he will see that there are such arguments for not allowing a general utilitarian defense in the practice for this sort of case. For to do so would make it impossible to ask for and to give a kind of promise which one often wants to be able to ask for and to give. Therefore he will not want to change the practice, and so as a promisor he has no option but to keep his promise.

Some qualifications are necessary in what I have said. First, I may have talked of the summary and the practice conceptions of rules as if only one of them could be true of rules, and if true of any rules, then necessarily true of *all* rules. I do not, of course, mean this. (It is the critics of utilitarianism who make this mistake insofar as their arguments against utilitarianism presuppose a summary conception of the rules of practices.) Some rules will fit one conception, some rules the other; and so there are rules of practices (rules in the strict sense), and maxims and "rules of thumb."

Secondly, there are further distinctions that can be made in classifying rules, distinctions which should be made if one were considering other questions. The distinctions which I have drawn are those most relevant for the rather special matter I have discussed, and are not intended to be exhaustive.

Finally, there will be many border-line cases about which it will be difficult, if not impossible, to decide which conception of rules is applicable. One expects border-line cases with any concept, and they are especially likely in connection with such involved concepts as those of a practice, institution, game, rule, and so on. Wittgenstein has shown how fluid these notions are.[26] What I have done is to emphasize and sharpen two conceptions for the limited purpose of this paper.

IV

What I have tried to show by distinguishing between two conceptions of rules is that there is a way of regarding rules which allows the option to consider particular cases on general utilitarian grounds; whereas there is another conception which does not admit of such discretion except insofar as the rules themselves authorize it. I want to suggest that the tendency while doing philosophy to picture rules in accordance with the summary conception is what may have blinded moral philosophers to the significance of the distinction between justifying a practice and justifying a particular action falling under it; and it does so by

[26] *Philosophical Investigations* (Oxford, 1953), I, pars. 65–71, for example.

misrepresenting the logical force of the reference to the rules in the case of a challenge to a particular action falling under a practice, and by obscuring the fact that where there is a practice, it is the practice itself that must be the subject of the uilitarian principle.

It is surely no accident that two of the traditional test cases of utilitarianism, punishment and promises, are clear cases of practices. Under the influence of the summary conception it is natural to suppose that the officials of a penal system, and one who has made a promise, may decide what to do in particular cases on utilitarian grounds. One fails to see that a general discretion to decide particular cases on utilitarian grounds is incompatible with the concept of a practice; and that what discretion one does have is itself defined by the practice (e.g., a judge may have discretion to determine the penalty within certain limits). The traditional objections to utilitarianism which I have discussed presuppose the attribution to judges, and to those who have made promises, of a plenitude of moral authority to decide particular cases on utilitarian grounds. But once one fits utilitarianism together with the notion of a practice, and notes that punishment and promising are practices, then one sees that this attribution is logically precluded.

That punishment and promising are practices is beyond question. In the case of promising this is shown by the fact that the form of words "I promise" is a performative utterance which presupposes the stage-setting of the practice and the proprieties defined by it. Saying the words "I promise" will only be promising given the existence of the practice. It would be absurd to interpret the rules about promising in accordance with the summary conception. It is absurd to say, for example, that the rule that promises should be kept could have arisen from its being found in past cases to be best on the whole to keep one's promise; for unless there were already the understanding that one keeps one's promises as part of the practice itself there couldn't have been any cases of promising.

It must, of course, be granted that the rules defining promising are not codified, and that one's conception of what they are necessarily depends on one's moral training. Therefore it is likely that there is considerable variation in the way people understand the practice, and room for argument as to how it is best set up. For example, differences as to how strictly various defenses are to be taken, or just what defenses are available, are likely to arise amongst persons with different backgrounds. But irrespective of these variations it belongs to the concept of the practice of promising that the general utilitarian defense is not available to the promisor. That this is so accounts for the force of the traditional objection which I have discussed. And the point I wish to make is that when one fits the utilitarian view together with the practice conception of rules, as one must in the appropriate cases, then there is nothing in that view which entails that there must be such a defense, either in the practice of promising, or in any other practice.

Punishment is also a clear case. There are many actions in the sequence of events which constitute someone's being punished which presuppose a practice. One can see this by considering the definition of punishment which I gave when discussing Carritt's criticism of utilitarianism. The definition there stated refers to such things as the normal rights of a citizen, rules of law, due process of law, trials and courts of law, statutes, etc., none of which can exist outside the elaborate stage-setting of a legal system. It is also the case that many of the actions for which people are punished presuppose practices. For example, one is punished for stealing, for trespassing, and the like, which presuppose the institution of property. It is impossible to say what punishment is, or to describe a particular instance of it, without referring to offices, actions, and offenses specified by practices. Punishment is a move in an elaborate legal game and presupposes the complex of practices which make up the legal order. The same thing is true of the less formal sorts of punishment: a parent or guardian or someone in proper authority may punish a child, but no one else can.

There is one mistaken interpretation of what I have been saying which it is worthwhile to warn against. One might think that the use I am making of the distinction between justifying a practice and justifying the particular actions falling under it involves one in a definite social and political attitude in that it leads to a kind of conservatism. It might seem that I am saying that for each person the social practices of his society provide the standard of justification for his actions; therefore let each person abide by them and his conduct will be justified.

This interpretation is entirely wrong. The point I have been making is rather a logical point. To be sure, it has consequences in matters of ethical theory; but in itself it leads to no particular social or political attitude. It is simply that where a form of action is specified by a practice there is no justification possible of the particular action of a particular person save by reference to the practice. In such cases the action is what it is in virtue of the practice and to explain it is to refer to the practice. There is no inference whatsoever to be drawn with respect to whether or not one should accept the practices of one's society. One can be as radical as one likes but in the case of actions specified by practices the objects of one's radicalism must be the social practices and people's acceptance of them.

I have tried to show that when we fit the utilitarian view together with the practice conception of rules, where this conception is appropriate,[27] we can formulate it in a way which saves it from several traditional objections. I have further tried to show how the logical force of the distinction between justifying a practice and justifying an action falling under it is connected with the practice conception of rules and cannot be understood as long as one regards the rules of practices in accordance with the summary view. Why, when doing philosophy, one may be inclined to so regard them, I have not discussed. The reasons for this are evidently very deep and would require another paper.

[27] As I have already stated, it is not always easy to say where the conception is appropriate. Nor do I care to discuss at this point the general sorts of cases to which it does apply except to say that one should not take it for granted that it applies to many so-called "moral rules." It is my feeling that relatively few actions of the moral life are defined by practices and that the practice conception is more relevant to understanding legal and legal-like arguments than it is to the more complex sort of moral arguments. Utilitarianism must be fitted to different conceptions of rules depending on the case, and no doubt the failure to do this has been one source of difficulty in interpreting it correctly.

An Examination of
Restricted Utilitarianism

H. J. McCloskey

It is my purpose in this paper to show that *restricted utilitarianism* is no more tenable as an ethical theory than is the better known *extreme utilitarianism* which it is intended to supersede.[1] According to restricted utilitarianism we justify particular actions by reference to general rules or practices and the rules by reference to the principle of utility. Hence according to this theory particular actions may be obligatory even though they are not productive to the maximum good possible.

This theory arises out of its exponents' dissatisfaction with extreme utilitarianism, according to which "it is always the duty of every agent to do that one, among all the actions which he can do on any given occasion, whose total consequence will have the greatest intrinsic value" (G. E. Moore). This is evident in the writings of its contemporary exponents and sympathizers, such as J. O. Urmson and John Rawls. Urmson, for instance, argues that restricted utilitarianism is much superior to extreme utilitarianism just because it escapes the standard, fatal objections to that theory.[2] This is why he regards it as important to show that the traditional

Reprinted with the permission of the author and editors from *The Philosophical Review*, Vol. LXVI (1957), pp. 466–485. What is here designated "restricted utilitarianism" is now more commonly called "rule-utilitarianism." For Professor McCloskey's further comments on this topic, see his book, *Meta-Ethics and Normative Ethics* (The Hague: Martinus Nijhoff, 1969).

1 The terminology is that adopted by J. J. C. Smart in "Extreme and Restricted Utilitarianism," *Philosophical Quarterly*, Vol. VI (1956), 344 [pp. 251–64]. All subsequent references to Smart's views relate to this article.

2 J. O. Urmson, "The Interpretation of the Moral Philosophy of J. S. Mill," *Philosophical Quarterly*, Vol. III (1953), 33 [pp. 151–60].

interpretation of John Stuart Mill as an extreme utilitarian is mistaken. Rawls argues along the same lines, illustrating in some detail the superiority of the restricted theory by reference to the objections that are urged against the extreme view in connection with punishment and the obligation to keep promises.[3] Rawls and Urmson in their respective articles are simply voicing an almost general feeling among contemporary utilitarians that the simple device of treating the Principle of Utility not as a justification of particular obligations but of general practices or principles provides a general solution to the traditional objections to utilitarianism. There are some grounds for this confidence; and it is significant that J. J. C. Smart, who seeks to defend extreme against restricted utilitarianism, does so almost entirely by pointing to inadequacies in the restricted utilitarian theory. Smart does not show that extreme utilitarianism can meet the objections that are commonly urged against it and with which the restricted theory seeks to deal. Instead, he concentrates on attempting to show that the restricted theory cannot meet any objections encountered by the extreme theory and that in its attempts to do so, it involves itself in absurdities; and only to a much lesser extent does he concern himself with showing that some of the more usual, but less telling, objections to extreme utilitarianism are not real objections. The most acute difficulties encountered by the extreme theory are those involving considerations of justice—for example, punishment; and it is of note that Smart fails to consider such cases and that he gives no indication how the extreme theory might be made to cope with them. On the other hand, in spite of Smart's contention to the contrary, the restricted theory does seem to assist utilitarianism in escaping many of these difficulties; but it is not completely successful in this, and it does encounter new and serious difficulties of its own. These difficulties are as fatal to the claims of the restricted theory as are the difficulties commonly urged against utilitarianism to the claims of the extreme theory. To bring this out, it is necessary to note and examine the main varieties of restricted utilitarianism.

Pure and mixed. (a) According to what might be called the

[3] John Rawls, "Two Concepts of Rules," *Philosophical Review*, Vol. LXIV (1955), 3 [pp. 201–29].

pure restricted theory, the principle of utility is the primary principle by reference to which "rules in practice" are justified. It is appealed to only when considering the rules in practice and never when discussing the rightness or wrongness of actions. Urmson explains restricted utilitarianism in this way, but I know of no utilitarian who, in an undeviating way, defends pure restricted utilitarianism. It is nonetheless an important position because many exponents of restricted utilitarianism write as if this is the view they wish to defend and as if they have not succeeded in distinguishing it from the other varieties. Smart concentrates his attention on this variety, probably for these reasons. (*b*) Secondly, there is the *mixed* variety. According to this variety, the principle of utility is the primary principle which justifies the "rules in practice," but it is also a rule or secondary principle which competes with the other rules. Stephen Toulmin most nearly of all the restricted utilitarians espouses this version, but it seems to be that to which practically all restricted utilitarians are forced by pressure of difficulties.

Conditional and unconditional. (*a*) *Unconditional* restricted utilitarianism is that which treats the rules as being rules which in themselves prescribe no exceptions or spheres in which they do not hold. (*b*) *Conditional* restricted utilitarian theories are those according to which the practices or rules are such that they allow, as not being covered by the practice, special types of cases which might at first appear to fall under the practice. An unconditional restricted utilitarian theory might be to the effect that stealing is never right. A conditional variety of the theory might explain the "rule in practice" as being "stealing is never right except by a starving man from a wealthy one and 'in similar sorts of cases.' " Most restricted utilitarians assume the unconditional variety, although under pressure some switch to the conditional variety. Rawls suggests that the latter is the more defensible variety, but he seems half-heartedly to go on and associate it with the mixed variety. The mixed and the conditional varieties of restricted utilitarianism are occasioned by the difficulties with which a pure unconditional theory cannot deal.

Rawls defends restricted utilitarianism by taking the activities of punishment and promise-keeping as examples which illustrate how the restricted theory can meet difficulties fatal to extreme utilitarianism. The following example brings out the nature of these difficulties as they may arise in respect to punishment.

Suppose that a sheriff were faced with the choice either of framing a Negro for a rape that had aroused hostility to the Negroes (a particular Negro generally being believed to be guilty but whom the sheriff knows not to be guilty)—and thus preventing serious anti-Negro riots which would probably lead to some loss of life and increased hatred of each other by whites and Negroes—or of hunting for the guilty person and thereby allowing the anti-Negro riots to occur, while doing the best he can to combat them. In such a case the sheriff, if he were an extreme utilitarian, would appear to be committed to framing the Negro. Stubborn, extreme utilitarians try to avoid this sort of embarrassing conclusion, but such is the dissatisfaction generally felt with their moves here that Rawls is rightly able to commend the restricted theory on the grounds that it, by contrast, offers a plausible utilitarian solution.

Rawls points out that we must distinguish between justifying a practice as a system of rules which are applied and enforced and justifying a particular action that falls under these rules. Utilitarian arguments, he contends, are appropriate with regard to questions about practices, while retributive arguments fit the application of particular rules to particular cases. As he reasons, "So firstly we should explain that A is put in jail because he is guilty, and that it is the practice to punish and put into jail those found guilty after a fair legal trial; and secondly, we should justify *the practice* of putting people found guilty in jail on utilitarian grounds."

This move, besides doing justice to the two important components in punishment—guilt of the punished and utility in the allocation of the punishment—seems to get over the difficulty that utilitarianism appears to involve unjust, illegitimate punishment of the innocent, because, as Rawls shows, punishing the innocent is condemned on utilitarian grounds as being contrary to a general utilitarian institution. The defense of utilitarianism on this point is not complete, however, until it is shown that the system of punishment is a better utilitarian institution than any comparable possible institution.

Arguing to this conclusion, Rawls sets out a contrast between the institution of punishment and an institution corresponding to that which critics of utilitarianism claim to be presupposed by the utilitarian theory. This institution Rawls refers to as *"telishment."* It consists in the infliction of suffering on innocent and guilty individuals alike for the sake of the general well-being, the victims being selected by senior state officials. Rawls argues of such an institution that it does not have the utilitarian justification punishment has, and from this he moves to the more general conclusion that "it happens in general that as one drops off the defining features of punishment one ends up with an institution whose utilitarian justification is highly doubtful." Rawls's point is that the critics of utilitarianism do not seem to see that their criticisms presuppose the setting up by utilitarians of an alternative institution to that of punishment, and that once this is appreciated and once the new institution of telishment is described in detail, this institution is seen not to have the same utilitarian justification that is possessed by the institution of punishment.

Rawls's reply to criticisms of the type urged by W. D. Ross and others of the extreme utilitarians' defense of promise-keeping is in effect that these criticisms hold only against extreme utilitarianism and not against utilitarianism as such.[4] Restricted utilitarianism acknowledges that not all promises which ought to be kept produce the best possible results. This, it is explained, is so because it is the practice and not the individual action falling under it which has a utilitarian justification. Since the practice which has this justification is one which involves the abdication of the right to weigh individual promises on the utilitarian principle, there is no difficulty over the obligation to keep particular promises which do not have the best possible consequences. Bringing out the nature of the practice of promise-keeping Rawls writes:

What would one say of someone who, when asked why he broke his promise, replied simply that breaking it was best on the whole? . . . It would be said of someone who used this excuse without further explanation, that he didn't understand what defences the practice, which defines a promise, allows to him. . . . The point of having the practice would be lost if the practice did allow this excuse. [pp. 214–15]

4 See W. D. Ross, *The Right and The Good* (Oxford, 1930), esp. chs. i and ii, and *Foundations of Ethics* (Oxford, 1939), esp. ch. v.

It is quite clear from the examples of promise-keeping and punishment that the restricted theory does escape some of the more usual objections urged against the extreme utilitarian theory. The former theory is able to offer reasons, within the utilitarian framework, for punishing only the guilty and for keeping those promises which it is generally felt should be kept, even when acting otherwise might produce valuable results. The restricted theory cannot deal with all the more usual objections urged against the extreme theory, however; and it itself is exposed to new objections. In brief, it fails to give reasons for keeping *all* those promises (and other obligations) which ought to be kept, but which on the extreme theory appear not to be obligatory; it implies obligations (for example, to keep promises) which in fact are not real obligations; it fails to assist the utilitarian position in meeting objections arising in respect of many activities, such as killing, the wrongness of which does not depend upon the existence of any institution; it involves a very paradoxical form of ethical relativism; and at key points the theory is vague and confused, and necessarily so. These objections may now be developed in detail.

(1) If the value of the institution or rule in practice is assessed on a utilitarian calculus, then it must be asked: Why should there not be exceptions to the institution also on utilitarian grounds in those situations in which the exception is not going to damage the institution? Exponents of the restricted theory speak as if to make exceptions on utilitarian grounds is to set up a different practice; but to punish an innocent person when and only when to do so is not to weaken the existing institution of punishment and when the consequences of doing so are valuable is not to set up what Rawls calls an institution of telishment. So even were it true that telishment is an institution that cannot be justified on utilitarian grounds—and this is by no means clear—it would still not follow that we should never telish. Similarly with promise-keeping and promise-breaking. The most that the restricted utilitarian can seriously contend is that if we knew that most people were going to treat promises as utilitarians are said to be in consistency bound to treat them and that the general practice and all the valuable results that accrue from having a practice of promise-keeping were to be thereby endangered, then the individual promise which has bad consequences should nonetheless be kept: whereas if we

know that the practice will not be endangered, that most people anyway are not utilitarians, and that there can be a general expectation that people can be counted on to act in certain ways in the future, then surely it is unreasonable to insist that even here the utilitarian principle itself cannot be invoked and that the promise should be kept. Yet if this point is allowed it follows that in our society, or at least in a society predominantly of nonutilitarians, utilitarians should not keep promises of which the consequences on the whole are bad. The only defense for conforming with the rule when the consequences of such conformity are bad would seem to be a causal one—that lack of conformity on this occasion weakens the practice, and so on. But this defense is possible only in rare, particular cases. Hence either there must be admission that very many promises need not be kept after all and that the restricted version is little better off than the extreme theory, or we get the absurd insistence on conformity with the rule, with no good reason for this being offered. The latter absurdity can be illustrated by amending an analogy used in another context by J. D. Mabbott and applying it in the context of restricted utilitarianism. The analogy then runs:

> The following dialogue at a bridge table will illustrate the fallacy. I am the third player on the first trick; the second player has played the ace. I hold the king. I remember that I have been told that the third player should play high. I whisper to my mentor behind me (the mentor representing the restricted utilitarian), "What do I play?" He says, "The king." "But it will do no good; the ace has been played." "Never mind that. You must play your king, that is the rule and you must conform with the rule." [5]

If the restricted utilitarian nonetheless denies this absurdity and insists that the rules of a practice should be kept where a breach will not harm the practice and will produce good results—that is, if he insists firmly that utility is a first principle and not a rule or secondary principle and that decisions must be reached by reference to secondary principles, then it follows from the pure variety of the restricted theory that all promises should be kept,

[5] Mabbott, "Interpretations of Mill's Utilitarianism," *Philosophical Quarterly*, Vol. VI (1956), 115 [pp. 161–68].

that the truth should always be told, and that the consequences are irrelevant simply because the first principle is irrelevant. And this conclusion is as objectionable as the other; the more especially as it seems also to imply that there are no duties where there are no rules in practice.

What seems to have happened in the development of restricted utilitarianism is that the restricted utilitarians have become confused between what are *in fact* accepted as good reasons in morals and what on their theory *should be* accepted as such. This is an important point and an important criticism. It is quite true, as the restricted utilitarians suggest, that we do regard it as giving a good reason for an action to point out that it is an instance of a general practice; but it does not follow from this that these same reasons should be regarded on the utilitarian theory as good reasons. Clearly on the utilitarian theory—the extreme or restricted version—to point to the fact that an action is an instance of a general moral practice is not always to give a good moral reason.

These various arguments which make up this first general objection to restricted utilitarianism would seem to be fatal to the claims of all varieties of the restricted theory.

(2) There are, of course, conflicts even between rules in practice. Even the restricted utilitarian has to face the conflicts of duties so commonly supposed to be fatal to the Kantian theory. There are either of two possible courses open to him. One is to argue that we should judge between the conflicting duties in particular situations on the grounds of the value of the consequences of the respective *actions*. But this either amounts to the extreme utilitarian position, or at least exposes it to extension along the lines of making the consequences always relevant, as after all they really are. Alternatively, the restricted utilitarian could choose between the practices on the basis of the value of the practices. This would seem to be the consistent move; but it leads to the absurdity of always preferring one practice to another. For example, if it were determined that truth-telling is socially more valuable as a practice than promise-keeping, then in any conflict between these two activities it would always be obligatory to tell the truth and break a promise. This clearly is absurd, and no serious moral philosopher, utilitarian or otherwise, would be happy to accept a theory which led to this

sort of conclusion. Further, there would remain the problem of what happens when two instances of the one rule conflict; for example, when two promises are in opposition, or when the truth at one level is incompatible with the truth at another level.

(3) This problem concerning the resolution of conflicts of duties brings to our notice another difficulty for restricted utilitarianism, namely, the problem of how one is to determine the utilitarian value of the various alternative practices. Take punishment, for example. Is it clear, as Rawls assumes, that an institution of telishment would be bad on utilitarian grounds? Something of the sort appears to have been the prevailing institution in Russia since the Revolution, and it is not clear that it has been contrary to the public good. While I am no admirer of the U.S.S.R.—on moral grounds—I am nevertheless disposed to believe that the very great advances in that country since the Revolution and the alleviation of human misery over such vast areas of the world would not have been possible without the aid of some such institution. Its utilitarian justification seems now to be diminishing, and the Russians appear to be acting as good utilitarians should, modifying the institution as the principle of utility requires. I may be wrong in this belief that such an institution had a utilitarian justification in the U.S.S.R.; at least it is arguable, but it is not seriously arguable that such an institution was morally unjustifiable in Russia whatever the empirical facts prove to be.

Further, we do not have to go to Russia to see that a system like telishment is possible, and possibly justifiable on utilitarian grounds. The people of Australia, guided by their prime minister, the Rt. Hon. R. G. Menzies, came very close to approving the introduction of a significant body of retrospective legislation. Punishment under retrospective legislation is punishment under quite a different institution to that in which one is punished only for offenses which are offenses at the time of the act. Punishment under retrospective legislation is a possible institution. The prime minister of Australia thought that it was a socially valuable institution. I am not qualified to judge whether he was right; but I suspect that he was right on the point of utility. Whether he was right on the point of utility or not, however, he was not so clearly right on the question of morals. But this is something a restricted utilitarian cannot afford to admit.

Similarly, laws such as those relating to punishment of habitual criminals, as well as those forbidding loitering with intent, alter the system from the kind which Rawls describes and which he suggests that we can justify on utilitarian grounds. The same sort of arguments would seem to be applicable concerning the institution of slavery in ancient Greece. The latter institution, for the greater part of the time it prevailed, seems to have had a utilitarian justification; but it did not have a moral justification.

What it is important to stress here, however, is the difficulty of settling a dispute of the following kind: Is punishment or telishment the more valuable institution? Such a question is not an a priori question but an empirical one for which apparently there are considerations supporting each alternative. I am quite uncertain as to the solution of the empirical question, and I suggest that if we are honest with ourselves we all must admit to such uncertainty; yet I, and I suspect most other people, am not uncertain in the same way about the moral wrongness of telishment, and this surely is significant. It suggests a direct insight into the obligatoriness and disobligatoriness of certain kinds of activities—direct insight that can give us the assurance in our moral judgments that we have, but which we could not have if they were dependent upon the findings of an empirical enquiry. Ross and other intuitionists have been accused of being dogmatists by utilitarian writers; but the charge is totally unwarranted in most cases and is much more appropriate when directed against the restricted utilitarian philosophers themselves, for they are dogmatic about empirical matters concerning which they have very little evidence. It is an amazing thing, when one considers the importance of morality, to find that restricted utilitarians do virtually nothing toward defending their assumption that the current moral conventions are, in terms of utility, the morally best conventions; and further that these same moral philosophers do nothing toward entering into a general empirical enquiry in this sphere. (Mill would be an almost isolated exception, if he could properly be regarded as a restricted utilitarian.)

So much for our third objection. It would hold equally well against all varieties of restricted utilitarianism.

(4) A fourth criticism relates to the vagueness of the key concept in the restricted utilitarian theory—the concept which is vari-

ously designated "social practice," "rule in practice," "institution," "principle," or simply "rule." This vagueness is an important feature of the theory, and once it is eliminated the theory becomes much less plausible.

Rawls explains the notion of "a rule in practice" thus:

> In the case of actions specified by practices it is logically impossible to perform them outside the stage-setting provided by those practices for unless there is the practice, and unless the requisite properties are fulfilled whatever one does, whatever movements one makes, will fail to count as a form of action which the practice specifies. What one does will be described in some *other* way.
>
> One may illustrate this point from the game of baseball. . . . No matter what a person did, what he did would not be described as stealing a base or striking out or drawing a walk unless he could also be described as playing baseball, and for him to be doing this presupposes the rule-like practice which constitutes the game. *The practice is logically prior to particular cases; unless there is the practice, the terms referring to actions specified by it lack a sense.* [pp. 222–23]

Rawls is here giving a correct account of one of the concepts of a "rule" required by the restricted utilitarian theory. One of the telling arguments of the restricted utilitarians is that various moral activities have their possibility and reality only in the context of a practice. Hence the need arises to ensure that there is a practice by conforming with it, at least on the whole.

Now, if Rawls is right—that the concept of "rules in practice" makes the practice logically prior to the action specified by it—then restricted utilitarianism is of assistance to the general utilitarian position in overcoming only some of the difficulties which beset extreme utilitarianism. Clearly not all of the activities claimed to be obligatory in their own right are such that they presuppose a general practice *to exist* as activities of a certain kind; and certainly they do not presuppose a general practice to be obligatory. Restricted utilitarianism arose out of an attempt to deal with the difficulties associated with the obligations relating to promise-keeping, truth-telling, repayment of debts, stealing, and punishment, and these are the difficulties the theory does appear to help to resolve. But there are other difficulties for extreme utilitarianism—difficulties associated with the obligations to perfect one's talents, to treat others as ends and not as means, not to kill, and so on. Whether or not there is a practice of not killing others whenever we wish to do so, it is still prima facie wrong to kill, although where there is widespread disregard of the obligation, it may be permissible to kill more than in a society in which the established practice is not to kill others. Further, murder and abstinence from murder are activities *logically prior* to a general practice and have a reality independent of a general practice in a way that promise-keeping does not. The same is true in respect of the duty not to treat others as mere means and of the duty to perfect our talents. These do not depend for their moral bindingness on their consequences, nor upon there being a general practice; hence if we are to treat others as means—and it is frequently necessary to do so—we need to have good reasons for doing so. The model of "rules" talk is promise-keeping and contracts generally. The "rules" talk is less effective with other prima facie duties, and with others again quite irrelevant.

The concept of a "rule in practice" elucidated by Rawls, while appropriate to a great deal of restricted utilitarian theory, is inappropriate for other parts of the writings of its exponents. A much vaguer concept is used. Clearly the sense in which the principle of utility can be thought of as a rule among rules cannot be the sense outlined by Rawls. The games analogy, popular with restricted utilitarians, brings out this confusion in the concept. It is a rule of football that if the ball is kicked between the center two posts at the end of the field it counts as a goal; and that a goal equals six behinds; that it is permissible to bump an opponent in the side but not in the back; that when a player is injured, and only when he is injured, he may be replaced by a reserve; and so on. It is a rule in practice, however, that a losing side replaces its weakest players in the last quarter, whether they are injured or not; that a team has a mascot; and so on. Now a careful consideration of the writings of restricted utilitarians brings out that there is an alternation between senses of rules corresponding roughly to these two senses of rule in football. For example, promise-keeping is a rule in practice in one sense; the next of kin caring for the aged is a rule in another sense of "rule"; and evading tax within the limits allowed by the law is a rule in practice in perhaps another sense again. Some points require one sense, some the other, and some, other senses again; but the theory requires a consistent sense.

Another sense of "rule" to be noted here is such that a rule is simply equated with the principle of an action. Some utilitarians talk as if the practice aspect of the "rule in practice" is unimportant—that it is the principle of the action that is the relevant consideration, and further that there are some principles which on utilitarian grounds should be universalized. Hence, irrespective of the empirical fact as to whether an activity is practised or not, there are some principles, so it is argued, which, if they were generally practised, would be justifiable on utilitarian grounds, and these are those with which we should conform. The sole virtue of this contention is that it escapes the absurdity of implying that what is right or wrong and what is a good or a bad reason depends on the prevailing customs. To establish this kind of view—that it is the principle which counts, where the principle is one which would have utilitarian justification if it were a principle in practice—it has to be shown that conformity with the principle will help to bring about its general adoption and that the value of the act on this account is greater than the value of the consequences of a breach of the principle. This will not be the case very often, however; certainly it will not be the case often enough to permit a utilitarian theory to be established along these lines.

This means that the practice is what counts; *and it means that what constitutes a valid moral reason in support of an action depends on the cultural practice;* although it is true that it also means that what constitutes a valid reason in support of the practice itself is universal, unchanging, and objective. But the first conclusion is plainly false. The Spartan youths surely, while not morally blameworthy, were certainly mistaken in their moral conduct; and so too is the Soviet official who, in accord with the institution of "punishment" that prevails in Russia, frames an innocent individual; and so too were the Greek slave owners, the recent Nazi concentration-camp officers, and the contemporary Russian slave masters. To point to the practice is not to give a valid moral reason for holding another man in slavery.

The logic of the expression "valid moral reason" needs to be noted here. On the restricted utilitarian theory its logic would appear to run as follows: "X was a valid moral reason for owning a slave in the fourth century B.C., but it is not a valid moral reason today." In fact the logic appears to be: *"X was thought to constitute a valid moral reason* for owning a slave by the Greeks of the fourth century B.C., but we see now that it was not a valid moral reason and that the Greeks were mistaken in the matter."

This point draws attention to a general difficulty for restricted utilitarianism, a difficulty which its exponents seem not to have considered because it has been concealed from them by the vagueness of their formulations of their theories. The difficulty springs from the fact that not all rules in practice are good utilitarian rules in practice nor the best utilitarian rules that could be rules in practice. What does the restricted utilitarian say about our duty in a society in which the rules in practice are not the best possible utilitarian rules, and perhaps not even rules justifiable at all on utilitarian grounds? The restricted utilitarian in fact seems to say nothing because he appears to have assumed that the rules in practice of Anglo-Saxon societies are the only rules that matter, and that these are good utilitarian rules in practice. On the whole they do seem to be good utilitarian rules, although many of them are by no means the best possible rules in practice. Examples of the latter probably include the prevailing rules relating to marriage, divorce, and sexual behavior generally; rules concerning the care of the aged by relations, if these may be called rules in practice; many systems of "punishment" in Anglo-Saxon countries; and the like. In any case, not all societies are Anglo-Saxon societies. Russia has its institutions of slave labor and "telishment"; Japan and the East their unutilitarian rules in practice. What is the moral agent's duty in these societies? The impression one gets from the writings of restricted utilitarians very strongly suggests conformity with the practice; and, after all, this is the impact this general account of ethics does have. Two answers are possible in terms of restricted utilitarianism, however, and both may be considered here.

We may consider first societies in which there are both rules in practice which have no utilitarian justification and other rules which should positively be condemned on utilitarian grounds. To suggest that there should be conformity with such rules in practice and that to indicate the rule in practice is to give a good moral reason for one's behavior would in most of these cases be to advocate blatant immorality. The Nazi rule in practice relating to treatment of Jews is a case in point; the Japanese practice of committing suicide to avoid dishonorable capture by the enemy is another case in point; and the many sacrificial practices of primitive religious groups are other examples. To point to the fact that one's action is in conformity with a rule in practice of one or other of these kinds is not to give an excuse or explanation which may exonerate the agent. Yet if it is suggested that the moral agent should not conform with these practices, what is the moral agent's duty in such a society? Should he be guided simply by the principle of utility itself, justifying his individual actions directly by reference to it? This is not an unreasonable answer, but it means that in such a society restricted utilitarianism is incapable of saving the general utilitarian position from attack along the lines indicated by critics such as Ross. Further, it means that it is up to the individual moral agent in each society to determine whether the various practices are justifiable utilitarian practices. Different conclusions will no doubt be reached by different agents about some of these practices.

Where the rules in practice are rules which have positive utilitarian justification but are nonetheless not the best rules in practice possible, the position is less clear. Some rules in practice are so much inferior to other possible rules in practice, even where the former have some utilitarian justification, that it is often positively immoral to condone the practice by conforming with it. Here the examples would depend on the sense of "rules in practice" used by the theory. On any usage examples are possible, but if the looser usage is adopted such that a rule in practice includes how people in fact behave and believe it to be clever to behave, then a multitude of examples becomes available. But quite apart from these cases, it is clear that conformity with the rule in practice, even where it is a good utilitarian rule or institution, such as telishment, is not necessarily the morally best action possible. If on the other hand it is maintained that conformity with the practice is only morally right where the rule in practice is the best possible utilitarian rule, then this same criticism may still be urged. In addition, two other criticisms become relevant. If we should be right in conforming only when the practice is the best possible utilitarian practice, we should not often be able, in order to have a good moral reason, to point to the fact that we are conforming with a practice. That is to say, the move that characterizes restricted utilitarianism could seldom be made; and equally important, it could rarely be known that it could be made. It is unlikely, however, that any restricted utilitarian would maintain that we should conform only with the best possible practices.

Most of the points made here as our fourth objection to restricted utilitarianism may be well illustrated by reference to sexual morality. In the sphere of sexual behavior we find a clear distinction between the moral rule in practice and the behavior in practice. Further, we find, as modern investigators such as Kinsey have confirmed, that within one community there are different moral codes, or in the language of restricted utilitarianism, different rules in practice. The state in terms of its laws and sanctions recognizes one system of rules in practice; but this system may not coincide with those of any one group within the state. Which of these various practices is the restricted utilitarian's rule in practice? To which does one have to point to have a good moral reason for one's behavior? Some of these rules in practice have a better utilitarian justification than others; some have little utilitarian justification by contrast with others; but all have some utilitarian justification, because practically any code of sexual behavior is better than none. Is conformity the right thing, and does it or does it not matter which of these rules or set of rules is the set of rules in practice?

These objections apply with equal force against all varieties of the restricted theory, although the objection relating to the equivocation in the use of the expression "rule" is of special importance in respect to the mixed restricted utilitarian theories.

(5) Finally, it needs to be noted that it is difficult, in terms of the criterion used by restricted utilitarians, to distinguish in the way in which we do between *nonmoral* and *moral* practices. The test of a moral practice—that it is a *moral* practice and therefore a basis for valid moral reasons—would seem to be either that it is conducive to good consequences or that it is thought so to be. If the former is the test, then many so-called nonmoral and even immoral practices, for example keeping to the left and possibly even slavery in the U.S.S.R., should be regarded as moral; and some so-called moral practices should perhaps be denied the name. If on the other hand the criterion is that the practice is generally thought to be productive of good consequences, then many important, genuinely moral practices would not qualify for the title, and some nonmoral prac-

tices would qualify. If we make the fact the criterion, we can seldom be sure that a practice is a moral practice; if we make the belief the criterion, then it would be surprising if many practices qualified. People just do not think or have opinions about the utilitarian value of institutions like promise-keeping, truth-telling, and so on. Further, it would seem to follow from the theory that many principles—the so-called prudential maxims—should be elevated to the level of moral practices; but clearly whether so elevated or not, prudential maxims would remain of a significantly different moral status from the principles of promise-keeping, truth-telling, and so on.

Many other objections could be urged against restricted utilitarianism; but the objections already developed are sufficient to bring out that the distinction between justifying a practice and justifying an action falling under the practice will not do for utilitarianism what the exponents of restricted utilitarianism claim that it will do. It does not provide a means of saving utilitarianism as a tenable ethical theory.

As we have seen, most of the objections indicated above are fatal not only to the claims of the pure version but of all versions of restricted utilitarianism. It is worth while, however, to examine briefly the more complex varieties, since it may be thought that they have special merits which enable them to provide a more sure basis for utilitarianism.

The mixed version, as we have seen, admits the principle of utility as a secondary principle while putting it up also as the primary principle which provides the justification of the secondary principles. It will at once be noticed that this complicates the account of the relation between the primary and secondary principles and obscures the concept of "rule" in the way already indicated. Clearly the sense in which promises are dependent for their reality upon the existence of the practice is different from the sense in which we can have a rule or practice of producing good. It is a theoretically possible version of utilitarianism, however, and one which escapes two absurdities to which the pure restricted theory leads, namely, that we should always conform with the rule and that we have no duties except those falling under the rules (in Rawls's sense of "rule"). Further, it is a version of which John Austin appears to have been an unwilling adherent and of which Toulmin is a luke-warm exponent. Toulmin's lukewarmness consists in the fact that while he is prepared to insist on the relevance of the principle of utility in all situations involving moral obligations, thereby treating it as a secondary as well as the primary principle, he is unwilling to treat it as a secondary principle of *duty*. Thus his particular the-ory is exposed to one of the absurdities of the pure theory—that there are no duties where there are no rules in Rawls's sense of "rule"—and also to the difficulties which are encountered by the mixed theory. These include the difficulties relating to the concept of rule and to the relation between the primary principle and the secondary rules. Toulmin suggests that this is the variety of utili-tarianism he is adopting in various places, including the section in which he discusses the issue of conflicts of duties.[6]

It is difficult to argue against this variety of the theory except in terms of the general objections to restricted utiliarianism already noted. This is not because of any special virtue of this variety, nor for the reason wrongly advanced by Smart—that this version repre-sents a collapse of restricted utilitarianism into the extreme theory—but simply because of its indefiniteness. In theory mixed restricted utilitarianism does represent a different theory from extreme utili-tarianism. In practice it is difficult to determine whether the two have been assimilated. Unless we are told how to weigh the practice against the consequences and how much weight to attribute to the practice qua practice, it is difficult to know how the mixed version works out in detail and whether its exponent has or has not fallen back into the outmoded extreme utilitarian calculus. Toulmin gives us no help in this matter, and the same seems to have been true of Austin. This means that no new objections relating specifically to this variety of utilitarianism can be developed here. Of those objec-tions already indicated, however, 1, 3, 4, and 5 may effectively be pressed against it.

The conditional varieties of restricted utilitarianism are also difficult to appraise. This is because they too are so vaguely stated that they could imply anything at all. My impression is that if all the exceptions and conditions hinted at by some utilitarians as being part of the practice are indeed part of the practice, then there is

6 Stephen Toulmin, *The Place of Reason in Ethics* (New York, 1950), pp. 147–148.

little left of the practice at all. It is difficult to see that we can do justice to the special cases in which we break promises with justification on utilitarian grounds by saying, as is suggested by exponents of these varieties, that we are really not going against the practice. We *are* going against the practice. When we make a promise we are not accepting an obligation to act in a certain way except where there are good consequences resulting from an alternative action; and where we do break a promise on this sort of ground we think of ourselves as having and facing a conflict, and not of puzzling over what the practice is. The conditional amendment of the theory seems to detract from all that is introduced into utilitarianism by restricted utilitarianism, namely, by the admission of the moral significance of promises (and the like) which have no direct utilitarian justification and which would appear to be overriden by utilitarian considerations. These varieties are too vague and elusive to discuss in detail, however, and their rejection must be based on the general objections to restricted utilitarianism already noted. Nevertheless, once they are made more precise, additional specific objections could be urged against them. It is worth recording here that it is probably not without significance that the most notable utilitarians have not only not adopted the conditional variety but have in fact positively denied its central thesis.

It is now necessary simply to point out that some sort of synthesis of restricted and extreme utilitarianism will not provide a solution to the difficulties which appear to be fatal to the claims of each theory. Extreme utilitarianism breaks down at points at which the restricted theory is unable to offer any assistance, for example, in respect to the duty to refrain from killing; and further, restricted utilitarianism, besides having fatal intrinsic defects, also has the defects of relating only to some duties and only to some societies, and then not to all the rules in practice in these societies. Utilitarianism therefore breaks down as an account of our moral obligations; and it breaks down because it is unsuccessful in accounting for the obligatoriness of those activities singled out by Ross as activities which are intrinsically obligatory.

Extreme and Restricted Utilitarianism

J. J. C. Smart

I

Utilitarianism is the doctrine that the rightness of actions is to be judged by their consequences. What do we mean by 'actions' here? Do we mean particular actions or do we mean classes of actions? According to which way we interpret the word 'actions' we get two different theories, both of which merit the appellation 'utilitarian'.

(1) If by 'actions' we mean particular individual actions we get the sort of doctrine held by Bentham, Sidgwick, and Moore. According to this doctrine we test individual actions by their consequences, and general rules, like 'keep promises', are mere rules of thumb which we use only to avoid the necessity of estimating the probable consequences of our actions at every step. The rightness or wrongness of keeping a promise on a particular occasion depends only on the goodness or badness of the consequences of keeping or of breaking the promise on that particular occasion. Of course part of the consequences of breaking the promise, and a part to which we will normally ascribe decisive importance, will be the weakening of faith in the institution of promising. However, if the goodness of the consequences of breaking the rule is *in toto* greater than the

Based on a paper read to the Victorian Branch of the Australasian Association of Psychology and Philosophy, October, 1955. Reprinted with the permission of the author and editor of *Philosophical Quarterly,* Vol. 6 (1956), pp. 344–354. Minor revisions have been made by Professor Smart. "Extreme" and "restricted" are used to designate what have now become more commonly known as "act" and "rule utilitarianism" respectively.

goodness of the consequences of keeping it, then we must break the rule, irrespective of whether the goodness of the consequences of *everybody's* obeying the rule is or is not greater than the consequences of *everybody's* breaking it. To put it shortly, rules do not matter, save *per accidens* as rules of thumb and as *de facto* social institutions with which the utilitarian has to reckon when estimating consequences. I shall call this doctrine 'extreme utilitarianism'.

(2) A more modest form of utilitarianism has recently become fashionable. The doctrine is to be found in Toulmin's book *The Place of Reason in Ethics,* in Nowell-Smith's *Ethics* (though I think Nowell-Smith has qualms), in John Austin's *Lectures on Jurisprudence* (Lecture II), and even in J. S. Mill, if Urmson's interpretation of him is correct (*Philosophical Quarterly,* Vol. 3, pp. 33–39, 1953 [pp. 151–60]). Part of its charm is that it appears to resolve the dispute in moral philosophy between intuitionists and utilitarians in a way which is very neat. The above philosophers hold, or seem to hold, that moral rules are more than rules of thumb. In general the rightness of an action is *not* to be tested by evaluating its consequences but only by considering whether or not it falls under a certain rule. Whether the rule is to be considered an acceptable moral rule, is, however, to be decided by considering the consequences of adopting the rule. Broadly, then, actions are to be tested by rules and rules by consequences. The only cases in which we must test an individual action directly by its consequences are (*a*) when the action comes under two different rules, one of which enjoins it and one of which forbids it, and (*b*) when there is no rule whatever that governs the given case. I shall call this doctrine 'restricted utilitarianism'.

It should be noticed that the distinction I am making cuts across, and is quite different from, the distinction commonly made between hedonistic and ideal utilitarianism. Bentham was an extreme hedonistic utilitarian and Moore an extreme ideal utilitarian, and Toulmin (perhaps) could be classified as a restricted ideal utilitarian. A hedonistic utilitarian holds that the goodness of the consequences of an action is a function only of their pleasurableness and an ideal utilitarian, like Moore, holds that pleasurableness is not even a necessary condition of goodness. Mill seems, if we are to take his remarks about higher and lower pleasures seriously, to be neither a pure hedonistic nor a pure ideal utilitarian. He seems to hold that pleasurableness is a necessary condition for goodness, but that goodness is a function of other qualities of mind as well. Perhaps we can call him a quasi-ideal utilitarian. When we say that a state of mind is good I take it that we are expressing some sort of *rational preference*. When we say that it is pleasurable I take it that we are saying that it is enjoyable, and when we say that something is a higher pleasure I take it that we are saying that it is more truly, or more deeply, enjoyable. I am doubtful whether 'more deeply enjoyable' does not just mean 'more enjoyable, even though not more enjoyable on a first look', and so I am doubtful whether quasi-ideal utilitarianism, and possibly ideal utilitarianism too, would not collapse into hedonistic utilitarianism on a closer scrutiny of the logic of words like 'preference', 'pleasure', 'enjoy', 'deeply enjoy', and so on. However, it is beside the point of the present paper to go into these questions. I am here concerned only with the issue between extreme and restricted utilitarianism and am ready to concede that both forms of utilitarianism can be either hedonistic or non-hedonistic.

The issue between extreme and restricted utilitarianism can be illustrated by considering the remark 'But suppose everyone did the same'. (Cf. A. K. Stout's article in *The Australasian Journal of Philosophy,* Vol. 32, pp. 1–29) Stout distinguishes two forms of the universalization principle, the causal forms and the hypothetical form. To say that you ought not to do an action A because it would have bad results if everyone (or many people) did action A may be merely to point out that while the action A would otherwise be the optimific one, nevertheless when you take into account that doing A will probably cause other people to do A too, you can see that A is not, on a broad view, really optimific. If this causal influence could be avoided (as may happen in the case of a secret desert island promise) then we would disregard the universalization principle. This is the causal form of the principle. A person who accepted the universalization principle in its hypothetical form would be one who was concerned only with what would happen *if* everyone did the action A: he would be totally unconcerned with the question of whether in fact everyone would do the action A. That is, he might say that it would be wrong not to vote because it would have bad results if everyone took this attitude, and he would be totally unmoved by arguments purporting to show that my refusing to vote has no effect whatever on other people's propensity to vote. Making use of Stout's distinction, we can say that an extreme utilitarian would apply the universalization principle in the causal form, while a restricted utilitarian would apply it in the hypothetical form.

How are we to decide the issue between extreme and restricted utilitarianism? I wish to repudiate at the outset that milk and water approach which describes itself sometimes as 'investigating what is implicit in the common moral consciousness' and sometimes as 'investigating how people ordinarily talk about morality'. We have only to read the newspaper correspondence about capital punishment or about what should be done with Formosa to realize that the common moral consciousness is in part made up of superstitious elements, of morally bad elements, and of logically confused elements. I address myself to good hearted and benevolent people and so I hope that if we rid ourselves of the logical confusion the superstitious and morally bad elements will largely fall away. For even among good hearted and benevolent people it is possible to find superstitious and morally bad reasons for moral beliefs. These superstitious and morally bad reasons hide behind the protective screen of logical confusion. With people who are not logically confused but who are openly superstitious or morally bad I can of course do nothing. That is, our ultimate pro-attitudes may be different. Nevertheless I propose to rely on *my own* moral consciousness and to appeal to *your* moral consciousness and to forget what people ordinarily say. 'The obligation to obey a rule', says Nowell-Smith (*Ethics*, p. 239), 'does not, *in the opinion of ordinary men*', (my italics), 'rest on the beneficial consequences of obeying it in a particular case'. What does this prove? Surely it is more than likely that ordinary men are confused here. Philosophers should be able to examine the question more rationally.

II

For an extreme utilitarian moral rules are rules of thumb. In practice the extreme utilitarian will mostly guide his conduct by appealing to the rules ('do not lie', 'do not break promises', etc.) of common sense morality. This is not because there is anything sacrosanct in the rules themselves but because he can argue that probably he will most often act in an extreme utilitarian way if he does not think as a utilitarian. For one thing, actions have frequently to be done in a hurry. Imagine a man seeing a person drowning. He jumps in and rescues him. There is no time to reason the matter out, but usually this will be the course of action which an extreme utilitarian would recommend if he did reason the matter out. If, however, the man drowning had been drowning in a river near Berchtesgaden in 1938, and if he had had the well known black forelock and moustache of Adolf Hitler, an extreme utilitarian would, if he had time, work out the probability of the man's being the villainous dictator, and if the probability were high enough he would, on extreme utilitarian grounds, leave him to drown. The rescuer, however, has not time. He trusts to his instincts and dives in and rescues the man. And this trusting to instincts and to moral rules can be justified on extreme utilitarian grounds. Furthermore, an extreme utilitarian who knew that the drowning man was Hitler would nevertheless praise the rescuer, not condemn him. For by praising the man he is strengthening a courageous and benevolent disposition of mind, and in general this disposition has great positive utility. (Next time, perhaps, it will be Winston Churchill that the man saves!) We must never forget that an extreme utilitarian may praise actions which he knows to be wrong. Saving Hitler was wrong, but it was a member of a class of actions which are generally right, and the motive to do actions of this class is in general an optimific one. In considering questions of praise and blame it is not the expediency of the praised or blamed action that is at issue, but the expediency of the praise. It can be expedient to praise an inexpedient action and inexpedient to praise an expedient one.

Lack of time is not the only reason why an extreme utilitarian may, on extreme utilitarian principles, trust to rules of common sense morality. He knows that in particular cases where his own interests are involved his calculations are likely to be biased in his own favour. Suppose that he is unhappily married and is deciding whether to get divorced. He will in all probability greatly exaggerate his own unhappiness (and possibly his wife's) and greatly underestimate the harm done to his children by the break up of the family. He will probably also underestimate the likely harm done by the weakening of the general faith in marriage vows. So probably he will come to the correct extreme utilitarian conclusion if he does not in this instance think as an extreme utilitarian but trusts to common sense morality.

There are many more and subtle points that could be made in connexion with the relation between extreme utilitarianism and the morality of common sense. All those that I have just made and many more will be found in Book IV Chapters 3–5 of Sidgwick's *Methods of Ethics.* I think that this book is the best book ever written on ethics, and that these chapters are the best chapters of the book. As they occur so near the end of a very long book they are unduly neglected. I refer the reader, then, to Sidgwick for the classical exposition of the relation between (extreme) utilitarianism and the morality of common sense. One further point raised by Sidgwick in this connexion is whether an (extreme) utilitarian ought on (extreme) utilitarian principles to propagate (extreme) utilitarianism among the public. As most people are not very philosophical and not good at empirical calculations, it is probable that they will most often act in an extreme utilitarian way if they do not try to think as extreme utilitarians. We have seen how easy it would be to misapply the extreme utilitarian criterion in the case of divorce. Sidgwick seems to think it quite probable that an extreme utilitarian should not propagate his doctrine too widely. However, the great danger to humanity comes nowadays on the plane of public morality—not private morality. There is a greater danger to humanity from the hydrogen bomb than from an increase of the divorce rate, regrettable though that might be, and there seems no doubt that extreme utilitarianism makes for good sense in international relations. When France walked out of the United Nations because she did not wish Morocco discussed, she said that she was within her rights because Morocco and Algiers are part of her metropolitan territory and nothing to do with U.N. This was clearly a legalistic if not superstitious argument. We should not be concerned with the so-called 'rights' of France or any other country but with whether the cause of humanity would best be served by discussing Morocco in U.N. (I am not saying that the answer to this is 'Yes'. There are good grounds for supposing that more harm than good would come by such a discussion.) I myself have no hesitation in saying that on extreme utilitarian principles we ought to propagate extreme utilitarianism as widely as possible. But Sidgwick had respectable reasons for suspecting the opposite.

The extreme utilitarian, then, regards moral rules as rules of thumb and as sociological facts that have to be taken into account when deciding what to do, just as facts of any other sort have to be taken into account. But in themselves they do not justify any action.

III

The restricted utilitarian regards moral rules as more than rules of thumb for short-circuiting calculations of consequences. Generally, he argues, consequences are not relevant at all when we are deciding what to do in a particular case. In general, they are relevant only to deciding what rules are good reasons for acting in a certain way in particular cases. This doctrine is possibly a good account of how the modern unreflective twentieth century Englishman often thinks about morality, but surely it is monstrous as an account of how it is most rational to think about morality. Suppose that there is a rule R and that in 99 percent of cases the best possible results are obtained by acting in accordance with R. Then clearly R is a useful rule of thumb; if we have not time or are not impartial enough to assess the consequences of an action it is an extremely good bet that the thing to do is to act in accordance with R. But is it not monstrous to suppose that if we *have* worked out the consequences and if we have perfect faith in the impartiality of our calculations, and if we *know* that in this instance to break R will have better results than to keep it, we should nevertheless obey the rule? Is it not to erect R into a sort of idol if we keep it when breaking it will prevent, say, some avoidable misery? Is not this a form of superstitious rule-worship (easily explicable psychologically) and not the rational thought of a philosopher?

The point may be made more clearly if we consider Mill's comparison of moral rules to the tables in the nautical almanack (*Utilitarianism,* Everyman Edition, pp. 22–23 [p. 62]). This comparison of Mill's is adduced by Urmson as evidence that Mill was a restricted utilitarian, but I do not think that it will bear this interpretation at all. (Though I quite agree with Urmson that many other things said by Mill are in harmony with restricted rather than extreme utilitarianism. Probably Mill had never thought very much about the distinction and was arguing for utilitarianism, restricted or extreme, against other and quite non-utilitarian forms of moral argument.) Mill says: 'Nobody argues that the art of navigation is not founded on astronomy, because sailors cannot wait to calculate the Nautical Almanack. Being rational creatures, they go out upon the sea of life with their minds made up on the common questions of right and wrong, as well as on many of the far more difficult questions of wise and foolish. . . . Whatever we adopt as the fundamental principle of morality, we require subordinate principles to apply it by'. Notice that this is, as it stands, only an argument for subordinate principles as rules of thumb. The example of the nautical almanack is misleading because the information given in the almanack is in all cases the same as the information one would get if one made a long and laborious calculation from the original astronomical data on which the almanack is founded. Suppose, however, that astronomy were different. Suppose that the behaviour of the sun, moon and planets was very nearly as it is now, but that on rare occasions there were peculiar irregularities and discontinuities, so that the almanack gave us rules of the form 'in 99 percent of cases where the observations are such and such you can deduce that your position is so and so'. Furthermore, let us suppose that there were methods which enabled us, by direct and laborious calculation from the original astronomical data, not using the rough and ready tables of the almanack, to get our correct position in 100 percent of cases. Seafarers might use the almanack because they never had time for the long calculations and they were content with a 99 percent chance of success in calculating their positions. Would it not be absurd, however, if they *did* make the direct calculation, and finding that it disagreed with the almanack calculation, nevertheless they ignored it and stuck to the almanack conclusion? Of course the case would be altered if there were a high enough probability of making slips in the direct calculation: then we might stick to the almanack result, liable to error though we knew it to be, simply because the direct calculation would be open to error for a different reason, the fallibility of the computer. This would be analogous to the case of the extreme utilitarian who abides by the conventional rule against the dictates of his utilitarian cal-

culations simply because he thinks that his calculations are probably affected by personal bias. But if the navigator were sure of his
direct calculations would he not be foolish to abide by his almanack? I conclude, then, that if we change our suppositions about
astronomy and the almanack (to which there are no exceptions) to
bring the case into line with that of morality (to whose rules there
are exceptions), Mill's example loses its appearance of supporting
the restricted form of utilitarianism. Let me say once more that I
am not here concerned with how ordinary men think about morality
but with how they ought to think. We could quite well imagine
a race of sailors who acquired a superstitious reverence for their
almanack, even though it was only right in 99 percent of cases, and
who indignantly threw overboard any man who mentioned the possibility of a direct calculation. But would this behaviour of the
sailors be rational?

Let us consider a much discussed sort of case in which the extreme utilitarian might go against the conventional moral rule. I
have promised to a friend, dying on a desert island from which I am
subsequently rescued, that I will see that his fortune (over which
I have control) is given to a jockey club. However, when I am rescued I decide that it would be better to give the money to a hospital,
which can do more good with it. It may be argued that I am wrong
to give the money to the hospital. But why? (*a*) The hospital can do
more good with the money than the jockey club can. (*b*) The present case is unlike most cases of promising in that no one except me
knows about the promise. In breaking the promise I am doing so
with complete secrecy and am doing nothing to weaken the general
faith in promises. That is, a factor, which would normally keep the
extreme utilitarian from promise breaking even in otherwise un-
optimific cases, does not at present operate. (*c*) There is no doubt
a slight weakening in my own character as an habitual promise
keeper, and moreover psychological tensions will be set up in me
every time I am asked what the man made me promise him to do.
For clearly I shall have to say that he made me promise to give the
money to the hospital, and, since I am an habitual truth teller, this
will go very much against the grain with me. Indeed I am pretty
sure that in practice I myself would keep the promise. But we are
not discussing what my moral habits would probably make me do;
we are discussing what I ought to do. Moreover, we must not forget

that even if it would be most rational of me to give the money to the hospital it would also be most rational of you to punish or condemn me if you did, most improbably, find out the truth (e.g. by finding a note washed ashore in a bottle). Furthermore, I would agree that though it was most rational of me to give the money to the hospital it would be most rational of you to condemn me for it. We revert again to Sidgwick's distinction between the utility of the action and the utility of the praise of it.

Many such issues are discussed by A. K. Stout in the article to which I have already referred. I do not wish to go over the same ground again, especially as I think that Stout's arguments support my own point of view. It will be useful, however, to consider one other example that he gives. Suppose that during hot weather there is an edict that no water must be used for watering gardens. I have a garden and I reason that most people are sure to obey the edict, and that as the amount of water that I use will be by itself negligible no harm will be done if I use the water secretly. So I do use the water, thus producing some lovely flowers which give happiness to various people. Still, you may say, though the action was perhaps optimific, it was unfair and wrong.

There are several matters to consider. Certainly my action should be condemned. We revert once more to Sidgwick's distinction. A right action may be rationally condemned. Furthermore, this sort of offence is normally found out. If I have a wonderful garden when everybody else's is dry and brown there is only one explanation. So if I water my garden I am weakening my respect for law and order, and as this leads to bad results an extreme utilitarian would agree that I was wrong to water the garden. Suppose now that the case is altered and that I can keep the thing secret: there is a secluded part of the garden where I grow flowers which I give away anonymously to a home for old ladies. Are you still so sure that I did the wrong thing by watering my garden? However, this is still a weaker case than that of the hospital and the jockey club. There will be tensions set up within myself: my secret knowledge that I have broken the rule will make it hard for me to exhort others to keep the rule. These psychological ill effects in myself may be not inconsiderable: directly and indirectly they may lead to harm which is at least of the same order as the happiness that the old ladies get from the flowers. You can see that on an extreme utilitarian view there are two sides to the question.

So far I have been considering the duty of an extreme utilitarian in a predominantly non-utilitarian society. The case is altered if we consider the extreme utilitarian who lives in a society every member, or most members, of which can be expected to reason as he does. Should he water his flowers now? (Granting, what is doubtful, that in the case already considered he would have been right to water his flowers.) As a first approximation, the answer is that he should not do so. For since the situation is a completely symmetrical one, what is rational for him is rational for others. Hence, by a *reductio ad absurdum* argument, it would seem that watering his garden would be rational for none. Nevertheless, a more refined analysis shows that the above argument is not quite correct, though it is correct enough for practical purposes. The argument considers each person as confronted with the choice either of watering his garden or of not watering it. However there is a third possibility, which is that each person should, with the aid of a suitable randomizing device, such as throwing dice, give himself a certain probability of watering his garden. This would be to adopt what in the theory of games is called 'a mixed strategy'. If we could give numerical values to the private benefit of garden watering and to the public harm done by 1, 2, 3, etc., persons using the water in this way, we could work out a value of the probability of watering his garden that each extreme utilitarian should give himself. Let a be the value which each extreme utilitarian gets from watering his garden, and let $f(1)$, $f(2)$, $f(3)$, etc., be the public harm done by exactly 1, 2, 3, etc., persons respectively watering their gardens. Suppose that p is the probability that each person gives himself of watering his garden. Then we can easily calculate, as functions of p, the probabilities that exactly 1, 2, 3, etc., persons will water their gardens. Let these probabilities be p_1, p_2, . . . p_n. Then the total net probable benefit can be expressed as

$$V = p_1 (a - f(1)) + p_2 (2a - f(2)) + \ldots p_n (na - f(n))$$

Then if we know the function $f(x)$ we can calculate the value of p for which $(dV/dp) = 0$. This gives the value of p which it would be rational for each extreme utilitarian to adopt. The present argument does not of course depend on a perhaps unjustified assumption that the values in question are measurable, and in a practical case such as that of the garden watering we can doubtless assume that p will be so small that we can take it near enough as equal to zero. However the argument is of interest for the theoretical underpinning of extreme utilitarianism, since the possibility of a mixed strategy is usually neglected by critics of utilitarianism, who wrongly assume that the only relevant and symmetrical alternatives are of the form 'everybody does X' and 'nobody does X'.

I now pass on to a type of case which may be thought to be the trump card of restricted utilitarianism. Consider the rule of the road. It may be said that since all that matters is that everyone should do the same it is indifferent which rule we have, 'go on the left hand side' or 'go on the right hand side'. Hence the only *reason* for going on the left hand side in British countries is that this is the rule. Here the rule does seem to be a reason, in itself, for acting in a certain way. I wish to argue against this. The rule in itself is not a reason for our actions. We would be perfectly justified in going on the right hand side if (*a*) we knew that the rule was to go on the left hand side, and (*b*) we were in a country peopled by super-anarchists who always on principle did the opposite of what they were told. This shows that the rule does not give us a reason for acting so much as an indication of the probable actions of others, which helps us to find out what would be our own most rational course of action. If we are in a country not peopled by anarchists, but by non-anarchist extreme utilitarians, we expect, other things being equal, that they will keep rules laid down for them. Knowledge of the rule enables us to predict their behaviour and to harmonize our own actions with theirs. The rule 'keep to the left hand side', then, is not a logical *reason* for action but an anthropological *datum* for planning actions.

I conclude that in every case if there is a rule R the keeping of which is in general optimific, but such that in a special sort of circumstances the optimific behaviour is to break R, then in these circumstances we should break R. Of course we must consider all the less obvious effects of breaking R, such as reducing people's faith in the moral order, before coming to the conclusion that to break R is right: in fact we shall rarely come to such a conclusion. Moral rules, on the extreme utilitarian view, are rules of thumb only, but they are not bad rules of thumb. But if we *do* come to the conclusion that we should break the rule and if we have weighed in the balance our own fallibility and liability to personal bias, what good reason remains for keeping the rule? I can understand 'it is optimific' as a reason for action, but why should 'it is a member of a class of actions which are usually optimific' or 'it is a member of a class of actions which as a class are more optimific than any alternative general class' be a good reason? You might as well say that a person ought to be picked to play for Australia just because all his brothers have been, or that the Australian team should be composed entirely of the Harvey family because this would be better than composing it entirely of any other family. The extreme utilitarian does not appeal to artificial feelings, but only to our feelings of benevolence, and what better feelings can there be to appeal to? Admittedly we can have a pro-attitude to anything, even to rules, but such artificially begotten pro-attitudes smack of superstition. Let us get down to realities, human happiness and misery, and make these the objects of our pro-attitudes and anti-attitudes.

The restricted utilitarian might say that he is talking only of *morality,* not of such things as rules of the road. I am not sure how far this objection, if valid, would affect my argument, but in any case I would reply that as a philosopher I conceive of ethics as the study of how it would be *most rational* to act. If my opponent wishes to restrict the word 'morality' to a narrower use he can have the word. The fundamental question is the question of rationality of action *in general.* Similarly if the restricted utilitarian were to appeal to ordinary usage and say 'it might be most rational to leave Hitler to drown but it would surely not be *wrong* to rescue him', I should again let him have the words 'right' and 'wrong' and should stick to 'rational' and 'irrational'. We already saw that it would be rational to praise Hitler's rescuer, even though it would have been most rational not to have rescued Hitler. In ordinary language, no doubt, 'right' and 'wrong' have not only the meaning 'most rational to do' and 'not most rational to do' but also have the meaning 'praiseworthy' and 'not praiseworthy'. Usually to the utility of an action corresponds utility of praise of it, but as we saw, this is not always so. Moral language could thus do with tidying up, for example by reserving 'right' for 'most rational' and 'good' as an epithet of praise for the motive from which the action sprang. It would be more becoming in a philosopher to try to iron out illogicalities in moral language and to make suggestions for its reform than to use it as a court of appeal whereby to perpetuate confusions.

One last defence of restricted utilitarianism might be as follows. 'Act optimifically' might be regarded as itself one of the rules of our system (though it would be odd to say that this rule was justified by its optimificality). According to Toulmin (*The Place of Reason in Ethics,* pp. 146–8) if 'keep promises', say, conflicts with another rule we are allowed to argue the case on its merits, as if we were extreme utilitarians. If 'act optimifically' is itself one of our rules then there will always be a conflict of rules whenever to keep a rule is not itself optimific. If this is so, restricted utilitarianism collapses into extreme utilitarianism. And no one could read Toulmin's book or Urmson's article on Mill without thinking that Toulmin and Urmson are of the opinion that they have thought of a doctrine which does *not* collapse into extreme utilitarianism, but which is, on the contrary, an improvement on it.

Suggestions for Further Reading

Books

Aiken, H. D. *Reason and Conduct.* New York: Alfred A. Knopf, 1962. Ch. 3.

Ayer, A. J. "The Principle of Utility." In *Philosophical Essays.* London: Macmillan, 1954.

Brandt, Richard. *Ethical Theory.* Englewood Cliffs, N.J.: Prentice-Hall, 1959. Chs. 15, 16.

Brandt, Richard. "Toward a Credible Form of Utilitarianism." In *Morality and the Language of Conduct.* Ed. by Hector-Neri Castañeda and George Nakhnikian. Detroit: Wayne State University Press, 1963.

Hare, R. M. *Freedom and Reason.* Oxford: The Clarendon Press, 1963. Ch. 7.

Hodgson, D. H. *The Consequences of Utilitarianism.* Oxford: The Clarendon Press, 1967.

Lyons, David. *Forms and Limits of Utilitarianism.* Oxford: The Clarendon Press, 1965.

Mandelbaum, Maurice. "Two Moot Issues in Mill's *Utilitarianism.*" In *Mill.* Ed. by J. B. Schneewind. Garden City, N.Y.: Anchor Doubleday, 1968.

McCloskey, H. J. *Meta-Ethics and Normative Ethics.* The Hague: Martinus Nijhoff, 1969.

Melden, A. I. "Utility and Moral Reasoning." In *Ethics and Society.* Ed. by Richard DeGeorge. Garden City, N.Y.: Anchor Doubleday, 1966.

Narveson, Jan. *Morality and Utility.* Baltimore: Johns Hopkins Press, 1967.

Rescher, Nicholas. *Distributive Justice.* Indianapolis: The Bobbs-Merrill Co., 1966. A complete bibliography on utilitarianism is contained in this volume.

Singer, M. G. *Generalization in Ethics.* New York: Alfred A. Knopf, 1961.

Smart, J. J. C. *An Outline of a System of Utilitarian Ethics.* Victoria: Melbourne University Press, 1961.

Toulmin, S. E. *The Place of Reason in Ethics.* London: Cambridge University Press, 1960.

Articles

Atkinson, R. F. "J. S. Mill's 'Proof' of the Principle of Utility," *Philosophy,* Vol. XXXII (1957), pp. 157–168.

Braybrook, David. "The Choice Between Utilitarianisms," *American Philosophical Quarterly,* Vol. 4 (1967), pp. 28–39.

Britton, Karl. "Utilitarianism: The Appeal to a First Principle," *Proceedings of the Aristotelian Society,* Vol. LX (1959–1960), pp. 141–154.

Broiles, David. "Is Rule Utilitarianism Too Restricted?" *Southern Journal of Philosophy,* Vol. II (1964), pp. 180–187.

Diggs, B. J. "Utilitarianism and Rules," *American Philosophical Quarterly,* Vol. I (1964), pp. 32–44.

Ewing, A. C. "Suppose Everyone Acted Like Me," *Philosophy,* Vol. XXVIII (1953), pp. 16–29.

Ewing, A. C. "Utilitarianism," *Ethics,* Vol. LVIII (1948), pp. 100–111.

Harrison, J. "Utilitarianism, Universalization and Our Duty to be Just," *Proceedings of the Aristotelian Society,* Vol. LIII (1952–1953), pp. 105–134.

Kretzmann, Norman, "Desire as Proof of Desirability," *Philosophical Quarterly,* Vol. VIII (1958), pp. 246–258.

Mabbott, J. D. "Moral Rules," *Proceedings of the British Academy,* Vol. XXXIX (1953), pp. 97–118.

Mabbott, J. D. "Punishment," *Mind,* Vol. XLVIII (1939), pp. 152–167.

Mandelbaum, Maurice. "On Interpreting Mill's *Utilitarianism,*" *Journal of the History of Philosophy,* Vol. VI (1968), pp. 35–46.

McCloskey, H. J. "A Non-Utilitarian Approach to Punishment," *Inquiry,* Vol. VIII (1965), pp. 249–263.

McCloskey, H. J. "Utilitarian and Retributive Punishment," *Journal of Philosophy,* Vol. LXIV (1967), pp. 91–110.

Raphael, D. D. "Fallacies in and about Mill's *Utilitarianism,*" *Philosophy,* Vol. XXX (1955), pp. 344–357.

Rawls, John. "Justice as Fairness," *Philosophical Review,* Vol. LXVII (1958), pp. 164–194.

Sprigge, T. L. S. "A Utilitarian Reply to Dr. McCloskey," *Inquiry,* Vol. VIII (1965), pp. 264–291.

Stout, A. K. "But Suppose Everyone Did the Same," *Australasian Journal of Philosophy,* Vol. XXXII (1954), pp. 1–29.

Stroll, Avrum. "Mill's Fallacy," *Dialogue,* Vol. III (1965), pp. 385–404.

Reference Guide to Selected Topics

Bentham, J., 2, 41, 44, 56, 99, 116, 142–50, 252

Deontology, 1

Epicurus, 44, 45

Hedonism, 2, 119–22

Hedonistic calculus, 35–38

Intuitionism, 4, 105, 133

Jesus, 55

Justice, 9, 78–101

Kant, Immanuel, 42, 89, 238

Metaethics, 8, 169

Mill, J. S., 3–11, 120–22, 123–40, 148–50, 151–60, 161–68, 190–92, 218, 252, 257

Moore, G. E., 124–32, 152, 161–64

Naturalistic fallacy, 8, 110–19, 122

Normative ethics, 8, 169

Promises, 211–15, 227

Psychological hedonism, 6, 116

Punishment, 202–11, 227, 234

Rawls, J. B., 167, 174, 175, 195, 231, 232–41

Ross, W. D., 163, 193, 210, 212–13, 235

Teleology, 1

Urmson, J. O., 161–65, 174, 201, 231

Utilitarianism
  Act (Extreme), 11, 173, 178, 251
  Rule (Restricted), 11, 173–99, 231, 251

Utility
  Principle, 15, 44
  Proof of, 72–78, 123–50
  Sanctions of, 64–72